The Youngest Billionaire (Large Print Edition)

Erin Swann

Because you don't always have to be a lady.

Cover design by Swann Publications
Edited by Valorie Clifton
ISBN-13 978-1-7917-1763-6

ALSO BY ERIN SWANN

The Billionaire's Trust
(Bill and Lauren's story) He needed to save the company. He needed her. He couldn't have both. The wedding proposal in front of hundreds was like a fairy tale come true—Until she uncovered his darkest secret.

The Youngest Billionaire
(Steven and Emma's story) The youngest of the Covington clan, he avoided the family business to become a rarity, an honest lawyer. He didn't suspect that pursuing her could destroy his career. She didn't know what trusting him could cost her.

The Secret Billionaire
(Patrick and Elizabeth's story) Women naturally circled the flame of wealth and power, and his is brighter than most. Does she love him, does she not? There's no way to know. When he stopped to help her, Liz mistook him for a carpenter. Maybe this time he'd know. Everything was perfect. Until the day she left.

Protecting the Billionaire
(Nick and Katie's story) They came from different worlds. She hadn't seen him since the day he broke her brother's nose. She never suspected where accepting a ride from him today would take her. They said they could do casual. They lied.

Picked by the Billionaire

(Liam and Amy's story) A night she wouldn't forget. An offer she couldn't refuse. He alone could save her, and she held the key to his survival. If only they could pass the test together.

Saved by the Billionaire

(Ryan and Natalie's story) The FBI and the cartel were both after her for the same thing: information she didn't have. First the FBI took everything, and then the cartel came for her. She trusted Ryan with her safety, but could she trust him with her heart?

CHAPTER ONE

Emma

"Just text me when you need to be rescued."

My heart fluttered.

That's all he said as he stood directly in my path and handed me his card. Piercing emerald green eyes appraised me, complete with full, thick eyelashes, the kind that should be illegal for guys to have. Tall, dark, and handsome didn't begin to describe this hunk. "Steven. Steven Carter, at your service." The words mesmerized me as I looked up to see them escape his kissable full lips that drew me like a magnet. I wasn't short, but he was well over six feet, with shoulders broad enough to make Atlas envious, along with a chiseled jawline to die for.

"From what?" I rasped, barely getting the words out. The dark-haired man blocking my way had me completely flustered. I had bumped into plenty of tall guys before, but right now, they all seemed like boys compared to this man. A real man. An eleven on the ten-point scale.

He nodded toward the dining area. "Your blind date, of course. You'll want to put that into your phone before you get back to your table, Miss...?" He stood there waiting, demanding an answer.

I should have shouldered my way past him back to my table without a word, but I didn't have the willpower. I lied and used my favorite bar name. "Tiffany. Tiffany Case." All that awaited me at that table, after all, was boring Gordie.

In college, my girlfriends and I would use fake names when we went out so we wouldn't get stalked by any of the guys we met. I had tried a few Bond Girl names and settled on Tiffany Case. She was a redhead, like me, and not as obvious as Pussy Galore. When I used my real name, Emma Watson, people didn't believe me anyway because they had seen Harry Potter and I looked nothing like her.

He licked his lips. "Tiffany. Lovely name. It suits you." Satisfied, he turned back into the dining area.

I more than glanced at his ass as he strode away. A lot more. I had slipped up. I couldn't ignore the sudden heat he caused in me. Surprised by him, I had forgotten I was using Miranda Frost for my *SuperSingles* date tonight. I had to remember I was Miranda to Gordie and Tiffany to Steven. Steven. I liked that name. The card was white with a gilded edge. Steven Carter and a phone number, nothing else. He had caught me on my second trip to the restroom. I couldn't stomach more than a half hour at a time of my date tonight. I lingered in the hallway for a moment as I fingered the card. Suddenly, tonight wasn't totally wasted. I added the stranger as a contact before stashing my phone back in my purse, along with the card. I pasted on a smile and made my way back to the table, where Gordie was waiting anxiously to bore me to death on the topic of insurance.

"And the difference with whole life is…" I zoned out as he droned on, digging into my meal with the occasional nod.

Cardinelli's was an expensive place, and I was damned if I was going to leave without getting to finish my lasagna. I just had to tough out another half hour of how marvelous it was to sell insurance. Life, home, car, pet, mortuary, you name it, Gordie sold it. There was something to be said for getting into your work, but this was supposed to be a first date. I wasn't doing a second with Gordie. He had lied about his height. He was shorter than me, even without my heels on. They all lied about something.

From my seat, I could see my mysterious green-eyed rescuer over Gordie's shoulder, and he held up his phone with a questioning look. Gordie had no clue as I smiled at Steven. I took another bite of my lasagna. The quicker I got this date over with, the better.

My phone buzzed on the table with a text.

MEGAN: I'm home

"If you need to answer that, I understand," Gordie said as I glanced at the message. That was sweet of him.

"It's just my sister telling me she got home okay."

Gordie smiled and put down his wine glass. "So is she checking to see if you need to be rescued from your date?"

Busted.

"No, we're good." He had guessed our code all right. If I didn't answer right away, she would call with an emergency that would give me an excuse to leave the restaurant. "She's just checking in." I texted her back.

ME: OK

I put the phone down. "How's your carbonara?" That got Gordie settled down. I felt bad lying to him. He wasn't handsy, and he didn't seem like an axe murderer or anything. He just couldn't help that he was less exciting than cold oatmeal. I flipped my phone on silent and put it in my lap. Just one more thing to do.

At school, I had become an expert in texting

under my desk without the teacher seeing, and now that was going to come in handy as I decided I felt more sorry for Gordie than anything else. I would amuse myself by texting the green-eyed hunk with the dark brown hair, even if he was sitting with that knock-dead gorgeous blonde.

ME: Not tonight thanks

He laughed with his date over Gordie's shoulder. And my phone vibrated in my hand. Good thing it wasn't on the table anymore. Gordie kept rambling on as I nodded.

STEVEN CARTER: So you go for the low IQ type

When I chanced a peek, Steven was looking directly at me. I smiled at him over my date's shoulder as I typed my response. Gordie smiled back.

ME: Why say that?

STEVEN CARTER: Any guy that spends all night talking about himself without finding out what

Finding out what? Steven was right about talking

all night. Gordie got that prize. A few seconds later, the answer appeared.

STEVEN CARTER: a beautiful woman like you has to say

His text didn't make any sense.

STEVEN CARTER: must have the brains of a mollusk

I giggled. Now it made sense. Gordie smiled, happy that I found something he said amusing.

ME: It wouldn't be fair and maybe I can learn something from him.

That was a stretch, more an outright lie. Maybe this is how Indian snake charmers did it. They talked to the cobras about insurance until they fell asleep. I called the waiter over and asked for some more iced tea.

Need more caffeine so that I won't doze off.

STEVEN CARTER: He's a moron nothing else worth learning

"Don't you like the lasagna?" Gordie asked. He had noticed that I wasn't inhaling my food anymore.

I lied. "I was just letting it settle a bit. It's very good. There is just so much, and I need some tea to wash it down." I couldn't eat and text at the same time. I dropped my phone in my lap and started back attacking my meal.

A few minutes later, Gordie was filling me in on the intricacies of insuring homes against fire in the foothills when my phone vibrated again.

STEVEN CARTER: Tuesdays and Thursdays are the only days for a first date

I had chosen Tuesday evenings because my sister Megan made it her mission to come over on Monday nights to 'help me' go through the website candidates. She thought I needed help finding a suitable date. She was right about my needing help, but guys like Gordie were not the answer. There was a serious lack of candidates at the museum where I worked. Most of them were ancient enough to have sailed over on the *Mayflower*, except for Jonathon, and he was gay. I had finally agreed to try the *SuperSingles* website, and so far, the results had been pretty disappointing. Gordie was busy quoting me automobile theft rate trends, so I had to entertain myself texting with Steven. Gordie had been talking so much that he hadn't gotten very far on his meal yet.

ME: Why?

STEVEN CARTER: Monday is no good - they only talk about the weekend games they watched

He had a point there.

STEVEN CARTER: Friday is out because they know you don't have work - they might expect a late night treat

No argument from me. Megan and I had already ruled out weekend nights as not first date-appropriate.

STEVEN CARTER: Wednesday you will get some comment about wanting to hump you because it is hump day

I giggled because that had really happened to me once, and the guy actually thought it was funny. Gordie gave me a slightly puzzled look before he continued. He didn't think what he was saying was giggle-worthy. I guess loss ratios were not meant to be funny.

STEVEN CARTER: Most important I'm here Tuesday and Thursday mostly

So the guy was here two nights a week. That would rack up some serious points on your credit card. I recalled seeing him here before, more than once, but he was always with that blonde knockout who was sitting with him again tonight. Some girls have all the luck. They have the looks and get the good guys, and the rest of us are stuck with the Gordies of the world.

STEVEN CARTER: Better luck next time maybe number five is your lucky number

ME: What makes you think this is number four?

STEVEN CARTER: I can count

He was right. Gordie was my fourth *SuperSingles* date in as many weeks. I put my phone away and smiled at the implication.
He noticed me.
Gordie caught my smile and thought it was meant for him as he started to try to sell me on buying whole life insurance for myself. A half-hour later, I passed on dessert and got out of the evening before I lost my sanity. Gordie was nice enough to pick up the check. He said it was deductible for him, but I thanked him sincerely nevertheless. Half of a big bill was still a lot for me. Gordie gave the valet his

ticket as we said goodbye and I walked toward my car. Valet parking was an extravagance I didn't need.

Mama always said, "You have to kiss a lot of frogs before you find your prince," but at least I got out of this evening without having to kiss this frog. On the way to my car, I took my phone out of my purse to call Megan and tell her I was heading home. It was still on silent, so I had missed the last text.

STEVEN CARTER: Have a nice evening Tiffany

I turned to look back at the valet stand, and he waved to me, with his date standing at his side.
What does his date think of that?
I waved back and dialed Megan.
He had waved.

* * *

Steven

I had my Bar Exam study material spread out in front of me in my little cubicle at the Ernst and Schwartz office in Santa Monica. It was easier to focus here than if I went downtown, but right now, I had trouble focusing because of her.

Tiffany Case. There was something familiar about

her name, but I couldn't place it. I pulled out my phone and reviewed the text conversation I'd had with Tiffany last Tuesday for the millionth time. She had said it wouldn't be fair to her dipshit date to cut it short. She had more fortitude than any woman I had ever met if she was willing to endure Dudley Dipstick all night just to be fair to him. *It wouldn't be fair.* The words stuck with me. *It wouldn't be fair?* Just who has moral standards like that?

I'd noticed her several weeks ago when she first came into the restaurant. She was a striking redhead with one-in-a-million sapphire blue eyes, and curves in all the right places. She was the complete opposite of the 'I only eat lettuce and carrots' under-nourished Hollywood wannabes that abounded in the LA basin. I could barely take my eyes off her that first night, and she had come back each Tuesday afterward. So far. For some reason, this girl, who was all class, got stuck going out with a string of complete dipshits. She had an air of innocence about her. If she was picking these losers, she was in serious need of a self-esteem transplant and a real man to show her what she was worth.

Last Tuesday, we were seated only two tables away, and I could hear the numb-nuts trying to sell her insurance, of all things. Seated across from a gorgeous woman and all he could do was go on and on about his insurance business. Blah, blah, blah.

My sister Katie almost had to restrain me from going over and dragging the guy out by his tweed blazer to save her from him.

Katie and I had a standing date to meet on Tuesday nights at Cardinelli's in Westwood. My brother Bill and his partner, Marco Cardinelli, had turned it into the premier place for fine Italian dining on this end of town. That was before my father died and left Bill to take over the company business. Now, Marco ran it singlehandedly while Bill was just an investor. The menu was great, and it was located midway between Katie and me. Every once in a while, Marco would give us a new dish he was working on to taste test. Katie loved that part.

The family was going in too many directions since Dad had died. He was the glue that kept us together, so I tried to fill in as best I could after his death with these family dinners.

I'd promised my dad before he died that I would become a great lawyer, something like Perry Mason, and help people in need. So far, that had amounted to three years of law school and now a first-year associate gig at E&S, as we called it. I still needed to pass the California Bar to be a real lawyer. So far, all they had me doing here was researching the most boring briefs and running papers down to the clerk's office. That and the occasional coffee run to keep me in my place. Being a first-year associate meant JD on my card instead of ESQ and a meager paycheck. For the firm, it meant billing me at the higher full associate rate to their clients and pocketing the difference. First-years were valuable that way.

Monica suddenly rounded the corner to my cube. "Want to catch lunch, Steve?" Monica Paisley was a partner at the firm and my boss for now. I was Steven to everybody else. She insisted on calling me Steve, her little power play.

"No, thanks. I still have some catching up on civil procedures to do." That was partly the truth. The other part was that I had no intention of spending any social time alone with Monica.

She waved goodbye. "Okay, rain check then."

"Sure."

Over my dead body.

To say that Monica had a reputation was putting it mildly. The rumor was that she had something on two of the senior partners. My guess was photographic evidence of past affairs with her. She used this leverage to keep them from putting a stop to her trolling in the first-year pond.

In the two summers I'd interned here at E&S, she had made boy toys out of three different first-years that I was aware of. One of them was flattered and thought she was kinky but fun. However, for the other two, it was something to be endured to avoid a bad recommendation. She was in her forties at least, with bleached blonde hair and boobs that were definitely fake, and she wore red high heels every single day, regardless of her outfit.

She had all the subtlety of a rhinoceros and was even less appealing. I considered getting a doctor's note with a nasty medical diagnosis that would keep her at bay when the time came. However, that was still on my to-do list. This was one time I was glad to have family money behind me. You didn't mess with a Covington because we had billions in resources and the connections to fight back. But if I used that leverage, it wouldn't stop her from exacting her revenge when it came time to write my recommendation, so it made more sense to just avoid her for the time being. Money couldn't buy me a way around the moral character recommendations I needed from a firm like E&S to get into the state bar. A fact she had reminded me of already by waving a gray envelope at me my first week here. The envelope was addressed to the Committee of Bar Examiners and contained two recommendations she had already typed up, one bad and one good. Which one she sent would depend, she had told me.

After Monica left, I couldn't get the words from last Tuesday night out of my head, nor could I stop seeing those eyes. *It wouldn't be fair?* Couldn't Tiffany see that it wasn't fair for her to have to deal with Dudley Do-No-Right Dipstick all night long when there were so many better men out there? Men who would listen to her, men who would ask her what she thought, what she was interested in, what she had done, and what she wanted out of life. A man like me.

At the end of the night, I was pleased to see that she was smart enough to have driven herself and be done with the douche bag.

I decided to risk texting her about tomorrow night.

ME: Got another date setup for Tuesday??

I waited, and when no response came, I finally got back to studying Civil Procedure. This was the section on the bar that killed the most careers, and I was not going to be one of its victims if I could help it.

Half an hour later, a response arrived.

TIFFANY: Not yet, but that is the plan. Will you be there?

ME: Sure, let me know when you need an out

I was careful to type 'when' not 'if' as I considered my next line.

ME:

Is this guy any better than the last moron

I didn't get a response. Shit. I'd overplayed my hand. I probably shouldn't have sent it. Mad at myself for pushing too hard, I went back to my study materials. All I saw on every page was Tiffany's enchanting smile and those eyes. I had to turn this around somehow.

TIFFANY: I won't know until tomorrow.

The text came at the end of the day. She was still talking to me... well, not talking, but at least texting.

Tomorrow evening can't come soon enough.

* * *

Emma

"That one. No, up one more." My sister, Megan, was looking over my shoulder as I scrolled through the possibilities for the fifth Monday night in a row. "Now that guy is hot, and a CS degree too. He probably makes a ton." The guy she picked out for me on the *SuperSingles* website wasn't half bad. However, he wasn't half good either.

Megan's experience with men had not translated into an ability to pick out winners. Hot to Megan meant clean-shaven. She had the mistaken idea that if a guy could learn to shave every day, you could teach him whatever else you needed to.

"He has possibilities," I mumbled.

Like none and less than none.

I popped another red M&M in my mouth and scrolled down farther. "He probably still lives with his mother." Computer guys often did.

"Emma, we've gotta get you laid, and computer geeks can be real steady too." That was Megan-speak for *I wasn't much of a catch myself, so I ought to set my sights a little lower.* Her thought was that if you went after the guy whom the other girls ignored, then he would be appreciative and a great guy who would cherish you and stick with you. So far, it hadn't worked out that way for her.

I huffed. "You can't trust a thing they post anyway. They're all liars, just to different degrees."

Braydon, Megan's latest catch, wasn't any better than her last three, and he once again disproved her theory. He was currently teaching Megan that a dorky guy could be an even bigger jerk than he was a dork.

At least she was getting some action, which is more than I could say for myself, but if dating a guy like Braydon was the price to get laid, count me out. Getting some had never been Megan's problem. Her self-esteem had always been low, and she was not very good at making a guy wait.

On the next page, I found a possibility and hit the *Like* button before Megan got a chance to veto him. Jason sounded nice. He had a math degree, he looked clean-cut, and although he wasn't moving the needle on the hotness meter, he seemed to be low on the dork scale. He had a job in financial services, if I believed his bio. He liked to bicycle and he had a dog.

"I like him," Megan said. "He has big hands. You know what that means." She laughed.

I ignored her. We went on for another half hour down the listings and I sent likes to another two guys before I got my first response. It was from Jason. With a little luck, a dinner was right around the corner.

"Tell him Cardinelli's tomorrow night," Megan insisted.

"Not again. It's kind of expensive."

"No shit Sis. If he can't afford the place, you don't want him anyway." That part made sense, I guess. "Look at it this way. You've got a fifty percent chance that he's a gentleman and he picks up the tab anyway and another fifty percent chance that you like him, so it's money well spent if you split the check. So you only have a one in four chance of having to pay for a wasted date."

"So far, your math isn't working. I had to pay twice already, and they were both a waste of time and good makeup." This didn't make any sense. I could find out if I liked the guy for a lot less at Round Table, but I didn't feel like arguing the point with my big sister. After fifteen minutes of back and forth with Jason, I had a date set for tomorrow night at Cardinelli's. I hadn't told Megan about the green-eyed hunk, Steven. She wouldn't have believed me anyway.

No way.

CHAPTER TWO

Steven

I arrived at Cardinelli's before Katie. A quick check of the dining room showed that I was ahead of Tiffany, so I moved to the bar with a view of the front entry and ordered a glass of Pinot Grigio. I waved over Katie when she walked in.

She climbed up on the stool across from me, her back to the entrance. "Bad day at the office, eh? Opting for a liquid dinner tonight?"

"Yes and no." She was partly right. "I just wanted to start slow is all."

She smirked. "Are we waiting for that redhead again?"

Was I that transparent?

"What redhead?" I said, feigning ignorance.

She waved the waitress over. "The one you drool over every time she comes in. The one you have had us skip a window table for so you could sit near her the last two weeks." She pointed her finger at me. "The one you corralled by the restrooms last week. The one you were texting with all during dinner last week. Ring a bell, Steven?"

I shrugged my shoulders. My sister enjoyed being a pain in the ass.

"The one you left in the middle of our dessert for so you could follow her outside. Is it coming to you yet?"

I couldn't ever keep a straight face with Katie. "I do not drool."

"Yes, that one." She chuckled. "Now give it up, little brother. What's her name?"

There was no sense trying to hold out on Katie. Ever since she made me cough up the name of the boy who had left her a note in middle school, I could never keep a secret from her. "You were done with your dessert anyway," I protested. Tiffany appeared over Katie's shoulder. Just the sight of her warmed my blood and sent a jolt of electricity straight through me. She met up with some shrimp of a guy in the front. Tiffany deserved way better than him. Way better.

Katie noticed the change in my expression and turned around in time to see Tiffany. She punched me in the shoulder and whispered, "Yes, that one, little brother. Now, what's her name?"

"Tiffany. Her name is Tiffany Case." I kept my

voice low as I watched the two of them enter the dining area.

Katie leaned forward. "Steven, you are so cute. You're like a little puppy dog, wagging his tail and drooling."

"I don't drool," I repeated.

"In all seriousness, Steven, listen to me." She grabbed my hand. "Be careful with her. Treat her like a real woman, not one of your normal bimbos. Got it?"

"What's that supposed to mean?"

"Steven, I know you. I can see it in your eyes."

"Katie, you're not the best source of dating advice."

"Shut up, you look just like Bill did when he met Lauren, so go slow and don't screw it up or you'll regret it."

The mention of Bill and Lauren stopped me cold. I'd been out at Columbia when it had happened, but Patrick and Katie had filled me in. Bill went off the deep end when Lauren left him. It nearly destroyed my brother. If Patrick hadn't echoed what Katie had told me, I would have thought my sister was messing with me. My oldest brother, Bill, was as solid as the Rock of Gibraltar. Nothing fazed him. I couldn't ever have imagined a breakup with a girl causing a bit of heartburn. He always had an inexhaustible supply of willing women, and he went through them like Dixie Cups.

Katie woke me out of my reverie. "Steven, if this one is different from those calendar girls, then you need to treat her differently, okay?"

Different.

I motioned toward the dining area. "Will you help me then?"

She climbed down from her stool. "Within reason."

That was good enough for tonight.

* * *

Emma

As I approached the restaurant, Megan texted to wish me good luck, informing me that Braydon insisted on a movie night, so she wouldn't be able to give me a rescue call. She was allowing Braydon to run her life again. Without a call from Megan, I would just have to hope Jason wasn't any worse than Gordie had been. I put my phone back in my purse after reviewing Jason's photo so I could recognize him. We had agreed to meet by the ficus tree just inside the door.

A man in a khaki suit stood up as I walked in. My heart dropped to the floor.

Why do they all have to be liars?

You were supposed to post a recent picture of

yourself, but Jason had a distorted view of *recent*. He was a lot older than his picture, with a significant paunch and a receding hairline. His profile also listed his height as average, but he was shorter than me. Jason's lies were the worst combination yet.

Jason led the way. All of my other dates had been gentlemen and offered to let me walk first. I guess in the new era of women's lib, I shouldn't have taken it as meaning anything.

At least Jason seemed to be less self-centered than Gordie last week, and he didn't drool like Bryce the week before, but he did talk quite loudly.

At his age, maybe he has a hearing problem.

He ordered a bottle of wine and bruschetta for an appetizer, announcing that dinner would be on him. That moved him up a notch in my estimation.

I started to tell him about myself. I told him how I'd worked in an art gallery after school before landing my current museum job. There were way more art history grads than there were good jobs. The gallery job paid next to nothing, but it was a start, and what else could I do? Work at Jamba Juice then move up to Starbucks? We were both Santa Clara University alums, so at least we had that in common.

He had gotten a math degree and moved into financial counseling.

"Is that like being a stockbroker?" I asked.

He frowned. "It's quite a step up from being a

stockbroker," he told me coldly.

I felt embarrassed that I'd insulted him without meaning to.

"Stockbrokers are just used car salesmen with better suits."

I had to laugh at his description. I didn't know any stockbrokers, but I'd met my share of slimy car salesmen. So far, it seemed this was going to be a pleasant evening after all, if I overlooked the outdated photo angle.

He smiled. I couldn't make out much from his eyes. There was no spark there. They were dull.

After glancing at the menu, which I'd almost memorized, I ordered the Chicken Fettuccine Alfredo.

"You don't really want the Alfredo. It's much too rich. The lady will have the Ensalata Regina," Jason told the waiter.

The waiter raised a questioning eyebrow in my direction. I smiled politely, biting my tongue, determined to not make a scene. My stomach turned. The waiter withdrew and Jason moved several notches up the jerk scale. With his paunch, he should be the one getting the salad, not me. I thought it but I didn't say it. I couldn't decide which was worse, his implying that I needed to diet or his trying to keep the bill down because he was paying. Either way, it was insulting. I shivered. I adjusted my sweater closed a bit more.

As the meal wore on and he downed more wine, things got worse. Jason was trying to impress me with stories of the Hollywood big shots he consulted for.

As if I give a shit.

He was getting louder as he drank more, with his glances at my breasts becoming longer and more lecherous. If any of his clients heard a recording of this conversation, they would probably fire his ass in a nanosecond. Discretion was not a word in his vocabulary.

He was the oldest of three. His two younger brothers from his mother's second marriage were MMA fighters. He got the brains, he said, and they got the brawn.

Who got the charm? Is what I wanted to ask, but didn't.

Then he implied for the second time that we would be going back to his place after dinner.

Not happening, dude.

My wine threatened to come back up. I'd said *no, thanks* already. I'd even been polite about it. He went down another notch.

He ignored me. The table next to us kept distracting him. Jason was constantly ogling the pair of giggling college-age girls with low-cut tops. He was probably trying to guess their cup sizes.

I rolled my eyes as he leered at them again. I just had to tough out another half hour to finish dinner and excuse myself.

I picked at my salad, not finding anything with any substance to it. The salad had a fancy name, but to me, it was just goat food, and not much of it at that. My date was quickly making me lose my appetite.

Jason bellowed on. He drove a Maserati.

Lame.

And he had the seats monogrammed.

Lame.

And he added a special sound system.

Lame.

I tuned him out. He mentioned for the third time that he was paying for dinner and we would be going to his place for dessert. He chuckled.

I couldn't believe it. This wasn't funny. It was getting nauseous. I decided that enough was enough. Implying that I could be bought for the price of a dinner was too much.

Screw you, Jason.

I was done here. I considered walking out but decided that there was a chance to salvage tonight if I could meet up with Steven again. I excused myself to go to the ladies' room. I half expected Steven to be waiting for me in the hallway. He wasn't.

Jason had barely noticed me leave as his head swiveled to watch the coeds giggle again.

What an ass.

In the restroom, I took out my phone.

ME: U here tonight?

STEVEN CARTER: Another moron?

ME: pls call I need out

I smiled as I turned on my ringer and returned to the table. I waited for his call to get me away from this disaster date and meet up with Steven instead. Jason was still trying to impress me with the famous people he knew.

Lame.

My phone dinged a text, which didn't faze Jason in the least.

STEVEN CARTER: Be just a minute

I only had to endure a little bit more of Mr. Monogrammed Maserati.

My Maserati blah, blah, blah, Senator, blah, blah, Hollywood, blah, blah, blah.

I started to count the references to himself as he droned on. I was up to sixteen since I had returned to the table.

* * *

Steven

I told the hostess what I wanted, and she managed to seat us out of eyesight, just behind Tiffany after they took a table.

Katie ordered us a bottle of Sauvignon Blanc. She was being a good sport about this as I listened as discreetly as I could.

I'd learned that Tiffany graduated from Santa Clara University.

The guy had no class. He was sitting across from the prettiest girl in the room and spent half his time watching two nearby half-dressed UCLA girls giggle and jiggle. When they ordered, I couldn't believe it. The dickhead changed her order from the Alfredo to salad, implying that she needed to watch her calories.

I wanted to get up and deck him, but Katie, sensing my aggravation, leaned over and whispered to me to calm down. When the dickhead started telling the whole room about his Maserati with monogrammed seats, Katie rolled her eyes and I almost burst out laughing. This went on for what seemed like forever.

I couldn't see how Tiffany had the self-control to put up with this for so long. However, she had said last week that it wouldn't be fair. She had to give the guy a chance. I waited for her to text me, but maybe she didn't know I was here. I considered sending her some kind of innocuous message but discarded the thought. I could get up and saunter by the window so she noticed me, or she might take a bathroom break to get away from this dipshit like she did last week's moron.

TIFFANY: U here tonight?

Katie's eyes lit up when my phone announced the incoming text. "That her?" she whispered.
I nodded and turned the screen so Katie could read it. I typed my response.

ME: Another moron?

TIFFANY: Pls call I need out

Katie grabbed at the phone to see the messages.

ME: Be just a minute

I'd formulated a plan this afternoon at the office, and just in case, I had called Marco to clear it with him if I wanted to implement it. It helped to be the co-owner's brother. I had also assured him that I would smooth it over with the customers so they didn't freak out.
Showtime.

* * *

Emma

"Good evening," I heard Steven say as he and his date came up from behind me with red aprons over their street clothes.

My mouth must have dropped to the floor. I'd expected a discreet phone call.

Steven bowed. "You two lucky lovebirds have just won tonight's drawing for a free wine tasting. "May I get your names, please?"

Jason was beaming. This was his lucky night. "Jason Biggs."

Quietly, I added, "Miranda Frost."

Steven paused for a few moments then made a note on his pad and raised an eyebrow to me. "Got it. Miranda and Wayson."

My eyes were drawn to Steven's. Those green eyes transfixed me again, and the evening improved one hundred percent.

"Jason," my date corrected him, snapping me out of my daze.

"Yes sir," Steven responded. "I am Steven, and the lovely Jill Masterson will be assisting me tonight." Jill nodded as Steven continued. Now I had a name to put with the pretty blonde's face. My heart sank as I realized how strikingly beautiful his date was. I'd only seen her from a distance before. I didn't recognize her from TV, but she was drop-dead Hollywood gorgeous. There was no way in hell I could compete with her. Jill had one of those faces that hardly needed makeup. Her dress under the apron certainly cost more than one of my paychecks. Her underwear probably cost more than my whole outfit.

Our previous waiter brought out four bottles of wine and glasses on a tray that he placed on a fold-out stand in the aisle. He handed Steven the corkscrew before retreating without a word. Whatever Steven had planned, it had been worked out with the staff somehow, and I was clueless. I would have to wait and see.

A questioning look crossed Jason's face. "Do I know you from somewhere?" he asked Steven.

"I don't think so, sir," Steven responded as he opened the first bottle of wine. "Perhaps the gentleman would like to tell us which of these four reds he prefers." Steven moved Jason's plate to the center of the table as he placed the four wine glasses in front of my smiling date. Being the center of attention suited Jason just fine.

Steven described the first wine as he poured out a large glass. Jason made a show swirling it, sniffing it, and tasting the wine. This was followed by two more glasses that Steven poured and Jason swigged.

Jason had no idea how silly he appeared trying to make a show of being a wine connoisseur.

Jill smiled at me and stepped in my direction, lifting several napkins off the wine tray.

As Steven poured the fourth glass, the lip of the bottle knocked the rim of the glass and the whole thing ended up in Jason's lap.

I squealed and pushed back as Jason gasped.

"Oh, so sorry." Steven fumbled with the glass. Jill quickly placed her napkins on the table, protecting me from the deluge hitting Jason.

"So sorry, Mr. Jasper. Let me help," Steven mumbled as he moved in with a napkin. The poor guy could not get out of the way as it looked like Steven's foot was behind the leg of his chair.

"You idiot," Jason screamed, drawing more than a few stares from the diners around us as he struggled to get up out of his chair.

"So sorry, Mr. Jester," Steven said, now towering over the struggling Jason.

Jason's face darkened to match the wine stains on his shirt. "It's Jason, you idiot," he yelled at Steven as he surveyed the damage to his suit. "Miranda, we're going to my place."

Fat chance that was happening.

I smiled courteously. "No, thank you."

Jill started to giggle.

Jason's eyes bugged out in disbelief. "Miranda," he pleaded.

Jason winced as Steven grabbed his arm. "I believe the lady said no," Steven told him forcefully. Steven then whispered something in Jason's ear that I couldn't hear.

Jason started mumbling to himself as Steven escorted him to the door.

Jill removed her apron and smiled at me as she offered her hand. "Name's Katie. So nice to meet you. I hope my idiot brother didn't get any on you."

My jaw went slack as I shook her hand. Her name wasn't Jill.

She was Steven's sister? Not his date?

I stood and surveyed my legs and shoes. "No, I think I'm good. Your brother?"

She laughed. "Yeah, somebody had to be his sister, and I drew the short straw."

A chill hit me. Jill Masterson was the name of the girl who got covered in gold paint in *Goldfinger.*

Steven figured out my deception.

Katie moved away from the table. "We would love it if you would join us." She moved to the table directly behind where I'd been sitting. "Trust me, he's not always this big of a klutz."

I hadn't seen them arrive.

She took a seat. Their table had three place settings but only two dinners.

Steven returned from escorting my ex-date out the door, and announced to the nearby guests, "I hope you enjoyed this evening's improvisational acting demonstration." He started to clap, and the crowd joined him for a short round of applause, and the previously shocked customers went back to their dinners, now somewhat more at ease, believing that this had all been playacting.

Steven pulled out a chair for me. "Sorry about the theatrics, but I wanted him to leave, not you," he said with a disarming smile. "I took the liberty of ordering the Fettuccine for you when Mr. numbnuts wouldn't let you have it."

I was so hypnotized by his lips as he said it that I couldn't manage a coherent response.

This man should have a warning label on his forehead.

They were seated directly behind me and had obviously overheard Jason, not that it was hard with his volume level. Not only had I been saved from another date from hell, but now I was having dinner with Steven the green-eyed hunk and his sister. On top of that, I got the Fettuccine that I'd wanted this evening.

They hadn't yet finished their dinners. He brushed his hand across my shoulder, moving behind me to reach his seat. His touch was electric and left a trail of tingles.

The heat rose in my cheeks as I glanced between them. Brother and sister. The resemblance was not close, but I could see it. Good looks certainly ran in the family.

The waiter returned with my entree. "Good job, Mr. C. That guy deserved it."

Katie and I both nodded, and Steven ignited me with his smile and those dimples again.

Katie giggled. "Monogrammed Maserati. What a

toad." She had that right.

"What did you say to him?" I asked Steven.

Steven wiped his lips with his napkin. "I just told him that if he didn't come quietly, he'd be getting blood all over his monogrammed seats."

Katie and I both laughed. I had no doubt that Steven could have made quick work of little loud-mouthed Jason.

Katie placed a hand gently on mine. "Tiffany, I haven't had this much fun in a long time, but I have to get going. Hope to see you again soon." She fixed Steven with a glare. "Now treat her right, little brother." With a wink to me and a cheek kiss to him, she was gone. She hadn't finished her dinner.

I waved to her as she left, and suddenly, it was only me and panty-melting Steven at the table.

"So, you're a *James Bond* fan?" He smirked and his dark green eyes paralyzed me in place. He stood and offered me his hand with a sincere smile. "Hello. I'm Steven, and you are…?"

I cringed. I took his hand. "Emma," I responded sheepishly.

Busted.

He pondered my answer and a smile tugged at the corners of his mouth. "Emma. That's a very beautiful name. It suits you. You shouldn't hide it."

The heat started in my chest and traveled up to my cheeks. My blush must have been obvious by now. What wasn't showing was the instant heat between my thighs. This man could make reading the dictionary sound sensual. Whereas Jason had leered at me, this man's gaze was pure admiration. I recrossed my legs.

It didn't help.

He leaned in. "Or would you like me to call you Plenty O'Toole?" He made an obvious show of shifting his eyes to my chest. "Or perhaps Pussy Galore?" He was going to have me leaking through my panties if he kept this up. This wasn't merely another guy. This was a man, and one who knew his Bond.

I pasted on my most innocent smile as I loaded some fettuccine onto my fork. "A practical girl takes precautions." Right now, practical was not a good description of what I was feeling. I recrossed my legs again.

He raised his wine glass. "So, Emma, tell me a little about yourself."

Not so fast.

I changed the subject. "Do you rescue girls from bad first dates every week?"

He took a slow, sensual sip from his wine glass before answering. "No, you're the first and only."

Fat chance.

He had no idea what he was doing to me. "Oh, then what makes me so special?" It was a bad idea. Saying the first thing that pops to mind might be good for a *Family Feud* contestant, but it was the wrong thing for a date.

Why did I think this was now a date?

He pinned me with that gaze of his. The piercing green eyes that I'd noticed in that first meeting in the hall peered straight into my soul. He pondered his answer for a moment. "I have wanted to meet you since the first time I saw you walk in here." He put his glass down. "Is that so hard to understand?"

The words took a moment to register. He had been watching me. "You don't know anything about me."

His grin expanded as the heat in my face went up a notch. "Let's remedy that, Emma." My name floated dangerously off his lips.

I took another forkful of food and chewed slowly, to calm myself, and glanced down at my plate, not answering his non-question.

"So what is a lady like you doing dining with morons?" he asked.

I finished chewing my mouthful. A lady didn't talk with her mouth full. "And just what makes you think I'm a lady?" I asked, afraid to meet his eyes.

He paused to take a sip of water. "It's not something you can hide. I know one when I meet one."

That was the best compliment I'd gotten in a long time. "Nice of you to say."

"So, what do you do when you're not out dining with morons?"

I was concentrating on eating the delicious fettuccine. "I'm an associate curator at the museum."

His eyes warmed. "Paintings or sculpture?" Was he just guessing? Or did he actually know that sculpture was a separate department from paintings?

I forked some more of my dish. "European paintings."

He quickly asked, "How did you get interested in art?" This was a complete change. The deepest question I'd gotten from my last several *SuperSingles* dates had been *What's your sign?*

I was slowly getting more at ease with this tall, imposing man. "My great-great-grandmother spent her early years in France and knew some of the painters of her day. She even sat for one. My mother also did a little painting before she got married, and I guess I thought it was in my genes. I started out as an art major in college. I had the interest but not the talent for it, so I switched to art history, with a double-major in psych."

"Interesting combination," he noted.

Interesting was not the normal response I got when people heard my choice of majors. "That was so I'd be qualified to work at Starbucks if I couldn't find a job in the art world." The line that a Psychology degree only prepared one to work at Starbucks was a common joke on campus.

He chuckled at that. "And that was at Santa Clara?"

He'd been listening.

"So, you overheard?" I asked.

He put his glass down. "More than enough to know that he was a jerk." He had that part right. Jason and Steven were as different as night and day. "The dipshit has no idea how to treat a lady."

It was the second time he had called me a lady. "And what makes you so sure I'm a lady?"

"Experience, tempered by judgment. You wasted an entire evening last week with boring Dudley Dipstick because you said it wouldn't be fair to him to cut him off too early. That, my dear, marks you as a lady." He grinned as he peered over his glass, his eyes meeting mine.

I had just been getting control of myself, and then he had to go and compliment me again. I couldn't control my blushing. "And you know how to treat a lady?" I asked coyly.

The lust in his eyes was simmering and unmistakable. His smile widened slowly but surely as his gaze fixed me in place like prey. "Just try me," he said softly. The predator in him was loose.

One word and he would devour me.

I was stricken with an intense desire to respond but helpless to come up with the words.

In an instant, it was over. The predator receded and the gentleman resurfaced. "And how do you manage to find such losers anyway?"

I had blown it.

"Well, my sister, Megan, has been coming over Monday nights to help go through the profiles on *SuperSingles.*"

"So, the sister who helped pick these losers for you? Has she managed to find a real keeper for herself?"

I almost spat out some wine with my laugh. "Not exactly."

He wore a knowing grin. "That's what I thought." He sipped his wine. "So, tell me, what are your criteria for picking out a date for the evening?"

"Criteria. Well, let's see. He needs to be honest and have a job."

"No slackers and no criminals then." He grinned. "Perhaps I should apply?"

My heart skipped a beat as I tried to hide my glee at his saying that. This man had a way of making me speechless, which was no easy feat. I recrossed my legs to try to control myself. "And, my number one rule, he can't be a lawyer."

A quizzical look crossed his face. "These criteria working well for you?" He already knew the answer.

I hesitated to admit it. "So far, no second dates."

He finished another bite of his food. "Good choice. For my money, none of those morons met the second date test," he said emphatically.

"And what test is that?" I asked.

He grinned as he picked up his glass. "For a second date, they need to be able to use their eyes to see you as a truly beautiful woman and use their ears to listen to you and learn about you as a truly wonderful person."

I could listen to this man dish out compliments like that all night long.

He sipped some wine. "But enough of them. I want to hear more about you."

I wasn't sure where to start. He already knew I went to Santa Clara. "After school, the only job I could get was as a sales associate at an art gallery. But I kept in touch with my professors from school every few months, and finally, one of them recommended me for this curator job at the museum." I started back on my meal.

"Most people don't have the tenacity to network like that."

It hadn't been easy for me. He was right about that. "Well, it paid off. This is a little museum, but at least I have my foot in the door now."

"And if you could have any job, what would that be?"

I didn't have to think to answer that one. "A senior curator at a major museum, like the National Museum in Washington. Well, actually, there are four museums on my list, including the MET in New York, the de Young in San Francisco, and the Art Institute of Chicago, and I would like to teach kids art in my spare time. That's what I'm going to do one day." That was the truth. I had a goal and I was going to get there, no matter what. I put my fork down. "Enough about me. What about you? What does Steven Carter want to be when he grows up?"

He peered down at his plate, spearing a piece of chicken. "Hard to say, exactly. I don't really like the idea of growing up."

I pointed my fork at him. "You're dodging."

His expression told me I'd hit a nerve. He hesitated before answering. "Right now, I'm just an office temp. But long-term, I want to end up helping people. That's my goal."

He didn't strike me as the office temp type. He was in a suit tonight, and not a cheap one. "An idealist?" I smiled as I picked up my glass again. "And what kind of job do you do to help people?"

"Right now," —he put his fork down— "I'm just a glorified gopher. Yesterday, I spent most of the day running packages back and forth. Today, I spent all afternoon looking over some books." He sipped some wine. "But all I saw on every page was your face, Tiffany… excuse me, Emma."

He was thinking of me and we hadn't even really met yet. That was either very cute, or he was serious stalker material.

A twinkle played in his eyes. "But I didn't know I was two names behind."

I learned that Steven and I both knew a lot of Bond trivia. Both of his parents were dead, and he was the youngest of five in his family, with three older brothers, Bill, Liam, and Patrick, and his sister, Katherine, whom I'd met earlier. He had an easygoing way about him, and unlike my last several dates, he seemed to have a genuine interest in me and what I had to say. As things went on, I learned he understood more about Impressionism and Post-Impressionism, which were my focus areas, than any non-art history person I'd met. His favorite artist was Renoir, as was mine. We talked about the museum's holdings and the gaps we had in our exhibits. He seemed quite interested in the museum.

Dinner with Steven had been easily the most stimulating time I'd had since, well, forever. Everything about him dripped testosterone, powerful but at the same time gentle, and he was interested in having a true conversation with me. The way he subtly devoured me with his eyes while remaining ever the gentleman was both intimidating and intoxicating. Twice, brief flashes of the predator showed in his eyes, but the gentleman quickly returned each time.

I'd finished my plate and was working on my fourth glass of wine, or maybe more. I lost count. "So, you have dinner here every week with your sister?"

He fiddled with the stem of his glass as a gentle smile formed. "Yeah, Katie and I have dinner most every Tuesday, and I've convinced my two local brothers, Bill and Patrick, to alternate meeting me here on Thursdays. Sort of my way of trying to hold us all together as a family since Dad died. Half the time, Bill threatens that he has too much work to make it, but I usually end up shaming him into it when he's in town." He really cared about his family in a very genuine way.

"And why here?" I asked.

He pointed around the room. "My brother Bill put this together. He's one of the owners." That tidbit explained how he'd gotten the staff to go along with his earlier charade. He had spilled wine on the floor, after all.

"I thought you said he worked and traveled."

He finished a bite. "I did, and he does. He and his friend Marco Cardinelli started this place, but since Dad died, Bill had to take on a real job, or at least that's the way Dad would have put it. So now, Marco runs this place, and Bill is just a co-owner."

I ended up filling him in a little on my mom and dad up north and my sister here in LA as we talked on. He told me stories of his childhood with his brothers and sister and summers spent backpacking in Yosemite. He laughed about the time they'd left their food too low and had it devoured by a determined bear. They'd had to hike all day with no food to get back to the main road.

We ordered gelato for dessert. I watched the slow way he sucked on the spoon as he took each bite. I couldn't help but visually undress him for the hundredth time. Everything he did made me hot and wet. I could hear my mother's voice tell me a lady lets the man make the first move. But what if I didn't feel like waiting forever? I had moved my hand to the middle of the table more than once, just short of reaching to touch him, but I hadn't gotten a response.

Before I knew it, the dining room was emptying and only one other couple remained.

"If Jasper Bigsnot drove you, I can offer a ride home."

I laughed at the way he twisted Jason's name. "No, I was smart enough to drive myself."

He rose and offered me his hand.

Finally, a touch. It was electric, sending more signals of lust straight to my core.

Get a grip, Emma.

I let him help me up, and after a few wobbly steps, I regretted the last glass or two of wine.

He put his arm around my waist and pulled me to his side to steady me. After we got out the door, he said, "I'll need your keys." His tone was commanding, not requesting.

"I can drive myself," I protested.

He squeezed my waist. "I always see that a date

gets home safely. Sort of a policy of mine."

Wow. He said I was his date.

I located the keys in my purse without any difficulty as we ambled toward the valet. I wasn't really that drunk. It must have been the heels.

He took the keys from me. "Tony, could you please do me a favor and follow me in the lady's car? I'll give you a ride back."

Tony drove my car. Steven helped me into his. After a little coaxing, Siri started giving him directions.

True to his word, Steven walked with me up to the door of my little apartment. As I fumbled with my keys, my eyes found his, waiting for him to make his move.

Hoping.

He smiled innocently.

I ignored my mother's advice about letting the man make the first move and stepped toward him.

That was all the invitation he needed. He pulled me into him. One arm snaked around my waist and the other behind my head as his mouth met mine. He pulled me closer and took control of the kiss. His tongue searched out mine, stroking me, teasing me, claiming me, and lighting my blood on fire as fireworks exploded behind my eyelids. He tasted of wine and pleasure and need. My breasts pressed to his chest as his hand followed my lower back to cradle my ass and pull me against him. His grip was firm, insistent, and powerful.

I melded my body to his. The heat of his body threatened to ignite me. Heat pooled between my thighs as his growing erection pressed against me. He smelled of spice and maleness. I'd been kissed by boys before, but never like this. This was a new experience. A man. A man with a hint of animal.

Things are going too fast.

Then, it didn't matter. I held him tighter. I twined my fingers in his hair as I held on for dear life. My heart was thundering against my ribcage. I relished the heat of him against me, the rod of his arousal pressing against my abdomen, the scrape of his stubble on my cheek. The smell of his hair. The taste of desire on his tongue. Time slowed, and the world dropped away as I was more drunk by the kiss than the wine. It didn't matter that we were in the hallway… nothing mattered, so long as he held me.

When he broke the kiss, I may have whimpered a bit. Things were fuzzy as passion clouded my brain.

How had I gotten so lucky?

In the space of a few hours, the night that started with another first date from hell had ended with the kiss to define all kisses. I held on tightly, my head pressed into his shoulder, not wanting to let go for fear that I would wake up and it would all have been a dream.

I trembled as his thumb traced the underside of

my breast.

He brought his hand to my face.

I pushed into his touch.

He lifted my chin with a finger.

I went weak as I gazed up into those luscious green eyes, awash with passion and desire.

"I think I'll call you Sugar. You taste so sweet." Then, he pushed me away. "Off to bed now, Sugar." His actions suddenly sent the opposite signal of the bulge in his pants. He kissed me on the forehead and turned me toward my door.

Somehow, I'd screwed this up.

Why didn't he want to come in? Was I a bad kisser? Maybe I should have squeezed his ass or grabbed for his belt buckle? But it was too late. He backed away down the hallway. "Is it okay if I call you, Sugar?"

"Sure," I mumbled as I turned the key in the lock.

He kept his eyes on me until I got the door open and went inside.

Once behind my door in the empty apartment, the loneliness hit me. I never felt lonely in my little apartment. It was my castle, my refuge from the world outside.

I grabbed a handful of M&Ms from the bowl on the counter. Things were too fuzzy to sort out right now. Move over, Tiffany, Miranda, and Emma. Here comes Sugar.

"Sugar," I repeated out loud to the empty room. *Sugar. I could get used to that.*

CHAPTER THREE

Emma

I hit it so hard my hand hurt. I'd gotten my annoying alarm clock to shut up on the first strike. Rubbing my eyes, I was waking up alone in bed again. I'd screwed up last night somehow. Not that I was a first date girl, but it had been a long time since I'd broken up with Todd. And that kiss, oh, my God, that kiss.

Todd. Just the thought of that lying, cheating sack of shit made me want to hit something. I stumbled toward the bathroom. My tongue felt like it was covered in fur and my head was throbbing. I should have switched to white wine last night. Red almost always gave me a next-day headache. The visage in the mirror looked considerably better than I felt right now.

After Tylenol and a shower, I was ready to face another day. Replaying last night in my head, I couldn't help but feel better. Lecherous Jason had taken a hike and been replaced by my green-eyed protector, Steven.

His last words hit me. "Can I call you Sugar?" Had he meant call me, call me, like on the phone? Or, had he meant call me 'Sugar' as a name? This morning, I wasn't sure anymore. I plugged in my phone, and after a minute, it told me I had a missed call.

I crossed my fingers and peeked.

Shit.

It was my sister's number. I'd left it on silent and missed her call last night. Probably checking on how the date with Jason went. She was so sure he would be the one. So far, she was zero for five in helping to pick those losers. I giggled. Steven had asked the right question. If Megan couldn't find a keeper for herself, how was she ever going to help me?

Megan was living with Braydon, of all people. Braydon, who had given her a baseball hat with a beer can holder attached to it for Christmas. He told her it was so he had a place to put his beer while she gave him a blowjob. What a jerk. She had laughed it off. She said he was crude, but at least he was her crude boyfriend.

How had her standards gotten so low?

Checking my phone further, I found that she had also texted me last night to set up lunch today, obviously eager to get the gossip on last night with Jason. I laughed to myself as I remembered Steven's name for him, Mr. Bigsnot.

* * *

This morning was a light day at the museum. Not much going on until Janice, my boss, handed a phone call off to me. "It's William Covington. He asked for you by name," she whispered, giving me the phone as if it was too hot to handle.

That was weird. I was so far down the org chart you'd need a telescope to find me. I put down the brown M&M that was destined for my mouth. Nobody called and asked for me. Nobody. I knew Mr. Covington's name, of course. Everybody at the museum did, but I'd never met him.

He had caused quite a sensation at last year's fundraiser. He had arranged for his date to win a prize at the end of the silent auction, and when she opened it, it was a magnificent engagement ring. He proposed to her right in front of the whole crowd. A true Cinderella moment. I had cried. Probably all the women in attendance cried. He was a true romantic, that one, and a big donor to the museum. He was also a personal friend of our Chairman, Mr. Benson.

Once on the phone, Mr. Covington asked if I could come by his office this afternoon to see a painting he wanted to loan to us. I agreed and made a note of the Covington building's address.

Janice was excited to hear the news.

"Why did he call you?" she asked.

"Not a clue," I told her. That was the truth. It bugged me for the rest of the morning.

Why me? I'd never met the man.

When I arrived for lunch with Megan, she had already ordered a burger for me with deep-fried green beans, her idea of healthy eating. I went to the counter and added a portion of real fries to the order. She could keep her green beans.

"You have this Cheshire Cat shit-eating grin on your face, so let's hear it. How was he?" She meant Jason, naturally.

I sat down. "Jason was a loser, even worse than last week. He changed my dinner order to a salad, then he goes and spends half the evening ogling a couple of college girls at the next table who were constantly bouncing up and down in their low-cut tops." I giggled and bounced in my seat to show her.

Megan laughed. "Well, you've got what it takes, Emm. It wouldn't hurt you to show a little cleavage yourself, you know." That was Megan's style. Low-cut tops, and even lower standards, had always gotten her laid. But was ending up with a guy like Braydon worth it?

Not for me.

Megan was right. I had curves, and I had a few Victoria's Secret push-up bras, but that didn't seem right for a first date, and my top last night hadn't been that baggy. "I wasn't the problem. He was," I told her.

She sipped her drink. "Well, you must be doing something wrong if you keep striking out." Megan didn't get it.

"I didn't strike out with Jason last night. I couldn't get past the yuck factor. You only strike out if you try to land a second date and can't." I smiled, remembering that the night hadn't ended poorly after all. "In the end, it turned out okay."

"I thought you said he was a bust. What are you holding back on your big sister?"

Lunch had arrived, and I started with a fry. "He was, but Steven wasn't."

She grew a mischievous grin. "And who is Steven?"

I laid it out for her as we ate our burgers. I told her about texting him and how he and his sister came to the table pretending to offer wine tasting and ended up giving Jason a wine bath.

Megan laughed. She agreed that the part with the wine was hilarious.

I told her that Steven and I spent the rest of the evening together, almost to closing time, and that I had enjoyed it so much. I described Steven to her, his mesmerizing green eyes, his chiseled features, the muscles, and the shoulders of Atlas.

"And?" she coaxed.

"And I was a little tipsy, so he drove me home."

"And? Tell me about the juicy part."

"What juicy part?"

"Tell me about the naked part." Megan could be so crass.

I looked away and grabbed a few fries. "We didn't get that far."

Shock registered on her face. "So, how far did you get?"

I continued chewing my fries, too embarrassed to answer. "We kissed." I didn't tell her that it was an earth-shattering kiss, at least in my book.

She frowned. "Sis, you've gotta up your game. Put your hand down his pants while he's kissing you and squeeze his cock. It gets 'em every time. Or at least rub him through his jeans. A guy wants you to want him. You've gotta make it obvious."

I checked my watch. I couldn't be late to the Covington Building, and this was about enough dating advice from my slutty sister for one day. "Have to go, Sis. I have to meet a potential donor in a little while."

She finished off the last green bean. "So you want my help next Monday?"

I got up. "No, thanks. I'll see where this goes first."

"Don't forget the pointers next time. Use your

hands."

I shook my head as I made my way back to my car. I checked my phone. My heart sank. Still no call or text from Steven. Megan was right. I need to up my game and take charge. I decided to go bold and text him first. After all, I'd instigated the kiss and that worked out.

ME: How's your day going?

I reached the Covington building twenty minutes later. My phone's message screen was still blank.
Was I being too pushy?
Maybe Steven didn't like pushy. I heard a lot of guys didn't, but there was no way to undo the text now.

Inside the building, I asked the guard at the desk for William Covington, the CEO of the mammoth company. That got me an invitation to wait for an escort up the elevator to the top floor. I straightened my suit and checked my lipstick. I checked my phone again. Still no response from Steven.

Jimmy from marketing came down to meet me. Mr. Covington's assistant was out at the moment so he had been sent to fetch me.

The office was huge, with a large oak desk, some chairs, a couch, and a separate small meeting table with its own set of chairs. William Covington stepped out from behind the desk to greet me. He was tall and just as handsome as I recalled from last year, with a vise grip of a handshake. "I would like to make a loan to the museum," he said matter-of-factly. He pointed to two paintings laid out on a meeting table near the window. The man was all business, but I guessed that was what to expect from the CEO of a big company like Covington. He thanked Jimmy, who waited outside.

Both paintings were Monets. I assumed he wanted me to pick. I remembered both of these works from my art history courses. They hadn't been seen in public for decades. Either one would make a great addition to our Impressionist room. They were similar in size and period, one a little older than the other. I glanced out the floor-to-ceiling window for a moment. If I had a view of the city like this, I wouldn't get a lot of work done.

"What do you think?" he asked.

I leaned over to inspect them. "I think they are magnificent. Which one were you thinking?" I was leaning toward the earlier one.

"Both, unless you don't have room."

I gasped. Nobody loaned us two grand master paintings at a time. Any museum that couldn't make room for a Claude Monet painting didn't deserve the title. "I'm sure we have room."

"I thought your impressionist exhibit could use some Monets." That was true. We only had one small one, and we were also lacking a respectable Degas. "And they are just gathering dust at the house." He made it sound like he had them stacked in a closet, and maybe he did.

To say Janice would be thrilled to get these was an understatement. She would go bonkers. I would have to peel her off the ceiling. "I can arrange to get them packed and picked up tomorrow, if that's okay," I said.

"Nonsense, Emma. Judy will get them wrapped and carried down to your car."

No way.

I shuddered. I couldn't carry a few million dollars' worth of paintings in my shitty little car. That was a really bad idea. "I think we should have the professionals move them."

He waved the suggestion away. "I need the table space this afternoon. You do have a car, don't you?"

"Yes, but..."

"Then it's settled." The man was clearly used to getting his way. He called Jimmy in and gave him instructions to get the paintings packed up right away as I scribbled out a receipt longhand for him. "Oh, and one more thing, Emma, if you have a few minutes to spare. My uncle Garth also has something for the museum that he'd like you to consider."

I was dumbfounded. Two grand masters and he

wanted me to look at something else. I thanked him profusely.

Jimmy led me through the halls to Mr. Covington's uncle's office.

Garth Durham, it turned out, was the company's CFO. He had a beautiful Degas on his wall that he wanted to loan to the museum as well. He mumbled something about it being in the way. The office was neat and spartan, with a lot of space. I couldn't see how the painting got in the way, but we didn't look a gift horse in the mouth. And just like that, Jimmy had their shipping people wrapping three priceless grand master paintings and packing them in the back seat of my dirty Camry. Janice was going to shit a brick when she saw these and learned that I'd driven them myself.

I guessed that arguing with William Covington would be an even bigger mistake than driving the paintings over. He was in tight with Lloyd Benson, who was Chairman of the Board of Directors of our museum. It was clearly safer to take my chances with Janice than to piss off a friend of Mr. Benson.

I drove like a ninety-year-old to the loading dock at the back of the museum and called ahead to get security to meet me. I didn't call Janice. I asked the shipping guys to be ultra-careful getting them upstairs to our office and to unpack them there.

As expected, Janice was beside herself and called the Director down to see the pieces I had *snagged*, as she put it.

I was an instant star. The Director asked us to get the pieces properly cleaned so they could go up promptly. As he left, he mumbled something about calling Mr. Benson right away.

The afternoon went by slowly as I kept checking my phone. Still nothing from Steven. A dull ache rose in my chest.

I should have waited for him to call me.

A lady would have waited.

* * *

Steven

I contemplated Emma as I stood under the blast of hot water from my shower head. Last night worked out both better and worse than I'd hoped. Better in that I got to save Tiffany, who turned out to be Miranda, who turned out to be Emma, from her latest mistake of a date, Mr. Bigsnot. And worse in that I only got a kiss out of it, but what a kiss. It was clear that a fire smoldered under the surface in that woman. I just needed a chance to uncover it. My dick came quickly to attention as that thought morphed into removing the clothes that covered that luscious body and admiring what lay beneath. I'd been fooled before, but she didn't appear to have dyed her hair. How inviting would that red bush look, or did she shave? That question was going to linger with me all day.

All dinner long, Emma had continued to amaze me. She was not only a very intelligent woman, but considerate and sexy as hell, although she didn't seem to know it. The way those deep blue eyes burned into me was almost painful. The way her long red hair framed her ivory face with those sultry eyes made her an exquisite sight. And those curves, curves that were meant to be held. I couldn't wait to take the softness of her breasts in my hands, to pull that ass close to me. Last night, my cock had swelled with anticipation all night long.

I'd made a mistake in not rationing her wine, though. She obviously couldn't hold her liquor. Being drunk put her off limits for the night. I did not, and would not, take advantage of a drunk woman, no matter how much she wanted it or how much I wanted or needed it.

Heeding Katie's advice had been difficult. Going slow was not my style. I had waited for Emma to give me some indication that she wanted at least a kiss, and by her door, she finally did. The kiss had been fantastic. She dressed demurely, but underneath that calm exterior was passion, a hunger for more, and I was going to give it to her.

I'd altered my usual schedule since she came into my life, or more accurately, since I saw her and wished she were in my life. Emma kept finding a way back into my mind. My little black book was stashed in a drawer and I was on a sex diet. My usual allotment of three or four dates per week had flat-lined at zero. My usual fast approach worked well with other women, and when it didn't, I instantly moved on to the next opportunity. They were all different, yet all the same. They giggled, they laughed, they fucked, and they left, some more willingly than others. However, none of them grabbed my attention for longer than a week or three. They were all so plastic. Not that they all had boob jobs, but they all seemed so phony underneath. I wasn't into one-night stands. It took longer than that to truly enjoy the talents a woman had to offer. The complication was that if they lasted for more than a night or two, they would learn my last name. That's when things always changed. That's why my cards had only my first and middle name. Not a lie, merely less than the complete truth. Being a single Covington was a blessing and a curse. Getting women had always been easy, but they always changed when they learned the name. They were no longer themselves. Men's brains were wired to chase beautiful women. Women's brains, it seemed, were wired to chase rich men.

There was something about Emma. At first, it was her face, her gait, her smile, and her laugh, and then it became the snippets of conversation I could overhear, but now it was much more. I needed to experience Emma, and I couldn't risk being shot down. I didn't want to move on to the next opportunity. I wanted her. If I moved quickly and scared her off, it would be painful.

Katie's observation that I looked like Bill when he met Lauren was scary. Bill had fallen hard for Lauren, and I'd learned that it almost killed him when she called off the engagement and disappeared. In the end, he got her back and had become the happiest I'd ever seen him, but the experience came close to breaking him.

Katie had a sixth sense. Katie called me when Bill started dating Lauren. She predicted that Lauren was the one. I hadn't met Lauren yet, so I blew it off at the time as stupid sister gossip. Katie had also been the one who had warned me about Victoria, a warning I didn't heed at the time and later wished I had.

* * *

I loosened my tie and switched off my phone before passing through security. This morning, I was assigned to assist in criminal court. We were handling the defense for Micah Goldsmith. He was accused of murdering his wife and daughter. It was a gruesome case that had made all the headlines. Today was the just the prelim to see if he would be held over for trial.

If the newspapers had their facts right, he was headed to trial and prison, or worse. Goldsmith had plenty of money and he could afford us. Monica had been overjoyed when she landed him as a client because he was going to be both high-profile and high-paying. Too often, the clients with the highest profile cases couldn't afford us, and the firm had to take them on at a greatly reduced rate or pass on them.

My job amounted to lugging boxes of files into court just in case we needed something and getting things set up before Monica waltzed in with Lenny, one of the firm's associates, in tow. She hardly did anything without Lenny as her backup. I couldn't see how everything I was lugging was related to the case, probably just for show to make the client feel he was getting something for all the hours he was being billed. That fit Monica's style.

This was a prelim, so there was no jury. Just us and the prosecutors facing Judge Vinson. That birthmark on his balding head and the hooked nose made the old judge appear sinister.

The gallery was filled with press types eager to hear any sordid details that came out.

Monica and the prosecutor started arguing motions in front of the judge. Today was going to be too boring for words.

After a few wasted hours, I switched on my phone at the lunch break. A message from my brother said that things were on track, but there was nothing from Emma. I considered calling her but decided against it and switched my phone back off. At least I'd avoided lunch with Monica. She was too busy babysitting the client.

Anything for more billable hours.

Several more wasted hours and it was over for the day. I gathered up my carload of boxes and headed back to the office. I switched on my phone as I started up the car and found a message from Emma that she had sent after our lunch break.

TIFFANY: How's your day going?

When I got back to the office, I would need to change her contact info to Emma now that I had her real name.

ME: Boring how about u

TIFFANY: Pretty hectic.

Back at the office with a hundred plus pounds of papers safely back upstairs, I checked my phone again. I hadn't gotten another text from Emma. It wasn't like me to be sweating this. I was always in charge, always setting the tempo. There were always more fish in the sea. Until now. I smiled as I updated her contact in my phone and contemplated what to do next. I settled on the one thing I was pretty sure we had in common. A movie night might be the right low-key way to start with her.

ME: Would Tiffany Case like to join me for some Bond - Diamonds are Forever

ME: Or would Miranda Frost like Die Another Day

I waited.

CHAPTER FOUR

Emma

I let out a huge breath. He had finally responded.

STEVEN CARTER: Would Tiffany Case like to join me for some Bond - Diamonds are Forever

STEVEN CARTER: Or would Miranda Frost like Die Another Day

I hadn't blown it after all.

ME: Either one. Where are they playing?

A minute later, I got the answer I was hoping for.

STEVEN CARTER: My place or I can bring the dvds to yur place u choose

I knew Megan would tell me to go to his place, so I did the opposite.

ME: How about my place?

STEVEN CARTER: Pizza or Chinese

ME: Pizza

STEVEN CARTER: On the way

Just like that, I had graduated from *SuperSingles* losers to movie night with a real man. I had no idea where he lived, but pizza had to take some time. This was pizza and a movie, so I needed to be casual. After a quick shower and light makeup, I chose some skinny jeans with sandals and a cute red top. I checked myself in the mirror. I undid another button. My toes needed to be repainted, but I didn't have time for that. I checked and rechecked my makeup. It had been less than a day but I was jittery with anticipation. I popped two M&Ms in my mouth as I waited for the knock on the door.

Steven arrived, his hands full with two pizzas, a bag from *DessertMagic*, and a half-dozen classic Bond movie DVDs. I was a little disappointed that he didn't make a move to kiss me when he entered. I sure would have enjoyed starting with a replay of last night.

His eyes appraised me. His smile told me he liked what he saw. "You look beautiful, Sugar." He put the pile down on the counter. "I didn't know what kind of pizza you like, so we have four choices here."

I got out some plates, glasses, and a bottle of wine I had chilled in the fridge, white this time, while Steven loaded a movie. We filled our plates and settled into the couch as Shirley Bassey started belting out the title song of *Diamonds are Forever*, a Sean Connery classic. Steven sat enticingly close to me, but not quite touching.

"Nice horse. Yours?" he asked, pointing to the picture of Lady and me on the wall.

"Yeah, that's Lady, the best Quarter horse in the state. She's retired now, hanging out in the barn at my folks' place." Daddy had taken it years ago of Lady nuzzling me in the barn. It was my favorite picture of her.

Steven asked about my day as the action began. As we ate, I filled him in on the sequence of events leading up to picking up the three loaner paintings at the Covington building and how they would augment our Impressionist collection.

"And what did you tell your sister about your date last night?"

As I told him about my day, I'd mentioned that we met for lunch but not anything else. "What?" I asked innocently.

70

He cocked an eyebrow. "You heard me, Sugar. You told me last night that Megan helped you" — he put air quotes around *helped*— "pick out those losers every Monday night. So you have lunch the day after, and she's not going to interrogate you?"

He had a point there. I'd told him about Megan's help last night. "Well, okay, I did tell her about Jason being a total loser." I finished my glass of wine. Steven was still working on his.

"Sugar, what else did you tell her?"

I got up and went to the kitchen. "Want another piece of pepperoni?" I refilled my wine glass.

"No, thanks. You know what I think? I think you told your sister about us, and you told her not to help you next Monday."

The heat rose in my cheeks and I couldn't keep a straight face. "You might have come up." I wasn't going to repeat Megan's advice under any circumstances. I returned to the couch and sat down next to him, our thighs and shoulders touching. The heat of his body through the fabric took my attention off the movie. I drank some more of my wine to cool off.

He turned and took the wine glass out of my hand. I'd downed half the contents since I'd poured it. "You've had your limit for tonight, Sugar."

I reached for the glass, but he kept it out of reach. "You're cutting me off?"

"That's right, Sugar. I don't want to take

advantage of a drunk lady."

He wants to take advantage of me? Sign me up.

Did that mean he left last night after just a kiss because he thought I was too drunk?

He placed his arm around behind me and pulled me into his side.

This was getting encouraging. I laid my head on his shoulder as we watched Sean Connery take on the bad guys. It seemed so right to have him here, his arm around me. My nipples hardened with anticipation. I closed my eyes and took in his intoxicating spicy male scent, feeling the rhythm of his breathing and the warmth of his body against mine.

His hand started to play with my hair and scratch my scalp, sending naughty tingles down my neck.

I placed a hand on his thigh and traced small circles on his jeans with my finger.

He leaned over and kissed the top of my head.

I was losing my self-control. He was teasing me, so close and yet so far. I snuggled closer as Sean Connery had another close call on the small screen.

"Ready for dessert, Sugar?" He didn't wait for my answer. He got up and went to the counter and opened the bag he had brought from DessertMagic. He pulled something out that I couldn't see and put it on a plate. "Close your eyes."

I did as he asked. The couch shifted as he sat. The movie was too loud for me to hear him moving about.

"Open up."

I opened my mouth and was rewarded with a spoonful of chocolaty goodness. It was decadently sweet and smooth. I opened my eyes as I sucked the spoon clean. He had gotten a piece of chocolate frosted chocolate layer cake with a strawberry filling between the layers.

He ate a spoonful and fed me another. It was yummy beyond description. "You need to get your daily dose of Vitamin C. 'C' for chocolate, that is." He put the dessert down on the end table next to him. "To properly enjoy this, you need to be lying down." He slowly pulled me over to lie on my back with my shoulders on his lap and my head propped up by his arm.

The throb of his cock against my back sent shockwaves all the way to my core. He had barely touched me and I was tingly all over. His eyes sparkled as they lingered on my cleavage. I was completely at his mercy.

He fed me a spoonful at a time. We traded little bites of the cake.

I sucked the spoon clean each time, as did he. As I watched him take each spoonful, I couldn't help picturing how those lips would feel sucking on me.

Another spoonful approached my mouth slowly as the hand behind my neck caressed my shoulder. As he removed the spoon, his arm brushed my breast again. My nipples pebbled even harder. His spell enveloped me. It suddenly struck me. He was seducing me. I'd never been treated like this. It was intoxicating. With his methodical gentleness, he was slowly ramping up my tension to an unbearable level as heat pooled between my legs. This was completely foreign. In college, seduction had meant a guy putting his hand under my shirt and starting on my back instead of moving directly to my breasts.

After several more spoonfuls, Steven playfully missed my mouth and got some of the chocolate on my cheek. "Oops," he mouthed.

I giggled like a high school girl.

He put the spoon down. "Hold still." He leaned over and licked the chocolate off my face. His free hand slid under my top, resting on my stomach and gently caressing the underside of my breast through my bra, scorching my skin with every stroke. "How did you like the cake?"

"Loved it." His lips drew me like a magnet. I curled my hand around his neck and pulled him down for a kiss.

His lips claimed mine as our tongues began a dance of their own. His cock surged beneath me. His hand came up to cradle my breast as he rubbed the bare skin above the bra line with his thumb, his touch leaving a trail of hot tingles behind.

I pulled myself up a little as I speared my hand

through his hair and pressed my mouth to his. It was impossible to keep the kiss simple and short, impossible to stop.

He effortlessly gathered me up in his arms and lifted me off the couch and set me back down lengthwise, lying beside me. He pinched and released the hooks at the back of my bra through my top as his tongue ravaged mine, and he moved to cup my breast in his hand, teasing my nipple with his thumb. Our mouths were still locked together, our tongues searching out each other and dueling for position.

He tasted of chocolate, white wine, and sex. His hair and neck smelled of a maleness and a spice that I couldn't place. The scent lit my body up. The explosions from the TV were in the background, but the predominant sounds were of the blood rushing through my veins and his breathing as the kiss grew more sensual, more tingly, more intense, more all-consuming.

He pulled away from my lips. "You're making it very hard to be a gentleman." His eyes were on fire with lust. He unbuttoned my top and I wiggled out of it.

I fumbled to work the buttons on his shirt with a single hand. I giggled. "Hard is good, but who needs a gentleman?"

He lifted up and pulled his shirt off, and we were skin to skin as he pulled my bra free.

I clawed at his back as we renewed the kiss, and his hand came to my breasts, cupping them, massaging them, and rolling my hardened, sensitive nipples between his thumb and forefinger, sending shockwaves through me.

He broke the kiss to move his mouth to my breasts, his tongue circling my nipple seductively, sucking on one nipple, followed by the other. His breath on my skin was hot as one hand moved between my thighs, urging my legs apart, while the other left my shoulder to trace over the top and side of my breast.

I whimpered in response. I finally took Megan's advice and rubbed his cock through his pants. The reaction was immediate. He quickly unbuttoned and unzipped my jeans, pushing them down enough to gain access to my mound. His hand slid inside my panties, and his fingers slid through my curls and started gliding along the length of my wet folds again and again, dipping a finger slightly into my entrance and back to circle my clit. He circled and teased my clit as I rubbed his cock through his jeans.

I arched my hips to get more pressure on my sensitive little bean, but he withdrew and continued to circle and tease, making me wetter by the minute. He continued to caress my breasts and lick and suck at my nipples as a finger entered me, slowly in and out and around, farther and farther. His thumb found my clit. He alternated kissing and sucking my nipples and then blowing softly, the cool air bringing shivers to my wet skin. A second long finger joined the first as he stretched me and continued circling my clit with his thumb.

I pressed into his hand, finally getting more pressure as he worked his thumb over and around my swollen bud, bringing me closer and closer to the edge. I clawed at his back and tried to pull him closer, but his mouth stayed focused on my breasts and kissing my chest, moving occasionally to my collarbone and my neck.

He pulled my chest to his as he sucked and bit lightly on my earlobe, his breath loud in my ear. He increased his pressure and tempo on my sensitive nub as he pushed me over the edge.

I was gasping for air, my pussy clenching on his fingers, my body spasming as he held me tightly. The waves of pleasure crashed over me, one after another, lights flashed against my closed eyelids, blood rushed in my ears, as I was helpless in front of the onslaught of my climax and the tremors in my core, an orgasm unlike any I'd experienced before.

I'd been with boys before, but never like this. In college, they had wanted to finger me and squeeze my breasts on the way to getting into my pants, but they were certainly all clitoral knowledge challenged. I had tried to teach Todd, but he was only interested in getting me on all fours so he could do me doggy style, and that never lasted long.

Steven pulled his hand from my pussy and gently stroked the hair out of my eyes and behind my ear. I could smell myself on his fingers. He smiled down at me, his green eyes glistening as he moved to kiss me again. A gentle, sensuous kiss. His fingers continued to stroke my ear as I relaxed in his embrace, my breasts pillowed against his massive chest. He broke the kiss and licked his fingers. "Sweet as sugar."

I giggled, lacing my fingers through his hair, and pulled him down for another kiss, tasting a bit of me on his mouth as I renewed my massaging of his hard cock through his jeans. I pulled at his belt buckle, unable to loosen it.

He knelt beside the couch. I thought he would undo his belt, but instead, he pulled off my jeans.

I kicked my sandals free. My panties followed, and I was completely naked to him.

He nudged my legs open and his eyes conveyed pure lust as they traveled every inch of my body. "You are even more beautiful naked than I imagined."

I should have been embarrassed that I was totally naked with my legs spread and the lights on in front a man I'd only really met yesterday, but instead, I felt oddly proud of the compliment. "We would have more room on the bed," I offered with a smile as I fixed my eyes on the bulging erection in his pants and reached for his belt buckle again.

He used the remote to switch off the TV and lifted me from the couch like I was a feather, which I definitely was not, and carried me to the bedroom.

I clung to his neck, breathing in his manly, spicy scent. He placed me gently on the bed and stood next to it as I attacked the belt buckle again, this time successfully, and unbuttoned his pants.

I was not prepared for what sprang out as I pushed his pants and his boxer briefs down. Now I understood what they meant by the phrase *well-hung*. I didn't have a lot of experience, but his cock was huge, a lot bigger than Todd's, but a lot of things were bigger than Todd's wiener. A whole lot of things. That was probably why he always turned the lights off. Steven's girth surprised me. I worried that I might not be able to take him in. I reached for him and stroked his gorgeous cock, pulling on it to get him to come closer.

He lay down beside me.

I teased the tip as I spread the drop of pre-cum over the dark pink crown. I was treated to Steven's soft moan.

His lips had reclaimed my breast, his fingers once again parting my folds.

"Does this feel good?" I asked as I clasped with both hands.

"Better than good. Way better."

After the way he'd made me come, I would do anything he wanted. Anything.

He was fingering me again and playing wonderful music on my clit. His lips worked one breast and then the other.

I continued to pull and stroke and twist, listening to his subtle groans as a guide of what to do, but I was losing the ability to concentrate on pleasing him.

He sent shivers through me with each twist of his fingers inside me. He paid equal attention to my swollen little nub as his fingers alternated with his thumb. He blew on my nipples after he kissed them, making each harder than before.

I had never really enjoyed having a guy play with my breasts as much before, but none of them had been as gentle and attentive as Steven was.

He kissed my ear and blew in it gently. Every little thing he did was better than the last.

I stroked his cock harder and more rapidly as his pressure on my clit increased and I neared another climax. I imagined his massive cock banging into me deeper than any man had before, and the image sent me quickly over the edge. Lights exploded, and my walls convulsed around his fingers again and again. My head was spinning as he pressed hard on my clit with each spasm of my climax and the surges rattled my bones. I cried out his name, unable to control myself. I had to let go of his cock and pull him closer as the spasms overtook me, exhausting me, leaving me breathless.

Now I understood the term *magic fingers*.

He had made me come twice, and I hadn't even gotten to feel his cock yet. He pulled his hand up and licked his fingers.

I guess that's his thing.

The way he licked my juices off them was fucking sexy as all hell.

I kissed him, again getting a taste of me on his tongue, as I tried to control my breathing.

I think this is going to be my new thing.

I didn't have any condoms. The guys had always provided those, and if I'd bought some, I wouldn't have known to get a Double-XL or whatever it took to sheathe Steven. Todd was always in danger of having the condom slip off. I hoped that Steven had brought one, or maybe a half dozen, the way the night was going. I pushed him over onto his back, which was not easy given that he was so much bigger and stronger than me. "Your turn." I straddled him.

He cradled the weight of my breasts in his big hands, massaging them with his thumbs.

My phone rang. It was the distinctive ringtone I'd assigned to Megan. I didn't care what she wanted right now. I had something I wanted. "It'll go to voicemail," I assured him as I slid my pussy over the length of his cock. The tip drove me crazy as I slid my clit over it again and again. Steven's huge smile and the fire in his eyes told me that sliding my wetness over his cock like this was driving him nuts.

He kneaded my breasts and pushed them together. He took a nipple in his mouth, teasing me.

The phone started up again. I ignored it. I pushed his head down so I could kiss him, gliding my slick slit over his rock hard cock some more. The phone went silent and then started up again. She never kept calling like this. "I'm gonna kill her," I mumbled.

"Who?" Steven asked as he tucked my hair behind my ear.

"My sister," I answered.

Steven pushed me up forcefully. "Family comes first. Always. Take it. I'm not going anywhere."

Megan's timing sucks.

CHAPTER FIVE

Steven

The phone call couldn't have come at a worse time. My cock was hard enough to drill granite. Emma was teasing me by rubbing her slick pussy along my length as I cupped her tits. She had the most marvelous soft mounds of real woman, no surgical enhancement here, topped with luscious pink nipples that hardened willingly. She made wondrous little whimpering sounds as I kissed them and blew on them.

When she told me it was her sister calling, I insisted she take the call. "Family comes first. Always," I told her.

She climbed off me to answer the phone out on the kitchen counter. After a minute, Emma returned. "I'm sorry, that was my sister, Megan, and she's... well, she had a fight with Braydon— Braydon's her boyfriend—and she wants to stay here for the night."

Just my luck.

I stood up and wrapped my arms around her. My rigid cock at attention pressed against her warm belly, and that was going to have to be good enough for tonight.

She slipped her hand between us and held my aching cock. "Sorry, how about tomorrow night?" Her was voice was heavy with regret.

I had dinner with Bill scheduled for Thursday. "Does Friday work for you?" I asked.

Her eyes clouded with disappointment.

I lifted her chin with a finger. "I have dinner with my brother tomorrow, and I have some studying to catch up on," I explained.

She pulled up on my cock, which made it hard to resist her. "Studying?" she asked.

I hadn't told her I was studying for the bar. There were lots of things I hadn't told her yet, but it had only been two days, after all. "Yeah, are we good for Friday night?"

We agreed that I'd bring Chinese over on Friday. At least those were the words we said. My nonverbal plan included a lot more of getting to know her luscious body, and her coy smile told me that she echoed the sentiment. I had an awkward time stuffing my still engorged cock back into my jeans. I didn't get the top button done. I kissed her hurriedly but took the time to breathe in a healthy lungful of her citrusy scent for the road.

Emma was frantic to get me out before her hysterical sister arrived, which was probably a good plan, given the bulge in my jeans.

On the way home, I relished her scent. I smiled to myself as I remembered her taste as well. She had kissed me each time right after I licked her juices from my fingers. What a turn-on. My dick, which I'd been getting under control, swelled again at the memory. She was one hot lady. There was a definite volcano inside this woman.

I turned on the radio as I pulled out into traffic. They were playing a Shania Twain song. Some of the lyrics struck me. *"First you gotta learn to listen, to understand her deepest thoughts." "If you want to get to know her, really get inside her mind." "If you want to move in closer, take it slow, take your time."*

I rolled Shania's advice over and over in my mind. And there was Katie's advice too. *Don't screw it up.* Big help that was. I hadn't told Emma yet that I was guilty of one of her three deadly sins. I was a lawyer, or at least almost a lawyer. I wanted her to accept me as Steven Carter, the guy who simply wanted to be with her, before I became Steven Carter Covington the frigging lawyer. Usually, it was being a Covington that screwed things up for me with a woman. It didn't allow them to be themselves. They instantly morphed into whatever they imagined I wanted them to be, sort of like bait to hook the rich kid and reel him in.

With Emma, I was going to have the complication that she and her sister had soured on lawyers for some reason. I guess it could have been worse. I would have to find the right time and the right way to tell her. This would take some thought.

As I lay in bed, I couldn't shake her memory. The sweet way she smelled, her marvelously soft breasts, and the way she called out my name when she came, clenching down tightly on my fingers. That was going to be so fucking good when it was my cock filling her. I could tell she was going to be tight, oh, so tight, and so wet. Hot didn't begin to describe her. Volcano was a closer word.

I was hard again visualizing her, and I wasn't going to get any sleep like this.

Why waste the memories?

I got up, retrieved a washcloth from the bathroom, and returned to bed. I started to stroke myself, all the while imagining it was her soft hands followed by her tight, wet pussy. After I was done, I cleaned myself off and rolled over to try to get some sleep.

Oh, Emma, you are going to be the death of me.

* * *

Emma

Megan had arrived moments after Steven left on Wednesday night. It was a good thing she'd called ahead. It would have been awkward times a hundred if she had knocked on the door when Steven and I were getting naked on the couch.

Braydon, it turned out, had come back drunk from his poker night. That wasn't new, and he had lost again, also not new, and he had taken it out on poor Megan. The unfortunate thing was that the triggers changed but the behavior didn't. Something would go wrong in Braydon's life and Megan would suffer for it. She hated him when it happened, but by the next day, she was resolved to make up with him and try again. I felt sorry for Megan that she had to endure this, but at least he didn't hit her. Megan refused to see the pattern. She was my older sister, he was her boyfriend, and he didn't cheat on her. End of discussion.

After venting for a while, Megan noticed the two wine glasses by the couch, and like a bloodhound after the scent, she dragged the truth out of me about Steven. Yes, he had been over, and how wonderful Tuesday and this evening had been with him. How truly different he was, and I went on and on. At least it cheered her up. She reminded me of her dating advice.

Thanks, Megan, but I have this covered.

This time had been no different from the last three fights with Braydon, and Megan was back at her place by Thursday night and Braydon was working late.

Steven and I had texted during the day Thursday, and we were still on for dinner tonight. I'd retrieved the three new Covington paintings from the restoration department and spent the morning taking measurements in the exhibit room to plan how our current pieces would move around in the exhibit to accommodate the new paintings. I finished my plan and handed it off to the preparations department to have them move the existing works and hang the three new pieces.

I had arranged to have Friday afternoon off to handle my search for my great-great-grandmother's painting. Great-great-grandmama Marie, on my mother's side, had once sat for a painting by the famous French painter, Pierre-Auguste Renoir, and that painting had been in the family for years when they lived in France. It had been lost in the war, and I was determined to find it for Mama someday. It belonged in our house.

Janice called as I started my work in the library after lunch. I needed to join her for an urgent meeting. It was hard to find things that Janice didn't consider urgent. Two weeks ago, I had to go out at rush hour to get more toner for the color printer. Such was life at the bottom of the pecking order.

I gathered up my papers and asked Siri to guide me to the address she had sent. It was the

Covington building that I'd visited earlier, picking up the three new additions to our exhibits. Janice met me in the lobby and explained that we were joining a rush audit of Covington artwork that a Mr. Perkins was running.

Thanks for upending my afternoon, Janice.

* * *

Steven

Friday morning came quickly. One thing about losing interest in dating other girls since I'd noticed Emma was that I was ahead of schedule with my studying for the bar. The firm wanted me to take a section of practice bar exam questions every two weeks, and so far, all was good on that front. But if last night's study session after my dinner with Bill was any indication, my study time wasn't going to be very productive now that I had tasted Emma. I couldn't get her out of my mind. My sweet Sugar.

We had texted and confirmed we were still on for Chinese and Bond tonight. I sent her another text after lunch asking if she had any favorite dishes she wanted me to pick up. I was waiting for an answer when Jeremy, another new first-year, stopped by. "Monica wants us to join her in the conference room."

Her Highness delighted in upending our

schedules with absolutely no notice. "But she told me to index the Weiss discovery items this afternoon."

Jeremy just smiled. "Not anymore."

I closed my notebook. "What gives?"

"Some rush project involving Covington," he answered.

That sounded like Monica. Everyone knew that she wanted to land Covington Industries as a client, and most of them thought that's why I was one of her first-years.

When we found her, Monica informed us that we had landed a job involving a potential investment in Covington. They needed a rush audit that the firm was helping with. The group of us were due at a meeting in the Covington building in an hour with the audit partner leading the engagement.

Once there, we were ushered into a conference room where we listened to a mostly bald beak-nosed man in a three-piece suit who introduced himself as Mr. Perkins from the auditing firm drone on. There were eight other people from his firm, four of us from E&S, and Uncle Garth around the table. The audit was to facilitate an investment infusion and was due in a week. This equated to the same as *yesterday*, judging by Perkins's use of the phrase *no time to spare* for the fourth time in as many minutes. Perkins was visibly relieved as the door opened behind us. "Janice, thank you for coming over so quickly," baldy said.

Another group had arrived.

* * *

Emma

Upstairs, an older balding man whom I assumed was Perkins called out to Janice and introduced us to the assembled group as we entered the conference room. I waved shyly when he said my name. He went on to explain why we were here, but when he recounted the value of the artwork, my breathing stopped. "Eight hundred and eighty-two million," the older man had said. For a moment, I wasn't sure I had heard him right. I composed myself and smiled to the large group sitting around the table.

Steven.

Steven was here. Now being called back into work this afternoon was looking a lot better.

The buxom older blonde woman with heavy makeup next to Steven placed her hand with her *Ferrari Red* nails on Steven's sleeve. She whispered into his ear, brushing her breast against his arm.

Cougar alert.

She kept her hand there much too long for my taste. I developed an instant dislike for this woman.

Her wooden smile showed the effects of too much Botox.

Mr. Perkins announced to the group, "I expect an audit plan from each of you by the end of the day."

"Emma." Janice tapped my shoulder.

I was so focused on the Cougar Lady clawing my Steven that I had missed what Janice had said. "Yeah?"

"Emma, you wait here while I talk to Mr. Perkins for a moment," Janice told me.

They were gathering in little groups. Several of the groups were centered around Perkins, but Cougar Lady, Steven, and two others were leaving, obviously not a part of the Perkins team, whoever they were.

Janice brought Mr. Durham, the company CFO, over. I had met him earlier in the week. He gave us several sheets containing an inventory of the artwork that we were to tally and evaluate. Our task was to authenticate and work with the legal team on determining provenance.

"And who's on the legal team for this?" Janice asked.

Mr. Durham pointed to the door. "They just left. Ernst and Schwartz sent over four people and they have been assigned conference room three. The partner's name is Paisley. She was the blonde lady over at this end of the table.

Rocks formed in my stomach. Cougar Lady was a

lawyer. I hate lawyers. That means Steven's a lawyer.

How could Steven do this to me? I told him I don't date musicians, politicians, or lawyers.

How could my day get any worse?

CHAPTER SIX

Steven

I turned around. Emma was entering the room with an older bleached blonde who had to be Janice.

Perkins continued. "These two ladies, Janice Standwick and Emma Watson, are from the museum. The company has eight hundred and eighty-two million in artwork on the books, and they will be providing the expert opinions for that aspect of our valuations."

I understood my father had accumulated a large art collection, but the total astounded even me.

It had startled Emma when Perkins announced the value, but she composed herself quickly. She glanced around the room. Her polite smile for the group grew extra bright as her scan found me.

Monica leaned over to whisper to me that I would be assisting her this afternoon.

Great, just what I don't need.

Perkins broke up the meeting and Monica led us down the hall to another conference room.

Emma and her boss, Janice, marched into the conference room a few minutes later. Janice told Monica how it was going to go. She basically told Monica to shove it. I couldn't help but smirk a little while Monica was being put in her place. It became hard to keep from laughing.

Emma avoided eye contact with me for some reason.

After they left, Monica was about to blow a gasket, but she had no tools to fight back with. She handed out some of the contracts we were tasked with reviewing and left in a huff.

The two of us and Scott, the associate who had gotten sucked into this with us, started to work on the contracts. The work was boring, but it went quickly as each of us traded contracts and made notes. Then we compared our notes to come up with a common summary of each one and to compare this against the contract summaries Covington had given to the accountants. We were the double-check on the company summaries. What the accountants did with them after that was for them to figure out.

The whole afternoon was like living in a fishbowl. The company employees would try to look inconspicuous as they walked by to sneak a peek at the lawyers camped out in their midst. Whatever this was about, they hadn't been told yet. All the while, I was looking forward to Chinese and Bond tonight with Emma. I couldn't wait to tell her how great it was that her boss had put Monica in her place.

We kept a careful eye on the time, and at five o'clock sharp, we trundled down to conference room three to get our parcel of information from the art experts. Emma stood in the background as Janice gave us a list of art and a folder on each, containing some purchase information that we were supposed to verify.

I smiled and nodded to Emma, and she ignored me. I'd thought the lawyer rule might be a silly thing that would be addressed easily once she got to know me, but the cold shoulder I'd gotten made it clear that I had misjudged.

Scott was senior, and he decided that he wanted to work on the folders while Jeremy and I trudged through more contracts. So that was that until one o'clock on Monday. Jeremy and I finished up with the contract that we were in the midst of by five thirty, when we called it a day.

I went by the room Emma and Janice had been in. No Emma. Her lack of even a smile in my direction earlier bothered me. I decided against a text. I need to talk with her in person. I stopped by Bill's office on the way out. He wasn't in.

* * *

Emma

Janice led the way as we searched for the legal team. We had passed conference room three, and they weren't there. "Naturally, they can't follow simple instructions," Janice noted. We found them in the larger conference room one.

The Cougar Lady, Paisley, greeted us. "Thank you for joining us, Miss Stanwick. We were just drawing up a plan of attack."

"Standwick," Janice corrected her. "Emma and I will be authenticating the art by order of location and handing them off to you in that order for your opinion on provenance, which we will then validate with our own research. We will give you a list at one P.M. and five P.M. each day, in conference room three down the hall, and later by conference call."

"I think we should discuss this first," Paisley objected.

Janice continued, "At each of the meetings, I expect your results on the list from the previous meeting."

I avoided looking at Steven.

Paisley was going to have none of this. "But…"

Janice cut her off. "If you have any questions, direct them to Mr. Perkins." With that, she turned and we marched out.

"Lawyers are just overpaid gasbags," she said as we walked off together. She had no idea she was echoing my sentiments at the moment. I never would have guessed that Janice and I had a dislike for lawyers in common.

"That's too kind," I added. I despised lawyers.

The first decent date I have in like forever, and he turns out to be a fucking lawyer.

A fucking lawyer?

* * *

Steven

With a quick stop at home, I changed out of my suit and into casual and grabbed some more Bond DVDs.

Loaded with two bags of delicious-smelling Chinese and another few Bond disks, I knocked on Emma's door. No answer. I checked my watch. I was on time, so I knocked a little louder. Still no answer. I didn't expect this to be easy. I hadn't been ready to tell her I was a lawyer yet, but that cat was out of the bag now. Tuesday and Wednesday night had been a good start, but I wanted her to get to know me better before I confronted her silly dating rules. I put the food down and texted her.

ME: I'm here with the food

SUGAR: Go away.

ME: And Bond

I expected issues, but I expected we could at least talk about it. It wasn't like I'd forgotten her birthday or anything. I didn't rate this kind of response after Wednesday night.

ME: You all right? I'm worried about u

She didn't respond.
I didn't hear anything through the door. I waited another few minutes before trying again.

ME: I got you cashew chicken

ME: And Mongolian beef

I knocked again. Still no noises from behind the door.

SUGAR: Not hungry.

ME: Please talk to me

I only had one ace to play.

ME: You are not being fair

I waited and hoped that playing the fairness card would get me an audience.

ME: The food is getting cold

ME: Leaving me out here is not fair

I heard her approach the door. The latch turned.
Her eyes were red from crying.
I wanted badly to hold her and make it better, but her closed stance told me not to try it. I came in and set the food down. "It's still hot. Want to eat first and talk later?"
She nodded silently and went to the fridge. She pulled out a bottle of wine and set it on the small dining table.
The curtains were drawn. I went to the window and pulled them open, letting in the early evening light.
She retrieved plates from the cupboard without a word.
Back in the kitchen, I noticed a bowl of M&M peanut candies. There was something odd about the bowl. I scooped out portions of the food onto the two plates. As I pulled the wrapper off the top of the wine bottle, I glanced at the bowl of M&Ms

again.

No yellow.

It was missing the yellow ones. All the other colors, but no yellow. "What's with the M&Ms? You order them special?"

"What?"

"You're missing the yellow. You eat those first?"

She gulped like I had said something wrong. "The yellows are for my sister."

I'd never heard of liking one color better than the next, but to each his own. "I had an exciting day today," I told her.

She didn't say anything.

"I got to watch my boss get put in her place by your boss. It was the most fun I've had in weeks."

She couldn't hide the corners of her mouth starting to turn up into a smirk. "She doesn't like lawyers either."

I located the corkscrew after searching three drawers. "Monica deserved it."

She smiled a little more. "Nobody likes lawyers." At least she was talking to me now.

I twisted in the corkscrew. "Monica is a real ass. She deserved even worse."

"I hate lawyers."

Now we were getting down to the nub of the problem, and it sounded worse than I'd imagined. The problem was more deep-rooted than I'd thought that first night.

"You didn't tell me you were a lawyer and you knew I don't date lawyers," she spat out.

I pulled the cork out. Refusing to acknowledge her anger, I smiled at her. "And you lied about your name."

She crossed her arms. "It's not the same. I was protecting myself."

I had seen almost a glimmer of a smile on her face for a second. "I was doing the same. Protecting something incredibly important to me." I smiled at her as warmly as I could manage. Smiles could sometimes be contagious.

"Protecting what?" she demanded.

I poured wine into one of the glasses. "As I said, something incredibly important to me. You have no idea how important." I kept my smile up at a megawatt.

She was trying to resist, but the corners of her mouth were turning up, just slightly. She was losing the battle. "Like what?"

I pushed the filled glass in her direction. "My chance to get to know a real lady with a screwed-up set of dating rules," I said.

A hint of a smile appeared, but she didn't take the glass.

I took the other glass. "It wouldn't be fair for me to be denied the chance to know such a beautiful and intelligent woman based on a meaningless label."

The hint of a smile grew to a grin. "I still don't date lawyers. I hate lawyers."

I poured the second glass. "Good thing I'm not a lawyer then," I responded.

That took her completely by surprise. Her look was questioning but cautious, as if I was about to spring a trap on her.

I motioned to the food. "Now eat. You agreed to eat and then talk."

She responded sternly. "I did not."

I offered her one of the glasses. "Did too."

She crossed her arms again, petulantly. "Did not."

I held the glass in front of her. "I told you the plan and you nodded your agreement."

She uncrossed her arms and took the glass reluctantly.

I carried the two plates over to the dining table.

She followed slowly.

I sat down and grabbed a piece of the Mongolian beef with the chopsticks and put it in my mouth.

She sat reluctantly and studied the food with a perplexed look on her face. She started to eat, clearly savoring the food. She was having trouble with the slippery cashews in the chicken dish. It wasn't easy to pick them up with chopsticks.

I grabbed one with my chopsticks and offered it to her. She opened her mouth and took it. One at a time, I picked up more and continued to feed them to her. The smile was slowly coming back. It was good to see her enjoying herself again.

She picked up some of the sweet and sour pork and started to feed me. We went on like this, feeding each other, and not making a mess of it either. Each time she closed her lips around my chopsticks, it became even more sensual than the last.

I fixed her eyes with mine. "I can't stay long. I'm behind on my studying for the bar." Not really true. "Ever since I met a certain beautiful redhead, I can't concentrate at all." That was the truth. I kissed the end of my chopsticks, without loading them with food, and offered the ends to her.

She kissed them and the corners of her mouth turned up in a small smile. She kissed hers and offered them to me. She picked up her wine glass.

I grasped my glass quickly and clinked it against hers. "To Chinese food and chopsticks." Then, I added, "To chopsticks and good friends." I offered her another chopstick kiss, which she accepted.

I filled our wine glasses again after we finished the food. I stood up and took her hand, leading her to the couch.

"I told you I don't date lawyers," she said as she sat down next to me.

I put my arm around her shoulder. "Good thing for me I'm not a lawyer then."

She didn't reject my arm around her, but she also

didn't move any closer. "So, you work for lawyers, but you're not one of them?" she asked.

I stroked her shoulder now that she was calmer. "I have a law degree, but I'm not a lawyer yet because I haven't passed the bar exam."

She huffed. "Typical lawyer talk. A distinction without a difference."

She was right. It wasn't very different. "If it helps, I don't like most lawyers either," I told her.

"Why did you have to be a lawyer anyway?"

Her question deserved an answer. "Being the youngest in the family, I didn't want to work in the family business. I would just be low man on the totem pole forever, and I promised my father that I would do something to help people. I couldn't stand the sight of blood, so being a doctor was out, and that left fireman and lawyer. I burned myself once as a kid, so fireman was out."

She contemplated the answer for a moment. "But you didn't tell me."

"I thought it would be better if we got to know each other without labels and preconceptions." I held her hand. "People have prejudged me my whole life, and I'm tired of it."

"What's to judge about you?"

I took my arm off her shoulder and faced her. "Let's play a little game. Trust me on this, okay?"

She nodded reluctantly.

"Do you have a scarf?"

She recoiled. "What?"

"Please, just go get a scarf. It's a part of the game."

A spark of concern flashed in her eyes. "I'm not letting you tie me up."

I laughed. "No bondage tonight, I promise."

The concern on her face was replaced with curiosity.

"Just get the damn scarf, Sugar."

She returned with a long floral print scarf.

I folded the scarf. "Now it's important for this that you just use your ears, so I'm going to blindfold you. You'll be perfectly safe. Okay?"

She nodded and let me tie the scarf around her head in a blindfold.

I put my hands on her shoulders. "Now I will say a word, and you say the first word that comes to mind. There is no right or wrong, just quickly say the first word you think of. Do you understand?"

She nodded.

"Cat," I said, starting simple.

"Mouse."

"Hawaii."

She thought for a moment. "Vacation."

"Remember, I said don't think, just react."

She nodded. "Okay."

"Ferrari."

She smiled. "Red."

"Lawyer."

"Scumbag," she hissed with a scowl.

"French."

The smile returned to her face. "Fries."

"Standwick?" I asked.

"Boss."

"Covington."

"Rich," she purred.

"Renoir."

"Impressionist," she said quickly.

"Tiffany."

"Case."

"Rich kid?" I asked.

"Spoiled."

I reached for and squeezed her hand for a moment. "We're done with this, for now." I pulled the scarf loose.

She blinked at the light hitting her eyes now. "So what was that all about? Now you want to be a psychologist?"

"No, we just proved what I was afraid of. That if I had told you everything about myself that first night, you would have pegged me as a rich, spoiled scumbag and never given me a chance to get to know you."

Her brows knitted, puzzlement in her eyes.

I grasped her hands in mine and captured her eyes with mine. "My full name is Steven Carter Covington," I said slowly.

Her eyes went wide. "*Those* Covingtons?" The

sound of her sharp intake of breath filled the room. "So, we were at your company today?"

This was the same reaction I always got. "No, not my company. My brothers run it. But that's exactly the point. I am sick and tired of being judged by my last name rather than for who I am."

She was processing the implications of what I'd told her. Her eyes lit up. "So were you were behind the paintings we got this week?"

"You told me Tuesday night what your exhibit needed, and I wanted to help."

Her eyes went wide. "Just like that?"

I got up and made a show of looking at my watch. "I need to go."

The corners of her mouth drooped. "Oh."

"I do, and since you think that rich kids are spoiled and lawyers are scumbags, you have to decide if you can be seen with a rich, spoiled, scumbag lawyer."

She stared at the ground.

I was being hard on her, but we couldn't let this problem fester. There was something in her past about lawyers that she wasn't telling me. I needed her to get past it, if she could.

We needed it.

I kissed her on the forehead. "Good night, Sugar," I said as I turned to the door.

I'll have to settle for a hand job of the self-administered variety tonight.

* * *

Emma

Last night after he left, I'd cried myself to sleep. Why did he have to turn out to be a lawyer? How could I tell Megan or Mama that I wanted to go out with a lawyer? Megan and I had learned when we were little girls that lawyers were the lowest of the low, and we had promised that neither of us would dishonor Elissa by associating with one, much less dating one. I dreaded this breakfast.

Megan met me at our favorite breakfast hangout, the International House of Pancakes. While the rest of Los Angeles favored egg white omelets with sprouts and lemongrass tea for breakfast, Megan and I grew up eating real food.

My heart was pounding as I sat down. I didn't know where to start. I recounted last night's events over my plate of buttermilk pancakes. "He said I needed to figure out how I feel about seeing a rich, spoiled, scumbag lawyer. And then he left," I told her.

Megan had cut her chocolate chip pancakes into precise tiny squares while she listened to me go on about last night. It was very un-Megan to not state an opinion at some point. "So, what are you going to do?"

I nervously watched her take a sip of her orange juice. "You know our rule against lawyers."

She put her juice down. "So I can see how you have a really big problem, Sis. You meet this guy who is a really bad dude because he doesn't tell you his whole name while you lie about yours. Twice, right?"

I nodded and peered down, playing with my pancake. I'd lied about my name, but I had to.

She continued. "And he takes you home after you drink too much and he's a douche because he's a gentleman, and instead of taking advantage of you, all you get is a goodnight kiss."

"Yeah, but..." I protested.

Megan held up her finger to stop me. She popped a small square of her chocolaty delight into her mouth. "And he doesn't care that you lied about your name, twice, so then he sets up this killer donation to your museum to help you, right?"

"Well..." I didn't know what to say to that. It had been more than nice to get those paintings.

She sipped her coffee as she contemplated for a moment. "Did he brag about it to you?"

"No," I admitted. I looked down at my pancakes. It sounded pretty un-scumbag the way she put it. I was losing my appetite.

She took another small bite of the chocolaty goodness in front of her. "And, he's so into you that he can't concentrate on his studying." She forked another piece of pancake. "We abso-fucking-lutely can't have that."

I slumped down in my seat.

"So when he brings you dinner and apologizes, you are mean to him because he has been acting so nice to you, and that has to fucking stop right now."

A chill overtook me. I was sounding crappier by the second, but she wasn't addressing that he was a frigging lawyer.

"And you invoke rule number one against lawyers and shoot him down, thinking you owe me that, and because of Ellisa"

I put my head down on the table. "Yeah, that's right. Why did he have to be a lawyer?" I said to the floor.

Megan was not helping me feel better. The way she put it, I had been acting pretty fucking stupid. "You look like shit," she continued. "You obviously worried about this all last night, so what you gonna do?"

I brought my head up. "I like him. I just wish he wasn't a lawyer." A non-answer was the best I had.

She put her fork down. "Emm, I gotta say, I'm totally with him. You gotta get your shit together. The man is not just his job, for fuck's sake. He promised his dad he would be a lawyer. His dad died, and now he has to follow through. End of story. You gotta decide if you want to get on that train and see where it takes you or call up fucking

Gordo or Jason or whoever."

My head hurt. I couldn't think. I put my head in my hands. "But you know we can't trust lawyers, ever."

"Give the guy a break, Emm. A lawyer killed Ellisa, I get it. I remember, and it hurts. But, that's in the past. It wasn't him. Honestly, sometimes, I think you just want to fuck your life up worrying about what might go wrong instead of living."

She was right. I did tend to second-guess myself a little. Steven was better in so many ways than any man I'd met in this town, and I was judging him by a label, just as he'd feared. On Tuesday, he had been my salvation, and by Friday night, he was my ruin, all because of what he studied in school.

Megan was down to her last few bites on her plate. "I'm just a waitress, so you won't follow my advice anyway." She waved her fork. She knew it was bullshit. Her advice had gotten me dates with Gordie and Jason and a few other frogs. "So, if you like him, why not keep seeing him? Pretend you didn't find out he's a lawyer and give him the Cosmo test."

More Megan sex advice was the last thing I needed. "No more sex tips."

She shook her head. "No, just dating advice. Maybe he is honest about being really into you. The Cosmo test is you make him do a bunch of stuff guys hate and see if he puts up with it."

I pushed my pancake around on my plate while I thought about it. "Like what stuff?"

"Make him join you at Yoga when the game is on TV. Take him to a knitting class, or a lecture at the university on dealing with PMS, or send him to the store to get you ultra-absorbent tampons. You'll think of something."

I laughed. My freshman roommate in college had actually lost her boyfriend when she asked him to buy her some tampons. "Okay, I'll think of something. Is it okay if I keep seeing him?"

Megan had the broadest smile. "Emm, you are so transparent. Of course you have my blessing. I always say fuck all the lawyers. If this guy makes you happy, go fuck yourself a lawyer. He's not the one that killed Elissa."

The mention of our dead twin sister sent a shiver straight through me. We didn't talk about her. We hadn't mentioned her name in years.

"Just one condition, Sis."

Megan was the best. She knew that I wouldn't move on Steven without her approval, and I was getting it. "Only one?"

"Okay, really two conditions. One, give him the Cosmo test, and two, I get to meet him before you fuck him." Megan could be so crude. "No sense breaking our rule if he's not seriously into you."

My heart was flying. "I'll think of something good."

I needed a plan.

* * *

Steven

Friday night, I'd left Emma with an ultimatum. This was new territory for me. The general script that played out was that once a girl found out who I was, it only intensified things. It never turned them off the way it had Emma. The Covington curse had always been that I could never tell if it was me or my bank account that a woman was interested in, and it always turned out to be the latter. The restaurants she wanted to go to would always migrate up the scale and the wine ordered would be more expensive. Any gift I gave would be judged differently. A rose would never be seen the same after they learned my name. Why wasn't it two dozen roses?

Why couldn't we just enjoy the simple things in life? That's why I drove a Ford, not a Ferrari. I was trapped by my name when it came to women. The one freedom I did have was the freedom to choose what to do with my time. I didn't need to work to support myself. None of us did. We all did jobs that we wanted to pursue, and I had chosen long ago to use my time and energy to come up with a unique way to help others. I truly meant it when I made my vow to my father, and I always kept my promises. I just hadn't found exactly how I would do it yet.

As I'd predicted, Friday night became a bust as far as studying went. Emma on the brain was not conducive to concentrating.

Saturday morning went better. I got halfway through a study section before Katie called to check in and remind me about the Sunday building project.

I spent an hour talking her ear off about Emma. She was a good listener. I explained the reaction I got from Emma when she found out I worked at E&S. "I know lawyers are not the most popular people around," I said.

"Ya think?" was her reply.

"But I didn't expect a reaction like that," I continued.

"Clearly, she had some traumatic encounter with a lawyer before that is causing this. Do you have any idea what it is?" Katie asked.

"Not a clue."

Katie was silent for a moment. "My best advice, little brother, is just go slow and show her that you are not the kind of person that she fears, and above all, don't get her anywhere near the people you work with or any other lawyer types. Something they say or do could set her off and she would associate you with whatever the pain is. So, take her sailing, or on a bike ride, burgers on a mountaintop, eat only at hole-in-the-wall hippie places. Do very un-lawyerly kinds of things. Surprise her and be the anti-lawyer."

"Should I ask her about it?" I asked.

Katie didn't answer right away. "I wouldn't. Just don't push. Be there for her, hang out a little. I know it's not your style, but let her set the pace and just be available. Dress down, be honest, be caring, listen, and don't be pushy. Lawyers are pushy. Be the exact opposite of what a lawyer is. She'll tell you about it when she's ready."

"Thanks, Sis."

"One more thing, little brother." She enjoyed calling me that entirely too much. "I could see in her reaction at the restaurant that she really likes you, so I'd guess she gives you a chance. She has the look of a woman in love. Just don't screw it up."

I went back to studying and waiting for Emma's call. The studying didn't go well. I made about half the progress I should have by dinner time. I reached for the phone more than once, but each time, I recalled the Shania Twain lyrics. *"If you want to move in closer, take it slow, take your time."*

Tonight was going to be another jerk-off session to keep me from going completely nuts. My dick reacted instantly when the image of Emma with the scarf tied over her eyes popped into my mind.

The next time I tie that scarf on you, Emma, it'll be the

only thing you're wearing, I promise.

CHAPTER SEVEN

Steven

Sunday morning had arrived, and still no contact from Emma. It felt wrong, but I was following Katie's advice to not push her. I hadn't called or texted. I was being un-lawyerly and also very un-me.

I checked my phone again. The waiting was driving me nuts. I cleaned up my breakfast dishes and started the drive down south.

My oldest brother, Bill, had gotten us involved in Habitat for Humanity last year when he was pursuing a business investment from the Benson Group. Since then, it had become an almost monthly event for the whole family. Today, we were joining a project in Hawthorne.

I had discreetly taken a picture of Emma with my phone, her bright blue eyes framed by that brilliant red hair and that gorgeous smile. The best curve of all on her was her smile. The picture appeared on the face of my phone as it rang before I was halfway to the construction site.

Finally.

"Good morning, Sugar. How are you?" I said hopefully.

"Hi." Her voice was hesitant. "Can we talk?"

"Sure, I'm driving right now. Go ahead. I'm all yours." I meant that in more ways than one.

"Maybe in person would be better."

Her wanting to talk in person was a good sign. "I'm going to be busy building a house all day. We can do it after, or better yet, Sugar, you can come down and join in."

"I didn't understand that. What did you say you were doing?"

"Habitat for Humanity, Sugar. I'm at a project in Hawthorne all day, and I'd like nothing better than to see your beautiful face in a hard hat."

"Well…"

I needed to make my pitch. "Sugar, I can guarantee there won't be any lawyers there, just good old regular people helping to build a house for a very deserving family."

She hesitated.

"It's for a good cause, Sugar, lots of sawdust and nails and sunshine. You get a free lunch, and even Katie will be there," I added hopefully.

She agreed and I gave her the address after warning her to wear comfortable clothes with long sleeves and closed-toed shoes. Finally, things were looking up. After last night, I'd been afraid I wouldn't even get a call from her and I would have to come up with a Plan B.

At the build site, I mentioned to my family as I found each of them that Emma was coming so they wouldn't be surprised, and I warned them to treat her well.

Katie punched me in the shoulder. "You sly fox, you. This is the perfect un-lawyerly kind of thing to invite her to."

Why didn't I think of that?

* * *

Emma

I told Siri the address Steven had given me and off I went. He said he was working at a Habitat for Humanity building project. I didn't see that coming. What was a scumbag lawyer Covington doing pounding nails on a Sunday when he could be playing golf or whatever else the idle rich did for recreation? I'd actually expected him to tell me he was busy studying for the bar. He had said he was behind schedule, after all. The man was full of surprises.

Steven had warned me to park on Howard Street

about two blocks away. Marching up to the build site, I could see why. Flatbeds with materials were everywhere and the lot was crawling with people. There had to be at least a hundred volunteers here. I had heard of Habitat for Humanity, but I'd never been to one of these before. I signed in on the sidewalk and was issued safety glasses, gloves, and a hard hat.

I set off in search of my lawyer man.

"Emma, may I call you Emma? So good of you to join us." It was the Covington CFO, Mr. Durham, who had loaned the museum the wonderful Degas.

I stopped in shock. "Mr. Durham," I managed to blurt out as I tried to recover my senses.

He surprised me with a quick hug. "Please call me Uncle Garth. Everybody does. Steven has had such nice things to say about you. I do hope you found a nice place to display my little Degas," he said rapid-fire.

Little was not at all the right description. His was one of the larger Degas paintings I had ever seen. "I can't thank you enough. Mr..., Uncle Garth. It's a wonderful piece and it should go on display very soon."

"Excellent, now let us go find young Steven. I know he is around here somewhere." He guided me through the throngs until we found Steven near the back. He was drilling holes in wood things, looking like he knew what he was doing. The lawyer was also a carpenter, house builder, or whatever.

"Sugar, you made it," he exclaimed. He gave me a quick family-like hug and thanked Uncle Garth for escorting me over. "You're just in time. We have to drill a set of holes in the framing along this wall for the electrical so those guys over there" —he pointed to a few people in the next section that was going to be a different room— "can put in the wiring. Wanna help?"

I had no idea how I was going to help. A paint brush I could handle, but power tools were not my thing. "Sure, what can I do?" I answered hesitantly.

He had me tighten up the headband on my hardhat that was starting to fall down over my eyes and put on my gloves. "I knew your red hair would be beautiful under a hard hat."

I laughed, but that was so cute I couldn't help but blush.

He was dressed in jeans and a tight long-sleeve blue Levi's shirt with the sleeves rolled up and a few buttons undone. He could pass for a hot construction calendar model, with bulging muscles barely constrained by the shirt. I liked this look a lot better than him in a suit. He turned away to pick up the drill. The jeans were tight enough to highlight that cute ass of his.

He handed me the electric drill. I'd seen my daddy use these plenty of times, but he had never trusted me to handle one by myself. "Use two hands, like this."

As soon as he mentioned hands, my thoughts ran back a few nights to his hands being all over me and what he could do with those magic fingers of his. I kept my mouth shut for fear I would say what was on my mind.

He reached around me and positioned my hands on the drill.

His body was warm against my back.

Coming here was definitely a good idea.

I had the fantasy of turning around and having my chest against his body instead and asking him to drill me. *Who was I kidding?* That was a Megan-style line, not something I would do. I giggled.

"What's so funny?" he asked.

"Nothing, go ahead," I answered.

"Now, place the tip of the bit lightly against the wood in the center of the piece." He moved my hands and the drill to do that while I giggled, visualizing about the tip of something else. "You have to stop laughing. This is serious. Now the next part is the tricky part. Let go, and let me show you."

I released my hands and he took the drill, still handling it from behind me with his arms draped around me. He was holding me even closer now. I caught an intoxicating whiff of his spicy male scent that went from my nose through my brain, turning millions of neurons off on its way to heat up my lady parts.

"When you pull the trigger, it gives a little kick as the bit comes up to speed quickly." He pulled the trigger.

I recoiled from the sudden noise. The drill screamed when it was running. A smile came to my lips as I felt something in his pants when I backed into him.

I wasn't the only one excited here.

"Then start to press into the wood, but keep a really firm grip on the tool."

My mind was in the gutter, imagining another tool I'd like to be holding right now. His proximity had warped my mind. I was turning into Megan. Horny and potty-mouthed and finding innuendo in every word.

"It sometimes gives a kick at the end and you don't want it getting away from you." That wasn't the only thing I didn't want getting away from me. He drilled a hole in front of me. He handed me the drill and moved back. "Now you try that on the next stud." Stud was a word he shouldn't be using around me right now. Not until I got a few more neurons back on-line.

It took me a few moments to coordinate enough brainpower to ask, "Where?"

He pointed to the next vertical piece of wood.

I got in position. When I pulled the trigger, the drill whined and tried to twist out of my grip. This was a lot harder than it seemed. I tried again and pushed it into the wood. It chewed a hole quickly, giving quite a jerk as it came out the other side, just like he warned me it would. I felt relieved. I didn't screw it up too much. I had drilled a hole. It wasn't in the center, but the wall was still standing.

We went on drilling holes around the room and into the next.

I'd learned studs was what we called the vertical pieces of wood. I drilled where he told me, and between us, we finished all the rooms before lunch. Some of the holes were different sizes for plumbing or something. He showed me how to change out the drill thingy that I learned was called a bit. Now I was a real carpenter or driller or whatever. I nearly lost my mind every time he said drill, but I kept my inner Megan in check and didn't embarrass myself all morning.

A loud horn sounded from the front of the lot.

"Lunch break," Steven announced. He took my hand and we found our way to the side yard. Holding his hand again gave me goosebumps.

"Emma, so glad you could make it." It was Steven's beautiful sister, Katie. She also gave me a quick hug before handing me off to William Covington, who insisted I call him Bill, followed by Bill's wife, Lauren, and Steven's other brother, Patrick. Uncle Garth wandered over after a few minutes.

Lauren started passing out sandwiches and drinks from a cooler as we took seats in camping chairs that she unstacked. "We have ham and cheese or tuna, your choice, and Snapple or Diet Coke."

I chose ham and cheese.

The group devoured Katie's sandwiches, followed by Katie's brownies with chocolate chunks. Katie and Lauren sat with me, and the guys sat in their own little group, ribbing each other, like guys always did, from the sound of it. We talked girl talk while the guys laughed and argued about sports.

"How did you all get started doing this?" I asked.

Lauren pointed over to another group farther back. "I think you might recognize the older gentleman in the brown shirt?"

I peered over. It appeared to be Lloyd Benson, the Chairman of our museum, of all people. I had only met him once, briefly. "Is that Mr. Benson?"

"The one and only. He's the one who got us interested in this last year, and now we all do it when we're in town."

When the horn announcing the end of the lunch break sounded, Steven and I went back to drilling holes where the foreman told us to, in the floor this time. Then we nailed plates over the wall studs at the level of the holes we had drilled. The hammer was a lot heavier than I expected. My arm started getting sore. Steven explained the plates were so the drywall screws wouldn't hit the electrical wires or the pipes in the walls.

Partway through the afternoon, Steven went to get some water for us and Lloyd Benson surprised me by wandering my way.

"Hey, Lloyd, she's taken." It was Steven returning with his water just as Mr. Benson reached me.

"Now don't forget to give Vincent a call," Mr. Benson said loudly to me as he walked away. A jab at Steven, no doubt. I'd never heard of Vincent.

"Who's Vincent?" I asked after Benson was out of earshot.

"Vincent is his son. He's an okay guy if you like midgets with bad teeth and worse breath."

I laughed. The two families were obviously good enough friends for practical jokes. Mr. Benson was messing with Steven.

Today was not at all what I had expected. I expected the construction volunteer types, but here were two wealthy families spending their day sweating their asses off and putting up a house for somebody they didn't even know.

When the horn announced the end of the workday, I still hadn't had any time alone with Steven to talk things over.

Katie joined me, washing up at the faucet out back. "So, how did you like it?"

"This was fun, but I think I'm going to be more than a little sore tomorrow."

"Yeah, that's pretty standard the first few times."

I rinsed my hands. "How often do you do this?"

"Almost every month, about nine times a year, I guess. I like it because you can really see that you've accomplished something at the end of the day, and it just feels good to give something back to the community, something of substance."

I had to know. "Does Steven bring all of his dates here?"

Katie touched my shoulder. "You're the first. None of us has ever met any of the girls he's dated since… let's just say it's been a long time. Here, give me your phone."

I handed it to her.

She started typing. "Now you've got my number. Call me some time and we can talk." She handed me back my phone as the guys approached.

Steven walked with me back to my car, talking in generalities about how the day was and asking how I felt about helping on the project and what I thought of his family members, but we didn't get to talk about us. When we were nearly there, his phone rang. It was his brother Bill, who needed help with something, and Steven had to go. "I'll call you later tonight," he said as he rushed back.

I didn't get so much as a kiss, and we hadn't gotten a chance to talk.

My luck sucks.

* * *

Steven

Bill sure had the worst timing. He called and needed help loading his truck just as I was walking Emma to her car. The first time all day we had been alone and able to talk. We needed to talk out this lawyer animosity problem of hers. I'd laid a real guilt trip on her Friday night. She needed to come clean with me and tell me what bugged her about lawyers, in general, so we could get past this. This was so stupid. It was like me saying I couldn't date girls with a last name longer than five letters. There had to be a way to prove to her that I wasn't the monster she feared.

All day long, it had been a struggle to be around her and not touch her, not hug her, not kiss her, not drag her into the back seat of my truck. Every time I peeked at her ass, I imagined bending her over the nearest table and fucking her brains out. When she turned around, I guessed how quickly I could pull her zipper down and spread her legs, or if I kept my eyes up, her tits tormented me. At least she wore a bra with some substance to it. If her nipples had poked through her work shirt, I would have lost it a dozen times today.

I wanted to sit with her at lunch and hold her hand, or more, way more, but the guys grabbed me and the girls sat in their own little group, probably gossiping about us based upon the occasional giggle emanating from their direction.

This go slow shit is really screwing up my game.

As I drove home, I went through the day in my mind. I could sense it when I wrapped my arms around her to show her how to hold and start the drill. She wanted me close. I had followed Katie's game plan, though, and I backed off. Emma had come to the job site and spent the day. She wouldn't have done that if she was intent on dumping me. I merely had to slay the imaginary demon in her mind.

How hard can that be?

Real fucking hard if I didn't know where it came from or the nature of the fear.

This was no good. I was talking myself in circles. For almost the first time in my life, I wasn't in the driver's seat with a woman. I had to wait for her to make a move. Respond un-lawyerly. What would a rational lawyer do? Then, do the opposite.

Un-lawyerly.

Back at my condo, the bar study materials laid out on the dining table called my name. I ignored them for half an hour, willing the phone to ring, to no avail. The damn thing remained blank and silent.

I sat down at the table and started in on the review section for rules of evidence when my phone magically came to life. It must be true, a watched iPhone never rings.

I turned the phone over, and it turned out to be Katie checking in. I told her about Bill calling for help with his truck that he didn't really need, and yes, I was pissed at him, and no, I didn't get a chance to talk with Emma, and yes, I agreed that Emma was a sweet girl, and no, I hadn't heard from her yet. Katie assured me there was nothing to worry about. She and Lauren had both had a wonderful time with Emma at lunch, and Katie expected to have a lunch date with Emma soon. In Katie's book, this was all great news. A girl has to be interested in a guy to want to talk to his sister. It kind of made sense in a girl kind of way.

An hour later, I was getting back into my groove studying-wise. Most of what was in the material had been covered in law school, but not quite in the level of detail I needed to know now. I could hear Professor Hargrove in my head as I dove into the section on searches with and without warrants. Hargrove had been a real stickler for detail, and that is what the law is all about. If the warrant had a flaw, the warrant could be invalidated and it would poison the admissibility of anything discovered in the search authorized by the faulty warrant. "Look at the details," he always told us. They could alter the course of the trial. Emma hates lawyers. Emma has a rule against dating lawyers. Where's the detail in that? Pretty black and white.

Now I recognized the detail I'd missed earlier. Emma said she and her sister had the rule against lawyers. The detail I had forgotten was Megan. She shared this rule with her sister, Megan. Megan must know the origin of the lawyer phobia. Now I had a way to discover the imaginary demon in Emma's mind so I could do combat with it.

Megan has the key.

At a little after ten, my phone came alive again with Emma's smiling face on the display. I breathed deeply to calm myself before answering.

"Hi, Sugar, I was just thinking about you."

Bad move. I am supposed to be playing it cool.

"Is that so?"

I didn't respond right away. "One thing you should know about me. I'm honest. I would never lie to you."

"That would be a first for a lawyer."

Shit, we were back on that again. "Go ahead. Test me if you don't believe me."

She hesitated. "And you have to tell me the truth?"

"Scout's honor." I waited.

Would she believe me?

"When did you first notice me?" she asked.

A direct question and an easy one. "A little over a month ago, when you came to the restaurant with a geeky nerd. You were wearing a black pencil skirt with a burgundy top and an oversized black purse."

"Wow, that's a lot of detail."

"You were, by far, the most beautiful woman in the room."

"Have you picked up lots of girls there?"

I told her the truth. "Never."

"Have you fantasized about me?"

Now we were getting into dangerous territory. I swallowed hard. "Yes."

"Touching yourself?"

"Yes."

"More than once?" she asked.

"Yes," I answered. "Now it's my turn. Did you have a good time today?"

"I sure did, but I can already tell that I'm going to be stiff and sore in the morning."

I had the solution. "A good massage tonight would help with that."

She ignored my not-so-subtle suggestion. "I was calling to ask…" This was sounding more promising by the minute. "Want to go to a movie tomorrow night?"

I smiled. "Sure thing, Sugar."

She invited me to join her for a movie down at the Century theaters.

Not as good as giving her a nice long massage, or Bond and pizza at her place, but I could work with this. We set a time and place to meet Monday night.

I went back to studying, but visions of giving Emma a massage kept interfering. That was the vision that I held in my big brain as my hand gave my little brain what it wanted.

She wants to try.

CHAPTER EIGHT

Steven

I arrived early to the theaters. It was Monday night and they were trying out a new retro concept where they played a dozen old classics twice a month on Monday. Tonight, they had *Die Hard*, a Schwarzenegger movie, *Dirty Harry*, *Casablanca*, the first *Fast and Furious*, *The Odd Couple*, and a few more comedies and chick flicks. It had been a while since I'd seen *Casablanca*. Bogart would be a good choice.

Emma, the picture of beauty, her long red tresses framing her smiling face with those deep blue eyes. She was bouncing toward me in a print sundress with spaghetti straps and sandals. Her broad smile foretold an enjoyable evening.

I was already figuring how to get her out of that dress later. Dresses were good, easier access to Pleasure Central than jeans.

She hugged me briefly. As I turned my head to

kiss her, she pulled away, still smiling and holding my hand. "I like Dr. Pepper." She combed her hair behind her ear with a finger. She twisted the ends of her hair. "If you get the popcorn and drinks, I'll get the tickets." With a giggle, she released my hand and turned to the ticket booth.

"Butter?" I yelled to her as she shimmied away with just the right amount of hip sway.

Over her shoulder, she answered, "A little."

I watched her enticing ass for a few seconds before turning to get the food. We hadn't picked a movie. A lawyer would have wanted to negotiate it. I didn't. Un-lawyer was the rule of the day. I followed my instructions and bought a large popcorn, light on the butter, two Dr. Peppers, and a box of Peanut M&Ms for her at the snack counter.

She was waving me to hurry up as I finished at the register. "Theater seven," she said as I reached her. She was bouncing for joy, and the bouncing her boobs did under that dress was getting me hard.

Number seven was toward the end of the corridor. The small electronic sign over the door said *Bride Wars*.

Just kill me.

The theater was remarkably full for such a crappy movie. And so far as I could tell, it was an estrogen fest. There wasn't another guy anywhere.

Emma chose seats near the front, two empty seats between groups of three women on the right and three young girls on the left. I got the side next to the giggling teenagers. There were lots of better areas to sit farther back, but I just smiled as I took my seat.

Emma started telling me about the plot of the film as I tried to listen to her over the banter of the teenyboppers, busily multitasking between talking to each other and texting at the same time. It seems they all thought Tommy somebody was gross, and Linda somebody had a stick up her ass, and Mrs. Tremont was mean, and Mr. Daggat was dreamy, and on and on and on.

It didn't seem so long ago that I'd gone to high school, but their jabbering bordered on being an alien language. If they ever grew up, they would learn that 'like' couldn't be every third word out of their mouths.

"I think you'll like it," Emma said. She had just completed summarizing the movie.

I couldn't lie to her, so I kept my mouth shut and nodded. Luckily, the previews ended and the teenyboppers put their phones away, limiting themselves to giggling and the occasional comment as the film started.

An hour and a half after it started, the credits were rolling down the screen and the audience was filing out. Emma and I stayed.

"This was a lot of fun, don't you think?" she asked.

"Sugar, anytime I get to spend with you is time well spent," I replied. That was the truth as far as it went, but I could think of fifty better ways to spend time with her. "The night is still young. Would you like to go out somewhere?"

She placed her hand on my arm. "Oh, I'm so sorry, Steven." A concerned look rose in her face. "I can't. Megan called and I promised to go see her tonight after the movie. But I would like to see you again soon. I have a really fun thing we can do."

Shot down again. She was avoiding alone time with me for some reason. "Katie had to cancel on me, so I'm free tomorrow or Wednesday."

She stood. "Wednesday night is perfect." The theater was almost empty except for the cleaning crew shuffling in between showings. "I have a surprise planned."

I stood. "You're not going to tell me what it is?"

She raised an eyebrow. "That would ruin the surprise, now wouldn't it? Dress casually, nothing you don't mind getting dirty."

We started out of the theater.

A surprise.

* * *

Emma

"The look on his face was priceless," I said into

138

the phone. I was filling in Megan on tonight's events. "When he had figured out I had bought tickets to *Bride Wars* instead of one of the action movies, or even *Casablanca*. It was just for a second, but you couldn't miss it. He would have rather been forced to chew glass than sit through that movie. Then when I picked out seats right up front next to some teenage mean girl high school types, his temperature must have gone up ten degrees."

"So, what did he say?" Megan asked.

"Nothing, he just watched the movie with me. He didn't grit his teeth, he didn't complain, at the end, he just said any time spent with me was time well spent."

Megan coughed. "Is this guy for real? Are you sure he's got the right parts in his pants? That's so sweet it's sickening."

I had to laugh. "Yeah, I know. And after, I told him I had to meet you. It was so hard leaving him. He looked so... sad."

"Be tough, Sis. I only had two conditions, remember?" she told me.

"Are you trying to torture him or me?"

"Who, me?" My sister couldn't pull off innocent to save her life. She understood exactly what I meant. She changed the subject by complaining about Braydon, as if it was something new.

After a half hour of bitching about Braydon, I was done for the night and we hung up.

The way Steven had made me feel last week was unreal. That man had the magic fingers and he had my number. Todd had rarely made me come, and never twice in one night. I couldn't remember if it had ever been twice in a week with him.

Lying in bed, I restlessly replayed the last week in my mind. I was only able to drift off to sleep after I fingered myself to an orgasm recalling last Wednesday night with Steven. The man with the magic fingers.

The next morning, I was almost out the door when Mama called. She wanted to talk about Megan. She was worried the situation with Braydon was getting worse. It took me half an hour to calm her down and keep her from coming down to visit and meddling in Megan's life again. A visit from Mama was the last thing either of us needed right now, and the call meant I was going to be late for work. Mama had the annoying habit of calling right before I left for work instead of in the evening, when I had time.

I drove faster than usual, got honked at twice for my trouble, and was still a little late for work. Today was not a good day to be late. We were hanging the Covington paintings this morning. But at least I didn't end up as LA's latest road rage statistic.

The preparation techs had already placed the Degas and were getting ready to hang the two Renoirs when I hurried into the exhibit room. The placement appeared perfect to me, and a quick check of the credit panels showed they had gotten the wording correct. One of the worst faux pas for a curator was to have a typo on the credit panel pointed out by a visitor. Janice and I were admiring how much better the exhibit looked now.

The last painting was being adjusted when Lloyd Benson, the museum's Chairman of the Board, walked in. "Good morning. I wanted to see our latest additions." He studied the artwork closely, one by one. "Magnificent pieces, Miss Watson. I understand you got those Covington boys to cough these up. Good work."

I had no idea he knew anything about the paintings. "I didn't really have anything to do with it, sir."

"Nonsense, young lady. I suggested it to them several times before, but you got it done. Excellent work."

I couldn't explain that it was due to my boyfriend, if that's what he was.

He moved closer and lowered his voice. "I gather that young Steven has taken an interest in you." The old man had quite a network of informants, but then again, he had seen me with Steven at the Habitat project.

I nodded, the blush heating up my cheeks.

"All I can say is that you won't find any better people than those Covingtons. For a family with their resources to be volunteering at Habitat like they do, that is really something. Most people would just write a check and be done with it. They have real character. You don't find that very often anymore." I didn't respond, but I thought the same applied to him as well.

Back in our little office, Janice had to embarrass me by telling the others what Mr. Benson had said. My stock around here was rising thanks to my maybe boyfriend.

When Tuesday evening came, terrible was not a bad enough word to describe my mood. This playing hard to get stuff was getting on my nerves. Why couldn't I call him and talk to him? Because Megan said.

Megan doesn't know everything.

I took in the space. It was my apartment, but tonight, everything reminded me of Steven. The cases to the Bond movies he had left were still by the DVD player. The couch brought back memories of that evening. I couldn't escape the memories. Megan had made me promise, and I owed it to her and Elissa to keep my promise. I turned on the DVR and started a *Bachelor* marathon with the volume up loud.

These Cosmo tests suck.

My phone rang, and I paused the DVR.

It was Mama. "Dear, I'm so sorry, but I have some bad news."

I cringed. "Is Daddy okay?" I managed to squeak out.

"No, dear, it's not your daddy." She paused. "I'm afraid that Lady has passed away."

I slumped down in my seat and the tears started. "What happened?"

"She didn't suffer, dear. She died in her sleep."

I couldn't stop sobbing.

"Daddy is going to bury her next to Mulligan by the fruit trees."

I was just sobbing and crying. I couldn't manage any words.

"I'm so sorry, dear. She's up in heaven now with Mulligan and Elissa."

My mother's mention of my twin sister's name just made it worse. I sobbed and cried on the phone with her for a long time, recalling all the memories. I promised to come up when I could to say a proper goodbye to my horse who was also my most special friend. There would never be another horse as kind and gentle as Lady.

I finally turned off the lights and cried half the night. I missed Lady so much. I cried myself to sleep.

CHAPTER NINE

Steven

Wednesday night came soon enough. As I arrived at the address she gave me on Pico Boulevard, what I found was a parking garage. Emma traded waves with me from the sidewalk as I drove in. The garage was parking for the community college.

She was dressed in faded jeans and a light blue V-neck shirt, with a satchel over her shoulder. Her hug was tighter and longer than Monday night. "I missed you," she said.

"I missed you too, Sugar." I squeezed her tighter, getting some of that citrusy smell from her hair.

She broke the embrace and started down the path into the campus.

"Do I get a clue?" I asked.

She ignored my question. "The professor told me I could bring you tonight to see if you liked it." So, a clue after all. We were going to class. She turned into the entrance to the art building, and we entered a large room on the first floor.

Chairs were in a semi-circle around a raised platform on the left. A few students and a few older than college-age women were already seated. They had pads of paper on their laps. Art class, by the look of it. "Good, we got here in time to get seats up front. She chose a seat in the center of the front row and had me sit next to her.

Some of the students had set up easels toward the back. Lauren grabbed oversized clipboards for us, and white lab coats, which we donned.

This must get messy.

She opened her satchel and took out large pads for the both of us and handed me a gum eraser and a long pencil. "As you can guess, this is a drawing class." Her eyes lit up. "I just love it. Mama was so good, she could have a made a living as an artist, but somehow, I didn't inherit her talent. Daddy says it was his fault."

She showed me how she held the pencil and started to sketch a cat freehand. It looked amazing to me, and she was quick. This was one thing I was not going to be any good at, but if she liked it, I was willing to give it a try. As the class filled up, I noticed this was once again going to be a testosterone-free zone. There was only one other guy among the crowd.

Then the model arrived, clothed only in a bathrobe. He dropped the robe.

Great. We are drawing a naked guy.

The model grabbed a chair and brought it onto the pedestal with him. He placed himself directly in front of Emma, one leg up on the chair, and struck a pose, his junk hanging down. He winked at her and smiled.

What an ass.

If he did it again, I might have to break my pencil off in his skinny little ass.

Emma blushed.

Who is this guy?

Emma started to sketch.

I started to fiddle with my pencil and drew a few lines.

It came so easily to Emma. The drawing on her board was quickly taking shape while mine made little headway.

The jerk model continued to stare at my girl and make eyes at her. He would smile when she glanced up from her drawing.

I tried to concentrate on my drawing but wasn't doing a good enough job to even get a prize at a grammar school competition.

Emma glanced at my board and gave me an appreciative grin. She had finished hers and was just touching up things. A really good drawing to my novice standards.

I looked up, and lover boy was mouthing something at Emma. I coughed. He stopped with a concerned glance in my direction. That's right, asswipe, you'd better cut it out. I gave him the ice-cold stare that said I was about to break him in two.

He got the message. His smile vanished.

The teacher started going around the class, making minor critiques here and there. "Excellent job, Miss Watson," was her comment on seeing Emma's effort. She took a quick look at mine and passed by without a word. She likely didn't have an hour to spare enumerating the failings on my board. She called for the next pose and we all moved to a clean sheet to start again.

Model boy took down the chair and moved forward on his pedestal, again almost directly in front of Emma. He smiled toward the coed to Emma's right and winked at her.

What a weasel.

We started the second drawing, and I was getting the hang of it, sort of. This guy was a horse's ass, so the drawing needed to reflect that, which made it easier.

The teacher called for a third and final pose after making her critique rounds again. Listening to her comments as she went around, it was apparent that Emma was the most talented in the room. No surprise there, from what I could see of her drawings.

Lover boy pulled a pad onto his perch and lay down on it facing the class, one knee up, his head propped on his cocked arm with that shit-eating grin of his, and his pathetic limp little dick lying on his thigh.

This is torture.

The class mercifully ended after the third drawing. It had been an hour and a half too long for me. Any more time with the skinny naked pervert leering at my girl and I would be adding murder to my list of achievements.

What a wanker

* * *

Emma

I waved to him as he turned into the parking garage. I waited with a dull ache in my heart. When I hugged him, I pushed a little, and he said he missed me too. My heart fluttered. I wanted to kiss him so badly. I almost called off the torture session I was about to put him through, but I'd promised Megan, and I owed it to her to go through with it.

He was curious, asking for a clue. I told him we were going to a class, which wasn't giving away much since we were on a community college campus. We were early enough to get seats up front, almost close enough to reach out and touch.

I sketched a cat for him and showed him how to hold his pencil while we waited.

Tonight was art class. More like male anatomy class, in a way. Although the class schedule said Drawing 220, Ms. Zewinski made it clear from the outset that since Mr. Gorham only used female models, she would only have male models in this section. This was to even things out, she said. All of the guys except for one switched sections the following week.

Our model tonight was Sean. He had been here a few times before. When he dropped his robe, Steven got the expression again, the one that said he'd rather be strapped atop an ant hill, but just for a second before reverting to his casual face.

Sean winked at me. What a douche.

When the class ended, we put the coats away and left the building. I took Steven's drawings to put them in my satchel. He had drawn rough approximations, just with one glaring issue. "You forgot the penis," I told him.

He pointed to a dot in the crotch area. "Right there. It's a micro-dick."

I laughed. "Compared to you, maybe." Next to this man, Sean did have a micro-dick.

Sean came out after us and met up with a waiting Marjorie, poor girl.

Sean stared in our direction. I made a point of wrapping my arm around Steven as we walked. "So, what did you think of the class?"

He didn't hesitate. "I think I enjoyed being with

you."

"So you liked it?"

"No way. One more wink in your direction by wanker dude over there, and I was going to pound him into the ground."

I laughed. "He can't help it. He's always been a douche." We started walking back to the garage.

Steven gritted his teeth. His protectiveness was hot.

We strolled in silence. His hand around my waist scorched my skin with desire. I skipped a step to get in stride with him. Our hips melded together as we walked. I only had to get through one more of Megan's Cosmo tests. "I was thinking..."

He stopped suddenly and faced me his hands on my shoulders. "Don't." It wasn't a shout, but he was firm, his green eyes hard.

My stomach churned. "Don't what?"

His face softened. His lips curled up into a smile. "Close your eyes."

I didn't comprehend fast enough.

"Just close your eyes, Sugar, and listen to me. Listen very carefully."

I held my eyes closed. "Don't give me another one of your psychology tests," I warned him.

He put two fingers to my temple. "You are thinking too much." He tapped my temple. "Too much."

I opened my eyes to protest. "But..."

"Closed, I said," he commanded.

I closed my eyes again with a huff.

"Listen to me. You are thinking too much and not feeling enough. Don't use this." He tapped my temple again. "Use this." He shifted his fingers to the swell of my breast over my heart. "I'm done being tested," he said coldly.

A cold vise closed over my heart. I might have pushed him too far. I kept my eyes closed. I couldn't bear to see him leave now.

His hand closed firmly on my shoulder. "Now it's my turn to test you."

He wrapped his arms around me, and in a heartbeat, his lips found mine.

His tongue teased me, and I opened to him. I grasped behind his neck and speared my hands into his hair, pulling him tightly to me. His spicy scent enveloped me. His arms welded our bodies together with a wicked force, his growing arousal making itself known against my belly. The blood was rushing in my ears.

"Get a room," someone nearby called out. We ignored them.

His hand moved to my ass and grabbed me tightly as I went up on my toes to reach as high as I could. He tasted like lemon drops and desire, sending instant heat between my thighs. He fisted my hair and pulled my head away, capturing my gaze with his. His green eyes were feral, predatory.

"You drive me crazy, Emma Watson."

I couldn't engage my vocal cords. My breath caught in my throat as the heat rose in me to unbearable levels. His fierce gaze drilled through me, erasing all lucid thought. Nobody had ever said anything half as hot to me. Holding him tighter was all that I could communicate. I couldn't lose Steven.

"But I'm done being tested." His voice was firm and harsh. He pulled my head closer, his nose almost touching mine. "You can choose to be mine even though I'm a lawyer, or not," he said in a low growl, "but no more games."

He still had a tight grip on my hair, but I pulled his head to mine, and this time, it was my mouth ravaging his. The nonverbal answer was all I could manage.

His response told me he understood. I wrapped my legs around him as he lifted me off my feet with his free hand under my butt. His other hand controlled my hair as he pulled my head to the side and nibbled on my ear. "You didn't answer my question," he said hoarsely. He lowered me and raised me again, rubbing my crotch over the steely cock in his pants.

I pulled at his hair to get access to his mouth again and resume our kiss. Our tongues and lips had not finished exploring each other. When I came up for air, I was finally able to speak. "Come to my place tonight and I'll show you my answer." Like

Megan said, fuck all the lawyers. It was time to fuck myself a lawyer.

We untangled ourselves after a few more moments. We walked the rest of the way to the garage, his fingers intertwined with mine.

He carried my satchel, hiding the bulge in his pants.

Screw Megan's tests.

CHAPTER TEN

Emma

We drove separately and I beat him to my place.

As soon as I opened the door, it struck me how messy my little apartment looked. I hadn't been expecting to have him over, so I threw the clothes littering my bedroom floor into the closet and shut the door. I straightened up the bed. I grabbed everything off the table and dumped it as quickly as I could in the dishwasher. I kicked the loose shoes by the coffee table under the couch as he knocked on the door.

I grabbed a bottle of wine from the fridge on my way to the door.

His smile as I opened the door warmed me all the way to my toes.

I set the wine bottle down. "I thought..."

He put a finger to my lips to stop me. "Sugar, remember what I said about thinking too much?" His voice was firm and the smile disappeared.

I nodded my response.

He brought his face close to mine as I readied myself for a resumption of our kiss on campus. He stopped short and whispered to me. "Tonight, I make the rules. Rule number one, you don't think. Do you understand?" He held my shoulders firmly.

"Okay," I whispered back.

"Rule number two." His voice became stern. He wasn't whispering anymore. The predator flashed in his eyes for a second. "You don't argue. Do you understand?"

"Okay." I was ready to do what the man wanted, whatever he wanted. I moved forward for a kiss.

He gave me a peck on the lips and moved past me.

My heart fell. A peck was all I got? After my all too obvious invitation for sex? I didn't know how I could have been more obvious. I wasn't thinking, I was feeling, and I felt let down. But I wasn't allowed to argue. So far, the rules sucked.

A bag from DessertMagic appeared from behind his back. "Have anything to eat around here? I brought dessert."

I managed a smile. The chocolate cake he brought last time had been heavenly. I opened the fridge.

He looked over my shoulder. "Oh, these are perfect," he said. He grabbed the package of jumbo bratwurst from the shelf.

"But I don't have any buns."

He kissed my neck and squeezed my butt. "I beg to differ, Sugar. You have marvelous buns."

I laughed. Maybe this wasn't going to be so bad after all.

"Where do you keep the frypan around here?"

I retrieved one from under the oven for him.

He started the stove and put two of the brats in the pan.

I got out some plates, set the table, and poured the wine. I handed him a glass.

He put it down and moved me in front of the stove. "You just stand here and don't move. You're going to get a sausage lesson. Right here, got it?"

This was silly. "I know how to cook a hot dog." I turned the flame up high.

He moved behind me. "You need to treat the sausage just right." His arms went around me, circling my waist.

This reminded me of him showing me how to handle the drill at the construction project. His closeness was tantalizing. He brushed the side of my breast as he moved his hands up my sides and back down. My nipples started to harden again.

"Sugar, you obviously don't know enough about sausage. Turn the flame down low. You have to heat them up slowly."

I adjusted the burner, but the heat that was building up wasn't only on the stove.

His arms were around me, and his hands slid up to trace the undersides of my breasts with tantalizing softness. "Lift up." He pulled my shirt off over my head as I raised my arms. This was quickly getting better.

I tried to turn around to face him.

"I told you, don't move." He spun me around facing the stove again. "Now stay there."

"You heat them slowly. That way, the sausage plumps up nice and thick. You do like them plump, don't you?" His fingers continued to move softly over my skin, leaving traces of tingles wherever they went.

I wiggled my ass against his crotch and found out I wasn't the only one heating up. "Thick is good."

He then pulled my sports bra up over my head. Now I was topless, but facing the wrong way. "You need to turn them so they heat all around."

I giggled as I located a rubber spatula in the drawer and used it to roll the brats over.

He started to massage my shoulders. "You're stiff."

I giggled. "Sometimes, a girl likes it stiff."

He continued to rub my shoulders and brought the bulge in his pants up against my ass. "Trust me, Sugar, it's stiff enough," he whispered in my ear.

"I'd have to see that to be sure," I shot back.

"There are other things that are good hard." He moved his hands around me to cup my breasts and

157

tease my nipples that tightened into hard little knots. "This is called an autonomic response. It means you can't fake it. They tell me the truth about what you're feeling." We both understood what he meant.

I turned the hot dogs some more and rubbed my ass against his cock. "And just what are they telling you now?"

"That things are warming up just fine." He continued to distract me by fondling my breasts and running his hands up and down my sides. He reached around me and undid my jeans. He pulled my pants down slowly and brought his hands back up, tracing the insides of my legs.

I trembled under his touch as he stopped just short of my pussy. I tried to turn around.

"Eyes front, Sugar, and no arguing," he said, thumbing my nipple and moving his other hand down my abdomen and through my curls to part my folds.

I gasped at the touch I had been yearning for. I rubbed my ass against him some more.

He circled my clit, teasing me. He kissed my neck and cradled my breast while dipping his finger in and out of me.

The heat inside me went up three alarms. I rubbed my ass against his crotch. I spread my stance to give him more room. I couldn't think about anything but his fingers and the big, thick cock I wanted. "Are we ready yet?"

He nibbled seductively on my ear. "Not quite." He was playing with my clit and making it hard for me to get any words out. He kissed my ear.

I was losing control. I turned off the burner, placed a hand on the counter to steady myself, and with the other started to rub his cock through his jeans. Stiff wasn't a good enough word for it. His movements were setting off so many nerve endings in my sensitive little nub, I couldn't concentrate.

He continued to work his hands and kiss my shoulders, my neck, and my ears. He wouldn't let me turn around. I locked my knees to keep from falling. My legs were trembling as his fingers moved inside me, and he tormented my clit with techniques they should teach in college.

I moaned my request to turn around. I tried to get my hand down inside his jeans but failed.

He wouldn't relent. His hand continued the magic finger treatment of my lady parts until he pushed me over the edge. My climax came suddenly, forcefully. His arm around my chest held me up as my legs trembled and my walls convulsed around his fingers. I was too weak to stand without his help. The blood rushing in my ears and my panting were so loud I couldn't hear what he whispered to me.

What?" I asked as I came to my senses.

He lifted me up.

I hung around his neck and rested my head on his shoulder.

He carried me into the bedroom. "I said, I think you're ready." He put me down on my feet beside the bed. He brought his hand to his mouth and licked his fingers with a wicked smile.

The tremors of my climax gently passed. My legs began to strengthen again. I pulled myself to him. I clawed at his hair and pulled myself up to reach him with my other hand behind his neck. My mouth found his for our hot little kiss.

His hand found my ass and pulled me up.

I wrapped both legs around him and held on, pressing my breasts to him as forcefully as I could. He no longer tasted of lemon drops. I could taste me and raw desire.

He broke the kiss. "Lie down," he commanded.

I put my legs down as he lowered me to the ground. I lay down and shifted myself to the center of the bed.

He pulled his shirt over his head, undid his belt and his jeans, and shucked them to the floor. The thickness and length of him amazed me again. He got on the bed.

I spread my legs.

He knelt between them, and his eyes feasted on my body.

I shivered. My pussy was open to him. I wasn't used to being in this vulnerable position with the lights on. However, Steven put me completely at ease.

"My God, Sugar, you're beautiful," he rasped. His cock twitched upward.

He retrieved a condom from his jeans. He ripped the foil with his teeth and handed it to me as he knelt on the bed and positioned himself with his cock over my chest. It twitched just above my boobs.

I hadn't done this before. I went to place it on the tip, but he stopped me.

"You have it backward," he said.

I flipped it over and started to roll the thin latex down over his cock. I struggled to get it down, but his soft moans of pleasure told me he didn't mind my fumbling my way through this.

He spread my legs wider. I pulled my knees up as he moved between them. His eyes fixed me with his gaze. "Tell me if it hurts."

My vocal cords were paralyzed by the predator in his eyes. I lay transfixed, unable to move, to respond. The heat of his breath ignited a flame inside me. The raw need behind his eyes aroused me even more than I thought possible.

He leaned closer. He reached down between my legs and positioned the tip of his cock at my soaked entrance.

I held my breath as I anticipated the coming sensation. I was scared of the size of him, afraid he wouldn't fit.

He pushed the tip an inch into my slippery entrance. He stopped, still, as I acclimated to his size. He pushed slowly a little farther, then out and back in just a bit more.

It hurt being stretched to the limit, but I dared not protest. I wanted this. I wanted him. I wanted all of him. We just needed to go slowly. I could see it in his face. I could tell it was costing him to go slow, to barely be inside me. He was so much bigger than Todd, and Todd had been a long time ago. Maybe I'd shrunk.

Did that happen?

He stopped, sensing my apprehension.

I pulled at his ass with my hand and my legs to urge him in.

He thrust in farther, and out, and in some more, continuing the subtle back and forth that slowly stretched my walls to take him. He was being so unbelievably gentle with me as we continued.

Before I realized it, I had taken all of him, and he slid in and out with pleasure quickly pushing aside the pressure and the pain.

He thrust harder and quicker, sending sizzling sparks along all of my nerves, and heat spiraled through my body.

The waves of pleasure rippled through me. I clawed at his back, pulling at him, willing him to fill me harder and deeper. I wrapped my legs around him and urged him in. All thought was replaced with feral desire and need. I rocked my hips into his thrusts.

I cried out his name as my toes curled and the spasms took over. I was unable to form the words I wanted to say to him. I wanted him to find his pleasure as I came down from my climax. "More." It was all I could say.

The animal returned to his eyes. He pounded into me with renewed force and quickly tensed up and found his release with a final groan before settling down on top of me, kissing my neck, my ear, and finally, my mouth.

Steven had shown me what a real man could do. I had reacted as never before. He had taken me to a place I didn't know existed. My boyfriend had the magic fingers and the magic cock.

He shifted his weight somewhat off me. His cock continued to pulse inside me. The heat radiating from my core relaxed me completely. I was exhausted and exhilarated. I listened to Steven's breathing slow and took in the smile of complete satisfaction on my boyfriend's face.

He kissed my nose. "Sugar, you are so fucking good it's unbelievable."

It's good to fuck myself a lawyer.

CHAPTER ELEVEN

Emma

Janice and I were in the lab, working through the latest group of paintings with the lab tech. Steven's father, Wendell Covington, had amassed enough art to start his own museum. It was unconscionable that one family would have so much when everyone else had to worry about making the rent. I got it, the Covingtons were rich, but this was at a whole level beyond rich. Some of the paintings were hanging in the family houses, and those were not in the audit, so we weren't checking them. Houses, as in more than one house, and the list was impressive, all the great masters. Most of the art was displayed in numerous corporate locations, and some were in storage because they didn't have enough wall space to accommodate it all. No wonder there was an audit. If anybody had told me a family in LA had more than nine hundred million in art, I wouldn't have believed them. Until now. Mr. Perkins's number only included the corporate art, not any of the art in the houses.

This morning's batch of five paintings had been in storage and brought over to us by armed delivery. We carefully unboxed them. Very carefully. We had the equipment to perform a vast array of tests in the museum lab but only the space for a few paintings at a time. Janice and I had finished with the microscopic analysis, the Woods Light, and the Infrared Reflectography. One of the paintings had been restored and touched up in minor areas, but nothing significant, and so far, things had gone well, with each of the items turning out to be exactly as described. Nobody had gotten a forgery past these people.

Janice was on her computer, making notes regarding the frontal examination of these five pieces, when I turned over the first painting to examine the back of the frame. We needed a sample from the stretcher to date the wood. That's when I noticed it.

The corner of the frame had a small area of writing. *R634* was what it said. The writing was not original.

A chill ran right through me. I shivered. Unfortunately, I recognized exactly what it was and what it meant.

This was an inventory mark from when the Nazis

stole this painting from the Rothschild family in France. The larger collections they looted during the war had been inscribed with letters denoting the families or museums and numbers for the item. The Germans were a meticulous people and extremely detailed in their recordkeeping. I'd seen this kind of mark before in my research. "Janice, you're going to want to see this and photograph it."

Janice came over from her computer with the camera. "My God, this was looted by the Nazis." Janice knew her stuff. She snapped a close-up of the marking. "It belonged to the Rothschilds. I think we might want to check the purchase history right away." The painting was a valuable Monet.

Janice leafed through the document folder for the painting. "It once went through Haberstock in Germany."

Unfortunately, I recognized the name. "He's known to have been a conduit for Nazi-looted art. Anything he touched has to be tainted."

I searched the *Commission for Looted Art in Europe* website. They kept a detailed database of Nazi-looted art from the war. I found the entry. "It's in the database as well, looted in France from the Rothschild family at the start of the war." This means the Covingtons had bought looted art, and probably knowingly. Anyone buying their quantity of European art would have known Haberstock's reputation and also would have known about the looted art database kept by the Commission.

We examined the other four paintings in this batch. Two of the four had similar markings. Mr. Covington had been hiding three looted paintings in storage for years.

Janice took the additional photos and added them to the batch. "Emma, don't say anything about this yet. I want to finish the entire inventory before we broach this subject with either Perkins or Mr. Durham."

We agreed to carry on as if nothing had happened for now. This would be a major problem for Covington, especially if the news leaked to the press. I took the wood samples for dating as we prepared for the next batch this afternoon.

I couldn't stop wondering if this was a good sign or a bad one. I'd been searching for my great-great-grandmother's Renoir for so long, and I had finally seen not one, but three of the looted Rothschild paintings, and this could get me closer to finding ours.

Our family had placed the painting along with some furniture with their neighbors, the Rothschilds, when they went searching for passage out of pre-war France. The plan had been to have the things sent once they reached safety. The war started before anything was forwarded to them, and the painting was lost in the war. It had been my mission to locate it if I could. It would mean the world to Mama to get it back in the family.

I was currently chasing down a lead on our Renoir that pointed to the LA area. If I were lucky, where there was one, there might be more. But this also meant Steven's family trafficked in stolen art. The thought made me nauseous. I crossed my fingers that Steven just didn't know.

One of the interns arrived with our lunch. Janice and I had taken to ordering Subway because we were in such a time crunch to finish this audit.

The afternoon paintings were routine, with no more back of frame markings.

I had trouble concentrating, though, thinking about the implications that Steven's father may have been involved in trafficking stolen art. Janice had ordered me to keep quiet about this for now, so I couldn't ask him, and if I did, I dreaded the answer.

They have Nazi art.

* * *

It was Thursday, and I knew Steven had dinner scheduled with his brother Bill tonight. I called him after work before dinner.

When he asked me how things went today for me, I lied and told him it was merely more of the same. He told me he had another boring day in court. He didn't bore me with any of the particulars, but one thing caught my attention. When he talked about his boss, Monica, the Cougar Lady Janice had put in her place on Monday. I could hear an edge to his voice. There was something there he wasn't telling me. I didn't press him on it, but it made me a little uneasy.

When I got home, I grabbed a microwave lasagna dinner out of the freezer and set out my search papers on the table. Meal in hand, I started to review my series of questions for tomorrow. I had Friday afternoon off again to spend on the search for our missing family painting. I was getting close. I could feel it. I needed to be organized and logical in my questioning tomorrow.

I composed myself, and four hours later, I thought I was well enough prepared for tomorrow afternoon's session, and I'd stared at my papers long enough to have everything memorized.

I checked my phone. It wasn't too late to call Steven, and I was done playing hard to get. He answered on the second ring.

"Hello, Sugar, I was just thinking about calling you."

"How was dinner with your brother?"

"Good, and tonight, Lauren and Katie both came along too."

I'd met Bill's wife, Lauren, at the Habitat project. "That's nice. I like them both. Very nice ladies."

"Yeah, and they like you too," he said playfully.

"So I came up?"

"That's why the girls were there. You and I were the main topic of conversation, or rather, inquisition."

"Really? So what did you say?"

He hesitated. "I said you were a little dull, and dumber than a rock because you were willing to spend more than two dates with me."

"You did not," I practically shrieked.

"Well, of course not. I said you are the smartest, kindest, sexiest woman I have ever met, and you drive me crazy every minute of the day that I'm away from you, and I constantly want to fuck you senseless, and you have the sweetest pussy."

I laughed. "That is very kind, but that doesn't sound like you either, so what did you say?"

"It should count because I was thinking it." That part, I hoped, was true. "Basically, I tried to give them as little information as possible. And I wasn't kidding that Lauren and Katie are big fans of yours."

"Are you just flattering me because you want to get into my pants again tonight?"

"Sugar, you know me so well. Is it working?"

I was flattered, and his talking dirty to me was getting me wet again. I wanted him to come over so badly, but my brain overrode my hormones. "It would be, except I have a big day tomorrow and I know I won't get any sleep tonight if you come over."

"Sleep is overrated."

He was making this super hard. "Raincheck?" I could think of something else that was probably getting hard.

"Okay, tomorrow night, seven o'clock at your place. Chinese or pizza?" he asked.

"Chinese. I like it when you feed me."

"You got it. Twenty-one hours from now and counting," he said.

I was getting hornier by the minute. We set the menu and dawdled on the phone as he tried to destroy my willpower by telling me all the wickedly nice things he wanted to do to me, which only confirmed that I wouldn't get any sleep if I relented. I had to settle for diddling myself while he talked dirty to me. He was so good at phone sex that it only took me fifteen minutes, and another three for me to hear his moans as he finished himself off while I told him how I was going to lick him and suck him next time I saw him. It took us each a few minutes to cool down, but I was certainly relaxed enough now to try to fall asleep.

"Next time, we should try this over Facetime," he suggested.

"No way, stud muffin. The magic is in the imagination," I answered.

Phone sex. I am definitely descending into Megan territory.

* * *

Steven

Thursday night had been dinner with Bill and Lauren. Lauren came along some of the time, but last night, she was on a mission. She and Katie were determined to learn more about my *'relationship'* with Emma, their words, not mine. That was odd, because ever since Victoria, I didn't have relationships. I only had dates or hookups or whatever you wanted to call them, but not a relationship. The word invoked images of something lasting, and Victoria had cured me of the fantasy.

Katie had called before dinner to encourage me to not screw it up, in her words, so now, their questions made more sense. The two were colluding. Bill had barely met Emma, but Lauren made it clear to him that she thought my Emma was a rare find. A real keeper, in her words. Bill chimed in that I should heed Lauren's advice because she had a keen sense of people and that was one of the reasons she had done so well at the company. Lauren blushed at this compliment, but I could tell Bill was being sincere, and he didn't give out such compliments easily. He trusted Lauren's judgment of people more than he trusted his own. Katie was equally complimentary of Emma.

Now the pressure really was on me to *not screw it up*.

I told them as little as I could get away with, certainly not that we had taken it to the next level the previous night. Certainly not that I had a mind-blowing night with her, and not that she drove me crazy and was the singular reason that I was falling behind on my studying for the bar. And not that I thought they had it wrong that she was a one-in-a-million find because I thought she was even better than that. I couldn't tell them that I hadn't even noticed another woman since I met her. Certainly not that she had tortured me with that chick flick and that stupid art class and that I would have endured another twenty of those humiliations to be with her.

No, I couldn't tell them any of those things last night. I had trouble grasping it myself. I was in completely uncharted territory.

When Emma called last night after dinner, I was unable to talk her into a repeat of Wednesday night. I told her sleep was overrated, but she was insistent that she needed sleep for today's work and we had to settle for phone sex. The words out of her mouth were such a turn-on I didn't need much hand action to come. It wasn't the same as being with her, but I had to settle for whatever I could get.

This morning, I got into work early to get some

morning study time in. That lasted until nine, when Monica dumped a case organizing task on me that would take all day. She made a point of waving her gray envelope in my face when she gave me the assignment. It was her little power play. *The bitch.* At least she hadn't tried to schedule a weekend retreat for the two of us.

The only break during the morning came when Lenny stopped by to tell me Judge Vinson had granted Monica the motions she wanted in the Goldsmith criminal case. Lenny said it like I should be excited. He was such a kiss-ass, and I could have cared less whether Monica got what she wanted or not. I was not on the case and I didn't care to be. Criminal defense seemed slimy to me. Lenny thought that it was exciting. Good for him. I guessed somebody had to do it, but count me out when it comes to defending a man who killed his wife and his daughter.

After lunch, piles of papers were spread across the table in front of me. I was in the third hour of trying to organize this project. The end was almost in sight. I could see a way to finish this before the end of the day.

Jeremy opened the door to the conference room I was working in. "Need to join Monica at a client's right away."

It was futile, but I asked anyway. "What's the emergency this time?"

"Some important deposition, she said, but if you ask me, she just wants to fill up the room to bump up the hours." Typical Monica. Two extra first-years at a deposition added considerably to the billable hours.

"Okay, I guess our time is hers to waste," I mumbled.

Jeremy gave me the address and took off as I rechecked my phone. Still no response from Emma.

I parked under the building and rode the elevator to the lobby, where they directed me upstairs. A little before two, I silenced my phone, and Jeremy and I joined Monica and Lenny in the conference room as she briefed the client. "Just remember, Tom, your best answer is always '*I don't recall.*' Don't give her anything, especially not anything concrete. Never answer anything more than what is asked, and don't volunteer any information. If a question is not clear and concise, ask them to repeat the question so you can be clear about what you are answering. And before you answer any question, any question at all, give me a chance to object. That will use up a lot of her time. She only has you for three hours, and since she is representing herself, it should be pretty easy to get her tied up in knots. We run out the clock and then you're done."

He shook his head and huffed. "Got it." He straightened his expensive suit and took a nervous sip of water. Big Tom Coulter was not used to being told what to do and having to do it for two or three hours straight. No surprise, sitting for a deposition was like going to the dentist. You didn't enjoy it. You just tolerated it because you had to.

Jeremy was right. He and I were only there to bump up the hours. Monica, her shadow, Lenny, and the two of us made four lawyers on our side, plus the court reporter, and she had said the opposing client was representing herself, so no lawyers on their side. Unnecessary overkill, typical Monica.

I glanced at my watch. Five after two. Five hours and counting until I saw Emma again, and three of those wasted locked in a room with Monica, listening to a boring deposition and pretending to take notes. As the lead, at least Monica would be busy looking after the client for those three hours.

I knew Tom Coulter. Our families bumped into each other occasionally growing up. His daughter, Celeste, had a crush on Bill in sixth grade. The Coulters didn't have Covington money, and their reputation was not stellar, but they were loaded by any reasonable definition, so he was a big client to the firm, no doubt. Monica would have to focus on keeping him happy. You didn't piss off clients like Tom Coulter if you wanted to stay a partner at E&S.

I heard the door open behind me.

The other side has arrived.

CHAPTER TWELVE

Emma

The phone sex had drained and relaxed me, but I still hardly slept last night. I was so worried about this afternoon. Now, I was dragging so badly that it took me three coffees to get through the morning working on another group of paintings from Covington with Janice. After lunch, I headed out to get a bite to eat before resuming my Renoir search. I didn't have much time, but I wasn't having Subway for the fifth time this week. I stopped at a Burger King on the way. They had tables large enough for me to lay a few things out to review before the session at two, and I was less likely to spill than if I'd stopped for Mexican. I only ordered a soda.

I entered the building a little before two with all of my notes and sat in the lobby composing myself and listening to some calming classical in my earbuds.

At two o'clock, a security guard escorted me upstairs. He opened the heavy conference room door for me.

Now was my chance to get some answers.

I stopped mid-stride.

Fuck.

It was the Cougar lady, Monica Paisley. She was the lawyer for the other side, and she'd brought along another three suits.

Double-fuck.

A court reporter sat in front of a steno machine in the corner. Thomas Coulter sat next to Cougar lady, smiling. I recognized the asshole from his company website. The suits on my side of the table turned around.

Steven.

Triple-fuck.

Steven was one of the lawyers opposing me.

How could he do this to me?

I shivered.

Steven quickly looked down at the table, avoiding my gaze, and abruptly gathered up his papers.

Cougar lady stood and offered me her card. "Monica Paisley for E&S, representing Mr. Coulter. We are ready to get started if you are."

I leaned across the table to accept the card. The door closed behind me. Steven had just left the room, and a questioning look by Cougar Lady to the other suits went unanswered.

My mind went blank. I wasn't sure what to do next. I took a seat across from Mr. Coulter. My vision blurred for a moment. Lightheaded, I opened the folder with my notes in front of me. I placed my phone in the middle of the table with the recorder app running.

Cougar lady put a recorder next to mine and announced the time, place, and case for the reporter, and we were officially started.

Now I would get some answers.

I asked a few perfunctory initial questions and then I got to it. "Mr. Coulter, were you in France in the summer two years ago?"

After a hesitant look to his lawyer, he said, "I don't recall." So he was going to make this hard.

"Do you have a daughter named Celeste Coulter?"

Again, he waited and glanced at Cougar Lady before answering.

She nodded.

"Yes, I do," Coulter answered.

"This is going to take forever if you can't even answer a simple question like that," I said.

"Objection," Monica shouted out. "That is not a question."

She rattled me. I composed myself and slid over three screen captures. "These are Instagram posts made by your daughter in France two years…"

"Objection, we have not validated that those posts are from Mr. Coulter's daughter." It was Cougar Lady butting in again.

I tried to keep my cool and continue. "These posts show you, your wife, and your daughter in France July, two years ago."

"Objection, not a question."

I kept pressing. "Is this you in these posts, Mr. Coulter?"

Coulter waited for Monica to object, but this time, she didn't. "It looks like it might be." The ass would not even admit the posts were of him.

"Did you purchase any artwork while you were in France during July two years ago?" I asked.

"Objection, we have not established that Mr. Coulter was in France two years ago. You don't have to answer that, Tom."

Coulter stayed quiet. She was really pissing me off.

I tried it a different way. "Where did you spend July two years ago?"

"Objection, relevance. We are here over a dispute of ownership of a painting, not where Mr. Coulter spends his summers."

This was getting tiring. I brushed my hair back and tried to regain my composure. We went back and forth on this for the next ten minutes without her letting him answer a single damned question.

Lawyers suck.

I slid my next piece of paper across the table. "Do you recognize this, Mr. Coulter?"

After the pause that had now become routine, he answered. "Can't say that I do."

"It is a receipt for payment from you to a Mr. LeMere for a Renoir and three other paintings in July two years ago."

"Objection, not a question, and that has not been verified."

I was starting to sweat. "Would you please read it for us, Mr. Coulter?"

He waited for Monica to nod her assent. "I can't make out what it says exactly, but I do see Renoir, but that's all I can get from this." The ass was now pretending to not be able to read.

We went around and around on that for a while and a few dozen other questions, with Cougar lady telling him not to answer most of them. Cougar lady objected that I was badgering Coulter because it was badgering to try to get a straight answer out of him. She objected relevance, hearsay, and specificity a million times. A complete fucking bitch. She wasn't letting me get anywhere. My blood was boiling. I kept hearing my daddy. "When you have a goal, just keep working at it and you'll get there." I wanted to pull out a Taser and shut the bitch up.

I pulled the magazine from my file. "Mr. Coulter, was your home featured in *Architectural Digest* last year?"

"I wouldn't know."

My top was sticking to my back I was sweating so much. "Mr. Coulter, do you live in Beverly Hills?"

He even paused before answering that one, the ass. "Yes."

I opened up the September *Architectural Digest* from last year to page forty-five and passed it across to Coulter. "Is this your house?"

"Objection, relevance. Don't answer that."

I continued anyway. My stomach churned with the frustration. "The article says that this is the Coulter residence in Beverley Hills. Is this your house?"

"Objection, he is not the only Coulter in the Beverley Hills area."

All through this, I got not one bit of cooperation. Cougar lady was being so unfair, and I was losing my cool. TV made this look so much easier. I swept my hair back again in an effort to calm myself. I silently counted to three.

I showed him the photograph of our family Renoir that Mama had given me. It was the only one we had. It was from before the war with my Great-great-grandmama in a room, in front of the Renoir on the living room wall. "This painting here is the same as that painting on page forty-five of that magazine."

Monica was getting red in the face. "Objection,

not a question, and we have not stipulated that to be Mr. Coulter's house, or verified the authenticity of that photograph."

Coulter fidgeted in his chair. He stayed quiet.

"You have to make him answer that," I spat out at Cougar Lady.

She calmly adjusted the papers in front of her. "If you were a lawyer, you would know that he doesn't have to answer irrelevant questions."

How could she say that? I wasn't a fucking lawyer, but so what? "I may not be a fucking lawyer, but I have the right to an answer," I blurted out at Cougar Lady. I could tell it was a mistake as soon as the words escaped my mouth.

"Any more swearing, young lady, and we walk. Let the record show that Miss Watson is hurling obscenities at the witness."

I can't let her get to me.

My stomach was telling me I shouldn't have had breakfast this morning. It was on the verge of depositing scrambled eggs all over their stupid mahogany table. He had to answer my questions. He just had to. "Do you own this painting?" I pointed to the one in my picture.

Objection, we haven't stipulated what painting that is."

Coulter smirked but didn't say anything.

I consulted my notes while I tried to calm down. I pictured Perry Mason, calm, cool, and collected, and summoned up my best impression of him. I couldn't let them get to me. "Do you own a painting that looks like this one?"

"Objection, insufficient specificity."

I couldn't take it anymore. "Do you own a Renoir?" I shouted.

"Objection, you're badgering the witness. Any more of that and we walk. Let the record show that Miss Watson yelled at the witness."

"I just asked if he owned a Renoir."

"Objection, that is not a question."

No wonder everyone hated fucking lawyers. "Do you, Mr. Coulter, own a Renoir?"

He looked to Cougar lady, who for once, did not object. "Not to my knowledge." That was it then. He was directly denying owning the painting. But even that was a sideways answer.

I boiled over. "This, here, is your house." I pounded the magazine. "And that painting on the wall is a Renoir."

"Objection, you are badgering the witness and you've been warned. Let the record show that Miss Watson has yelled at my client again after being sufficiently warned. We're done here. Mr. Coulter will not be answering any more questions."

"He didn't answer any to start with," I hurled back.

Cougar lady stood up. "We're done. Miss reporter, please show the deposition finished at two thirty P.M."

I stood and stared her down. "I have until five. We are not done yet."

She gathered up her papers. "Yes, we are. I will not allow you to badger my client. Mr. Coulter, you may leave."

Two minutes later, I was alone in the conference room wondering what had gone wrong.

Asshole lawyers.

They proved the legal system had everything to do with money and nothing to do with fairness. I gathered up my things and left the building, cursing lawyers under my breath. I had been working toward this afternoon for a year, and now, I'd blown it. I'd fucked it all up.

Now I'm never going to find the painting.

* * *

Steven

The opposing client was Emma.

What the hell is going on?

I hadn't caught any sign in her face that Monica knew about me and Emma. She was just being her normal asinine self.

Neither Jeremy nor I had been briefed on the case prior to being summoned by Her Majesty. The folder in front of me, though, contained the complaint against the Coulters that had been filed last year. I took the folder and left the room as soon as Monica started to introduce herself.

Once down in my car, I opened the folder to review the papers. For a non-lawyer, the complaint was well-drafted. Emma believed Tom Coulter had purchased a painting stolen from her family by the Nazis in the Second World War. As I read on, I learned she had traced the painting to a French art dealer, and she had evidence that Tom Coulter had purchased it from the dealer two years ago.

I was completely stuck. Emma was going to have another reason to hate lawyers if Monica had anything to say about it. Monica would be ruthless, and she would tie up poor Emma in an endless string of motions, and Monica had bragged last summer that she also had friends in the sheriff's office happy to target someone with a half-dozen traffic tickets just to ruin their day. *Fair* was not a word in Monica's vocabulary.

I drove back to the office and resumed working on the project Jeremy had interrupted a few hours earlier.

Monica barged in less than an hour later with her usual tact. "What the hell was that all about? I wanted you in that deposition."

"I know that woman socially. I can't be associated with the case," I said calmly.

"A girlfriend?"

I didn't answer.

"Maybe we can use that to our advantage," she suggested wryly.

"No way."

Her eyebrows shot up. "Then definitely, a girlfriend. How interesting," she said. Her face lit up as though she had just found a hundred-dollar bill on the floor.

I had no intention of discussing anything in my personal life with her. "I've known Tom Coulter a long time. Our families are friends. If he finds out that you put anyone on the case that is friendly with the opposition, he will dump this firm in an instant and personally fry your ass. Is that what you want?"

Monica's smirk quickly disappeared and was replaced with a frown that told me she hadn't considered that angle. "I guess you were right, then, to step out." The potential of losing a major client was not worth any amount of messing up my life. She vanished as quickly as she had appeared.

I texted Emma to see if she was okay. I didn't get a response.

When I completed the afternoon project, I didn't bother changing out of my suit. I went straight to the Chinese restaurant on the way to Emma's. Hopefully, she would still want to see me.

I knocked and she came right to the door. A good sign.

Her eyes were red and her mascara had run. "How could you be working for that crook?" she sobbed. She swung the door open to let me in.

At least we weren't going to yell through the door. That was a good sign. I put the food on the floor and held her by the shoulders and gazed straight into her teary blue eyes. "Sugar, I'm not his lawyer. I got called in at the last minute to fill a chair. I didn't even know it was you on the other side." I pulled her in and hugged her tightly, closing the door after me with my foot.

"It was horrible. Your boss was horrible. I've been working so hard on this, and now I screwed it up and I'm nowhere." She sobbed in my arms.

I kissed her on the top of her head. "Sugar, I'm sure you didn't screw up anything."

She sobbed. "Yes, I did. It was my one chance and I didn't get any of the right answers."

I kissed her on the head. "Sugar, will you let me help you?"

"You can't. You work for them, for her, that fucking bitch," she spat out.

"We can agree on that." I squeezed her close for a second then led her over to the couch. "Sit down and tell me all about the case."

She plopped down, wiping her nose.

I sat on the coffee table facing her so she could see how intently I was listening to her story. "Let me start. I am not your lawyer, and I'm not giving you any legal advice, but I'm your friend, and I would like to hear about your problem, and I might be able to suggest some things that would end up helping you, Okay? I'm here to help."

She nodded and wiped under her eyes with a tissue from the end table. "It started a long time ago."

I lifted her hand and kissed it.

She continued. "My great-great-grandmother Marie was painted by the famous French painter, Renoir. My grandmother told Mama she suspected Marie was his lover. Anyway, he gave her the painting and it was passed down in my mother's family." She opened the folder on the coffee table and handed me an old photograph. She sniffled. "It's the painting on the wall in the back."

The photograph was very old, but still clear. The painting was quite small, but any Renoir was priceless.

"Our family placed the painting and other things with neighbors when they were coming to America just before the war broke out. The painting was taken by the Nazis and lost for decades. I managed to track it down a few years ago to a dealer in France. He gave me this." She showed me a handwritten note. "It is the receipt for selling the painting, along with three others, to a Mr. Coulter. He had been a regular buyer, but all the dealer could remember was that the man was from California."

I didn't understand enough French to decode the entire thing, but the total at the bottom surprised me. "Isn't one hundred and twenty thousand Euros for a Renoir and three others a little on the low side?"

"By a factor of more than ten. Mr. LeMere, the dealer, knew he was selling stolen merchandise. And based on the price, Coulter did too." She wiped her nose. "I spent a year calling all the Coulters I could find until I came across this." She pulled out an *Architectural Digest* article. "Here." She pointed to a painting on the wall in the magazine. "There it was, in full color, right on the wall in the Coulters' dining room in the magazine. So I called him. He denied having any painting like it. So that's when I started the suit."

"So, he told you he didn't have the painting anymore?"

"No, he said he never had anything like it, but I hadn't told him I had a picture of it on his wall."

"So what did he say today? I assume you showed them the article."

"Your boss was such a bitch. She kept objecting to everything I said, and I never really got any answers from him. She just yelled objection at everything I asked." She sobbed.

I didn't know if she would know that lawyers always recorded depositions, and most often videotaped them. "Did you record the meeting?"

She nodded, wiping her nose.

"Good girl. Can I hear it?"

"But I was so pathetic," she whimpered.

I squeezed her hand. "Emm, I can't believe that."

She took out her phone and tapped on it until it started to play back the deposition. She upped the volume as I listened.

As the recording went on, I had to smile. Emma had been very persistent, but she just didn't know the rules. I moved to the couch and put my arm around her shoulder and pulled her in to lean on me. I was quiet until it finished.

"See? I didn't get any answers," she sobbed.

I pulled her chin over to look at me. "Sugar, let me tell you what I heard."

She sniffed and wiped her nose again, nodding.

"You had them scared. You have more evidence than they expected you to have, and Monica was just trying to throw up roadblocks and confuse you. She was not allowed to object to most of the things that she did, and if you had called the judge during the deposition, he would have backed you up and forced Coulter to answer the questions."

"Call the judge?"

"Yes, if the two sides can't agree on something like these objections, they can answer under protest and ask the judge to later strike the answer, or the judge can be called on the phone to intervene. For example, Monica objected to two of your questions as asking for hearsay. Well, that's allowed in a deposition, not prohibited the way it is at trial, but you wouldn't know that. What I hear on this tape is that you got railroaded by Monica and that Coulter was not responsive to your questions. A lawyer might tell you that you have a few options now. One would be to take this to the judge and have him order another sitting for the deposition."

"Really?"

"What I hear is that they are scared of you."

A smile appeared for the first time. "Really?" she repeated. She wiped under her eyes again. "But in the end, he said he didn't own a Renoir."

"There are a few ways he could say that. One, he could have sold it to someone else after you filed this suit. Two, he could have given it to a relative as a gift. Three, he could try to claim he didn't know it was a Renoir. You needed to follow up with did he ever buy or own a Renoir?"

"So, I didn't ask the right questions?"

"These people are tricky. They don't answer the question with the same forthrightness that you ask it."

"So you think I have a chance?"

"Sure, it's not over yet. Let's say he was honest and he sold it. You could still find out where it went next. Anyway, I have a law school buddy who owes me big time. I'll get him to help you with drafting your petition to the judge and sitting in on any other depositions. He's quite good at this stuff. He'll make sure you get your answers, and it doesn't hurt that his dad is a judge."

"But I can't afford a lawyer. I already told you that."

"Trust me, this won't cost you a dime. He owes me a lot more than this. But don't believe any of the stories he tells you about me. They're all lies."

She hugged me and cried. She didn't deserve what fucking Monica had put her through. She really didn't.

I kissed the top of her head. "Some food will help."

She sniffled and nodded.

I went to the counter and brought the food over. We ate the Chinese with forks this time. It was less fun than the chopsticks, but it kept us from spilling on the couch. She got a half-full bottle of wine from the fridge, and we polished it off, followed by another one with the meal. Emma's mood improved with some food in her stomach, or it could have been the wine. She couldn't hold her liquor at all. She was completely drunk after two glasses of wine. She didn't slur her words, but she couldn't walk straight when she took the plates to the sink.

After dinner, she selected a Bond movie and we cuddled. She was so drained she fell asleep on my shoulder before the movie ended. I turned the volume down with the remote and enjoyed the sensation of her next to me and the citrusy smell of her hair. I didn't want to wake her, but she couldn't sleep like this all night. After enjoying the feel of her against me for a while longer, I carried her groggy body to the bed, pulled her shoes and her pants off, and pulled the covers over her. I stripped down to my boxer briefs, turned off the lights, and slid under the covers next to my woman. She snuggled up against me and I put my arm around her, listening to her breathing turn slow and steady. She was dead tired, and she was mine. This was the first time since Victoria that I was in bed with a woman and going to fall asleep without fucking her first. I should have felt cheated, but I didn't.

It just feels right.

CHAPTER THIRTEEN

Emma

A hint of the coming morning slipped by the curtains as I opened an eye. I had a full bladder and had to pee. My tongue felt like I had licked the bottom of a bird cage and something was poking me in the ass. Steven lay in bed with me, his arm around my waist, his warm body against my back. I slowly understood what was poking me.

I wiggled out from under him to get to the bathroom. I should have peed before getting in bed last night, but I hadn't gotten myself in bed, that much was obvious. I had my top and my bra on. I never slept in a bra. At least he had taken my shoes off.

"Morning, Sugar."

"Morning to you too, Mr. Horny."

"So you noticed?"

I called back from the bathroom. "Kind of hard

to miss."

"I was thinking, last night was the first time in a long while that I fell asleep with a woman without, you know, doing anything first."

"So, being a gentleman is a first for you?"

"Very funny. It was sort of cute listening to your little snorts as you fell asleep."

"I do not snort," I yelled around the corner.

"How could you possibly know?"

"I'm a lady, that's how." I went back to the bed as he used the bathroom. I took off the rest of my clothes and got under the covers, waiting for him. "Am I not pretty enough?"

"I told you, I don't take advantage of drunks," he yelled back.

I pushed the sheets down to my knees. "I'm not drunk now."

As he rounded the corner, I could see it in his face, even in the low light.

The predator had returned. His eyes were carnal, wide with lust. "And what does the lady have in mind?" The bulge beneath the towel betrayed him.

I reached for the towel and pulled it off. "I don't want to be a lady." I grasped his cock and pulled him down to me.

He lay down with me and I pushed him over on his back. I straddled him and leaned forward, rubbing the tips of my breasts lightly over his chest. "My turn to take care of you."

Every time I'd put my body in his hands, pure pleasure had been my reward. This morning, he was getting paid back.

He put his hand down to put his finger between my legs, but I moved down to where he couldn't reach me and kissed his balls.

I looked up to see the smile that told me I was starting out right. It was my turn to give him what he needed. I had almost no experience with this, but Megan had told me in her slutty way that all guys wanted to be sucked, and I was going to find out if that was true with Steven.

His fingers stroked my hair.

I grasped his cock with both hands and it expanded in my grip. I kissed the tip, then licked the length of the underside to a delicious moan from him. I grabbed it again with both hands and stroked up and down, twisting one way and then the other.

I rubbed his cock against my cheek as he closed his eyes and his legs tensed. I licked him again before taking the tip in my mouth. His musky scent and taste turned me on. I took more of him in my mouth and sucked lightly as I withdrew to the tip, gliding my lips over him. I took him in again and pressed my flattened tongue against him, moving up and down, taking as much as I could. I placed both hands below my mouth, twisting with each stroke. I tasted the drop of pre-cum.

His moans increased as I tightened my grip.

I let saliva escape the seal of my lips and pulled it down with my fingers to lubricate his length. The room faded away as I concentrated on moving over him and licking and blowing on the tip when I released my lips, twisting his length with my hands, pulling him to me. The reaction of his cock and the moans he gave me signaled he was getting what he needed.

I kept my focus on stroking and sucking and altering my movements and my pace to his increasing moans.

My man was all about control, but this morning, I was in control.

He didn't say a word, but his eyes communicated his desire. He wanted more.

I cupped his balls, licked his length, and sucked on one hairy ball and then the other before returning to his rock-hard cock. I worked him faster with my hands and took him in and out of my mouth, spitting, licking, and sucking as his moans became deeper and he tensed up. He was on the verge.

I needed my man to come for me, to let go of his control, to lose himself to me.

He gripped my shoulder and my head as he tensed up. He was close. He jerked up and into the back of my throat for a moment.

I gagged. He was so deep. I pulled back and

sucked and stroked. I cupped his balls, and the stream came into my mouth as he shook. I sucked and swallowed, and swallowed again. I'd never swallowed it before. Actually, a man had never come in my mouth before. As Steven opened his eyes, the look of contentment greeted me.

This morning, he had surrendered to me.

After breakfast, Steven called Mike Salois and arranged for me to meet him next week to go over the case. I wanted it to be Steven who was helping me, but I understood that he wasn't allowed to because his firm worked for Coulter.

"Why is he willing to do this for you?" I asked Steven.

"Because he owes me big time." He didn't seem to want to tell me anymore, so I didn't push.

Steven went home to study and I went into work. It was Saturday, and I had to join Janice to finish the last of the local Covington art. There had also been some in San Francisco, Boston, and New York. We contracted out the examinations of the East Coast pieces, and the results were due Monday. Janice was going to do the San Francisco art on Monday with the help of the de Young Museum staff. We had become quite proficient at this and finished early with the last three pictures.

I wonder what Mike owes Steven?

* * *

After finishing the Saturday morning work with Janice and our lab tech, I joined Steven for an afternoon by the beach. We went to the Santa Monica pier, where he took me on the Ferris wheel and the carousel. We played Skee-Ball. He beat me every time. He celebrated like a little kid. It was endearing to see him have fun like this. He rented us bikes, and we pedaled down the beach sidewalk toward Venice Beach. The sun and sea breeze were so refreshing. I'd forgotten how much fun you could have with the simpler things in life.

We stopped at a little taco stand in Venice for a late lunch. Steven told me he and his brothers came here a lot when they were in high school. You could see the sidewalk a long distance in each direction. People thought it was fake when the movies and TV shows always make a point of showing girls in bikinis rollerblading down the sidewalk in southern California, but they actually did that here along the beach in Venice.

Steven told me his brother Bill thought this was the best girl watching location on the entire beach.

Not what I need to hear.

His brother was probably right, based on the last few babes who had skated by.

Now I had to endure lunch at the equivalent of a strip club, where prettier, skinnier girls whizzed by every minute. All of them with perfect tans and bikinis skimpier than my underwear.

He ordered fish tacos and I got chicken.

We took our chips and salsa to a little table with an umbrella. It had an old red and white checkered plastic table cloth, the kind you could wipe up easily.

I watched another bikini babe roll by. "Why does Mike owe you big time?" I asked.

"Because I promised not to date his sister." His mischievous grin gave him away.

I'd expected an answer like *He wrecked my car*. "Seriously? You know I can't tell when you're lying, big guy. What's the real reason?"

His grin disappeared. "Maybe later."

"We said no secrets. I want to know."

He hesitated. "I saved his sister back in college."

Now it sounded a lot more serious than *He wrecked my car*. "Saved how?"

"From being raped," he said in a low voice. Not exactly the conversation you wanted heard by the nearby tables.

I shuddered. "Oh, my God." I wasn't prepared for an answer like that. That was heavy.

He kept his voice low. "She was drunk and ended up at an off-campus party with some bad dudes."

I took Steven's hand, not to comfort him, but because I was getting anxious about the story myself.

He continued. "Mike was out of town, so she texted me for help. Patrick and I had to bust a few heads, but we got her out of there safely." His expression was pained.

"So you were a hero."

He hung his head. "No, that ended up making me a criminal. One of the guys I beat up was the brother of a cop. I ended up with an assault conviction because I broke the asshole's arm."

It didn't make any sense to me. "But…"

He interrupted me. "Charged and convicted. Black and white. A criminal. End of story."

"Does that hurt your becoming a lawyer?"

He finished his chip. "Yes and no. It's complicated."

The guy behind the counter interrupted the story by calling our number.

Steven retrieved the tray with our food. "Mike's father is a judge. He helped me get the conviction sealed, and in California, that means that I don't have to tell them about it, so I can take the bar exam and get my license." He took a bite of his taco and chewed for a bit before continuing. "But in New York, where I went to law school, and most other states, they ask, and I have to tell them about it, which means it is somewhere between hard and impossible to get a law license."

"That's not fair," I complained.

Another few bikini distractions whizzed by

without Steven even noticing. They could have been topless and he wouldn't have noticed. Well, maybe he would have noticed them then.

He finished chewing another bite. "Convictions where violence is involved are frowned upon. It calls into question your moral character. So here I am, back in sunny California, where I can get my license because they don't ask and I don't have to tell."

I didn't like what they did to him, but what did I know? "But that's not fair. If you were defending his sister, how do you end up the criminal?"

"Sugar, that's the thing about the law," he said. "It's a set of rules that are meant to be fair to most of the people, most of the time, but in the end, the rules always win out over right and wrong. That's just the way it is. Fair isn't part of the equation."

It sucked that he was right about that, so now the rules said he could only be a lawyer in one state out of fifty, but at least it was my state.

Another bikini model rolled by a few feet from us. They were all so nearly perfect I was losing my appetite.

We slowly ate our tacos and talked about his time in college and a bit about his brothers and his sister, Katie.

Then he dropped the question. "Tell me the real story why you and your sister won't date lawyers."

I froze. I hadn't expected it, and the story was a

painful one. "Maybe another time."

He wouldn't let me off like that. He insisted. I'd made him answer my question, so I had to explain.

I took a deep breath. "Megan is not my only sister."

He sat quietly, just listening.

"I had a twin sister named Elissa. She was killed by a drunk driver."

"I'm so sorry," Steven said.

"Megan and Elissa were walking back from the store. I was at home. The guy hit them both. Elissa was killed and Megan was pretty badly hurt. She still has two pins in her leg."

Steven was listening intently.

"The other driver was a lawyer in town."

Steven nodded.

My eyes started to tear up. "The witness said that after he hit them, he stopped the car to get out, but then he got back in his car and just drove off to let her die."

He took my hand. "I'm so sorry, Emm."

I dabbed a napkin at my tears. I went on. "When they took him to trial" —I sniffled— "he got some bigshot lawyer to defend him, and he got away with it. We never understood why or how." My tears were starting to flow. "When they left the courthouse, the two lawyers..." I almost couldn't bear to say it.

Steven rubbed my hand.

I sobbed. "They high-fived each other like they had just won a game or something."

"That's terrible," Steven said.

"We've both hated lawyers ever since." I sobbed. I couldn't hold the tears back any more. "Elissa loved the yellow M&Ms. When we were little, I would save the yellow ones for her." I wiped my eyes with a napkin. "That's why I don't eat the yellow ones. They were always for her."

He came around the table and hugged me and stroked my hair. "I'm here for you, Emm."

When I recovered, he sat back down and I changed the subject to Megan, and I filled him in on her life with Braydon.

The conversation didn't sit well with him. The disgust in his eyes was palpable, and it was clear that he thought Megan should move on. I had the same opinion, and I had told her so more than once.

"What if I have a little chat with this Braydon douche? He isn't a cop or anything, is he?"

I could see from the anger in his eyes that it wouldn't be a pleasant conversation for Braydon, and a trip to the hospital might be the result. "You can't do that. Promise me you won't do that. Megan would kill me. It's her life to screw up is what she always tells me."

Steven dropped the subject, but it clearly still bugged him.

I'd planned to set up a lunch with Megan and

him. I had promised her she could meet him, after all, but with his current attitude toward her relationship with Braydon, it would probably not be a good idea just yet. I asked him to tell me a little about his sister, Katie. She had seemed so nice at the restaurant.

He explained she was in accounting and working on her CPA certification. She was working really long hours at one of the big accounting firms. "It's sort of like indentured servitude. To be a CPA, you not only have to have the college courses and pass the tests, but you have to get one of these firms to sign off that you have worked enough hours in the field. So, each of these people coming out of the schools has to work for one of these guys for like two years to pass the experience requirement."

"Two years?" It seemed like a lot.

"Yup, so they work them like dogs, sort of like galley slaves, where the partners of the firm are beating the drum and these newbies are doing the rowing. Then, when the two years are up, a lot of them leave, and they replace them with fresh meat from the colleges. Anyway, Katie is still in that two-year period, so she's really working like a dog."

It sounded pretty hard. I didn't envy her.

The whole time we were there, dozens of bikini babes were rolling by, all tanned and fit, and most of them in bikinis so small the fabric could fit in a thimble. Steven barely even glanced at them. He had his eyes glued on me.

I noticed them, but he didn't. He really knew how to make a girl feel special. I'd never been on a date before where I understood so clearly that I was the center of attention and the only thing in the world my date cared about. It sent tingles down my spine just thinking about it. He couldn't have paid me a higher compliment.

We dumped our meal trash and strolled down to the water. We played tag with the waves a while before turning our bikes back toward the pier. A perfect afternoon between the pier, the taco stand, and time walking along the water.

He spent some time trying out alternative nicknames for me. He almost decided to change it to *Kitten*. Luckily, he settled back on *Sugar*, which was fine with me. I could already hear Megan's laughter when she learned my nickname was *Kitten*. The pussy jokes would never end.

Steven was driving me back home when my phone rang.

It was Janice. Her mother had been in an accident, and Janice was off to Phoenix to be with her, so she was going to need me go to San Francisco for the Monday examinations at the de Young Museum.

"Road trip, Sugar?" he said after I explained the call to him. "I'm drivin'."

Bossy much?

"No way, I'll fly Monday morning. It's easier," I objected.

He looked over at me and smiled. "Road trip. We'll leave early tomorrow, and that way, there will be plenty of time to visit with your folks."

I did want to see them, but he couldn't know where they lived. "I think you had too much sun today. What makes you think they live in San Francisco?"

"You told moron number three your family lived in Gilroy, the garlic capital of the world, and you hadn't seen them in a while."

He was right. I had said that to Bryce. "That's creepy. Did you bug the table or something?"

"I was at the next table." He tapped his ear. "Good ears. We can stop in Gilroy on the way up. It'll be fun."

It was impossible to move him off the idea of driving up. Steven said he could work on his computer Monday morning and it would be no problem. We would drive back Monday night, so I resigned myself to two long days in the car. At least his car had working air. My car was marginal in that regard.

Road trip.

CHAPTER FOURTEEN

Emma

We left early and made good time. Sunday morning traffic was predictably light. It was a typically beautiful California day, some low clouds pushing in over the beach and a clear sunny day inland. We took US 101 along the coast, which took a little longer but was much more scenic than I-5 through the central valley. We talked as the trip went on, and the sprawl of Los Angeles gave way to mountains and coastline.

"So tell me about Todd." That came out of nowhere. "You said his name in your sleep."

Oh, shit, was that true?

"He was just a guy." I went on to explain how I'd met him, how he had cheated on me, and how we broke up. I must have sounded pathetic. My stomach turned when I recounted how I had found out about him.

Steven smiled in my direction again. "Moron. Any guy that would cheat on you is at least five beers short of a six-pack." Thankfully, he dropped it after that and didn't bring it up again.

As we closed the distance to Gilroy, I grew more nervous. My father, the rancher, was a laid-back guy who could put anybody at ease if he wanted to. But every time I'd brought a boy home, the ex-Marine in him intimidated the hell out of them. Not a single one had passed muster with Daddy as acceptable boyfriend material. The prospect of his driving off Steven had me terrified. "I think we should pass on stopping by my parents'."

"Nonsense, Sugar."

"I don't think we have the time."

"It's family. Of course we have the time. Family always comes first. What's the problem?"

I was starting to sweat. "My father can be a little difficult."

"Yeah, so what? What father wouldn't feel protective of a beautiful daughter like you?"

"More than protective. He was a Marine Gunnery Sergeant and well…"

"Enough said. He wants to know if I'm good enough for you. Don't worry, Sugar. He's not going to scare me off." That was easy for him to say. None of the boys who had met my father stayed with me for more than another week.

As we passed Pismo Beach and headed inland, I

called ahead to let them know we were stopping by. Mama was thrilled to hear the news and no doubt headed straight out to the market for barbecue fixings. *Let no opportunity for entertaining go to waste* was her motto.

We stopped in town before heading out to the ranch to pick up some flowers for Lady's grave. Ever since I left for school, I had enjoyed returning home, an oasis of calm in the world, where all we worried about was the land, the animals, and the weather. I was returning to my roots, but today, it had a foreboding feel to it, and not just because Lady had died.

Steven stopped the engine in front of the old ranch house and rushed around to open the car door for me. Mama came out and waved.

I introduced them before we went inside.

Stepping through the door, I could see Daddy was not going to behave himself. He had his Winchester rifle on his knee pointed in the direction of the door and pieces of several guns on the coffee table in front of him.

Steven strode right up to him. "Pleasure to meet you, Gunny. Steven Covington." He extended his hand, and Daddy got up and shook it for a very long time.

"Nice to meet you, Son." Daddy was grimacing, not a good sign.

"Nice Winchester you have there, an 1894?"

A rare look of surprise crossed Daddy's face. "You know your rifles, Son."

"I'm sure you could teach me a thing or two, Gunny."

Daddy grunted and handed Steven a pistol. "Could you give me a hand and break that down for me? I can't seem to figure it out." Steven quickly disassembled the gun and put the pieces on the towel on the table. He threw a knowing smile in my direction. Steven knew he was being tested. There was no way a gun confused my daddy.

Mama grabbed me and we went into the kitchen. "Best leave them be, dear. You can't change who your father is, so just be at peace with it."

I hugged her. She cared so much. Mama had vegetables on the kitchen island that she had been chopping. I grabbed a chef's knife and attacked the bell peppers, keeping my voice low. "Mama, I like this one a lot, and I don't want Daddy to chase him off."

She rinsed off a second knife in the sink and joined me with another cutting board. "If he is a good as you think he is, there's no need to worry. Your daddy won't be able to chase him away if he wanted to." That had a ring of truth to it. "Now tell me a little about him."

I went on to tell her how Steven was a really nice guy and that we met not long ago, and he was a lawyer. At which point, she turned a jaundiced eye to me.

"And Megan knows this?"

"Yes, Mama, and she approves."

She let out an audible sigh. "Well, you two are old enough to make your own decisions, I guess, but I would be careful if I were you. You know what they say, a tiger can't change his stripes, so if you don't like stripes, don't fall for a tiger."

"Mama, he's not like that."

We went on preparing the meal while the men finished in the other room and left to go outside.

We followed a little while later to light the grill when shots rang out from the other side of the barn. I could only hope Daddy was showing off and not putting holes in my brand-new boyfriend.

Mama placed an arm around me. "Don't worry, dear. Boys will be boys. You can't expect them to handle guns and not want to shoot them. It's just something genetic. Your daddy was a Marine. He'll be safe about it."

I gathered up the flowers I'd bought and took them out to the orchard where Mama told me Daddy had buried Lady. I started to cry. There was freshly turned dirt next to Mulligan's grave. Mulligan had been Elissa's horse. He died two years ago. Mulligan had taken such good care of Elissa, just the way Lady had always looked after me. We were blessed to have had such kind, gentle animals. I sobbed as I put the flowers down on Lady's grave.

My tears were flowing freely down my cheeks and onto my shirt.

Daddy knew horses, and he had picked them out for us, perfect horses for the little girls that we were at the time. We didn't start out with ponies. Daddy put us up on these big Quarter horses and told us we would grow into them, which we did.

My nose was running along with my tears. I missed them so, Lady because she had been so special to me for so long, and Mulligan because he had been such a special part of my bond with Elissa. My twin sister and I had always ridden together until that day she was taken from us. All the long rides we had together came rushing back to me. We would take sandwiches and ride out the back gate up into the hills, just the two of us, or rather, the four of us.

The dinner bell rang. I said my goodbyes to Lady and Mulligan and wiped my nose and cheeks with my sleeves.

Mama had an old ship's bell that she rang to call us in from the pastures when we were young, and she rang it today to call us all in. She had prepared chicken and vegetable kabobs grilled on the barbecue with coleslaw and biscuits on the side. We set the table inside. This time of year could be problematic keeping the yellow jackets away when they smelled meat on the table.

Steven and Daddy dusted themselves off as they

came in the back door. Whatever it was they were doing had involved the horses. Steven had horse hair on his sleeves and jeans, but luckily, no bullet holes in him.

Steven must have noticed the redness in my eyes. He grabbed a tissue and wiped under my eyes and gave me a long hug. The kind of hug I needed right now.

Daddy pulled out Mama's chair for her. "Steven, here, is a pretty good shot." Daddy had never said that before about anybody.

Steven grinned as he pulled out my chair for me. *Daddy called him Steven.*

* * *

Steven

When we passed through the door, her father had a Winchester pointed at my knees. A little higher and I would have started to worry. "Pleasure to meet you, Gunny. Steven Covington."

Her father stood. He was wearing a red USMC tee shirt, and he clearly had kept himself in good shape since leaving the corps. He took my hand and started to squeeze as he shook it.

Two could play that game. I gripped his harder

and harder as we continued to shake.

"Nice to meet you, Son." A crinkle finally appeared around his smile as I was giving it all I had, and he gave up. He hid his hand from the women as he opened and closed his fist.

I hoped I hadn't actually hurt the old man. I expected I had passed the test.

I recognized the rifle. "Nice Winchester you have there, an 1894?" It was the same model of lever-action rifle that my grandfather had introduced us to as kids.

"You know your rifles, Son."

"I'm sure you could teach me a thing two, Gunny." I had no doubt about that.

He smiled as he handed me an automatic. "Could you give me a hand and break that down for me? I can't seem to figure it out." Emma had warned me a few tests might come my way.

Good thing I was a Bond fan. This was a Walther PPK, 007's gun of choice. I released the magazine, put it down, and pulled back the slide. The chamber was empty, but I'd been taught to always check. I decocked the hammer, pulled the trigger guard down and to the side, and pulled the slide back and up, removing it from the gun. The spring came off next, and I laid the pieces down on the towel for him.

The women had retreated to the kitchen.

A slight smile formed at the edges of his mouth.

He had expected me to fumble with the gun for a while. The Walther had a very unusual slide retention mechanism.

Score two for me.

"How'd you know the rifle was an 1894?" He asked me.

"The magazine strap changed with the 1894. My granddad had one."

He now sported at least a half-smile.

Score three for me.

"Wanna shoot it?"

"Sure, I think I can remember how."

"First, I've been cleaning these guns and we need to put 'em back together. Think you can help me with that?"

"Happy to, Gunny." I put the Walther back together in just a few seconds. He had three other pistols taken apart on the towel. This was another test. He had clearly mixed up the parts to the three guns on purpose. There was a Colt 1911, a Sig, and a Glock. It was a good thing our self-defense teacher, the Master Chief, had exposed us all to multiple makes of guns. My training kicked in and I got them all reassembled without a hitch.

The Gunny's expression showed I had surprised him.

Score four for me.

"I musta' mixed up the parts," he mumbled.

Fat chance.

He gathered up the .45 and the rifle. He handed me some boxes of ammo from the drawer and we went outside. Stopping in the barn, he asked me to grab a box filled with empty coke cans. We set the cans on a fence up near the hillside and walked halfway back to the barn.

He offered me the rifle and a handful of bullets. "Think you can hit one of those from here?" This was his way of challenging me.

I loaded eight rounds into the magazine. It had been forever since I'd done any shooting with Granddad's Winchester, but we weren't too far out. The stock of the old rifle was cold against my cheek as I lined up the sights. I hit the first can low and adjusted for the next three. Four shots, four cans down, just barely. I handed the rifle to the surprised ex-Marine. "Your turn, Gunny."

Now the pressure was on him. Sweat started to show on his temple. He took his time steadying himself up and fired. We ended up tied, four each. "You're a pretty good shot with a rifle, Son. Were you ever a Marine?"

"No, Gunny, I never had the honor."

"How are you with a sidearm, Son?"

It seems I still had another test coming my way. "Fair to middling, Gunny."

He slapped a clip home on the Colt and slowly plinked three cans with six shots, which was excellent shooting with a handgun at this range. A broad smile formed on his face. He figured he had me now. He ejected the clip and reloaded it from his box of ammo. Fresh clip in place, he handed me the warm gun.

My first shot went wide. I had forgotten how heavy the recoil of the .45 felt compared to the lighter 9 mm guns I'd practiced with. When I fired the last of my six shots, the fourth can fell.

He slapped me on the back. "Son, are you sure you were never a Marine? You sure shoot like one."

"My granddad and my uncle were Marines. Does that count?"

He laughed. "It means you come from good stock." We started to walk back toward the barn. "So, Steven, your granddaddy the Marine, he the one that taught you to shoot like that?"

"No, that was Master Chief Dudley, an ex-SEAL. My father thought we should all learn a little self-defense, and that included shooting."

"A navy man, huh?" He was clearly disappointed I'd learned from a Navy man instead of a Marine.

Inside the barn, he showed me his horses. I helped him to brush them down. He was a real animal man. He had a gentle way with the horses. He was working on Doc, and I was getting the dust and dirt off Dusty, who certainly lived up to his name. "Steven, what do you do for a living?"

No sense trying to hide it. "I went to law school, and I'm studying for the bar now to be a lawyer."

He continued to brush Doc's legs. "You know, most people think lawyers are scum."

"Yeah, I get that a lot."

"So why do you want to be scum?" He made scum sound even worse the second time.

"Because I promised my father before he died, and I always keep my promises." That was the truth.

He moved back to brushing Doc's back while he thought the answer over for a bit. "That's a good reason," he said finally. He untied the horse and led him back into his stall.

We threw the horses some hay just as a bell started ringing in the direction of the main house.

"That would be the food calling us," he said.

I brushed myself off as we walked back.

He put his hand on my back. "Steven, I would sure hate for Emma to get hurt, if you know what I mean."

"No need to worry, Gunny. She means the world to me." The meaning of his warning was not lost on me.

He opened the house door and we were greeted with the aroma of barbecue. He stopped inside the front door. "I'm glad we had this talk, Steven."

I could see that Emma had been crying and the flowers she had brought in weren't on the front table anymore. I guessed she had been saying a tearful goodbye to her horse. I grabbed a tissue, wiped her eyes, and held her tight to me, rocking lightly back and forth. I didn't say anything. She just needed time to heal the hurt in her own way.

The Gunny pulled out Mrs. Watson's chair for her and I did the same for Emma. We sat down to a feast of BBQ chicken and vegetables with slaw and biscuits. The conversation was normal family fare until Emma's mother turned it to the family painting, which evidently meant a lot to her. "Emm tells me that you think she has a good chance with this lawsuit she has going on?"

It wasn't exactly what I had told Emma. "All I can say is that from what I heard of the deposition and the material Emma showed me, she has them running scared, and I have a friend who will help her with the filing that should get you an answer as to where the painting is."

Her creased brow indicated it wasn't quite the answer she had hoped for. "And we can get it back?"

I paused. "I sure think so, Mrs. Watson."

"Oh, that would be wonderful." She went on to tell me the history of the painting, pretty much as Emma had already described but with the emotion that showed how much it meant to her.

I hoped I hadn't committed more than Mike and I could deliver.

By the time we had finished the meal and the apple pie Mrs. Watson had baked, it was time to get back on the road to San Francisco.

Once in the car, Emma couldn't wait to grill me. "What happened with Daddy?"

I smiled at her. "Nothing much, just guy stuff."

She grabbed my hand. "It wasn't nothing. He called you Steven when you came back."

"Yeah, so?"

"He never calls anyone anything but Son," she said.

"You think I passed the test then?" I asked.

Emma was ecstatic. "Duh?" She squeezed my hand. "What did he say?"

I kept my eyes on the road. "The only thing he said was I'd better treat you right, or else."

She sat back in her seat, giggling. "That sounds like Daddy."

I smiled. My girl was with me, she was happy, and that was the best feeling on earth.

I passed the test.

CHAPTER FIFTEEN

Emma

The fog was coming over the hills as we approached San Francisco. The farm and ranch land of Gilroy had changed to the sprawling suburbia of San Jose, and then the crowded urban environs of San Francisco itself. Steven had booked us a room at the Ritz-Carlton. A package was waiting for me at the desk when we checked in.

Opening the door upstairs, I nearly fainted. Plush was an understatement, and the view was like a postcard. I'd never stayed in a hotel where the bathroom had a heated towel rack. Now I knew where the term *Ritzy* came from. It was a suite with a separate bedroom and living room. A vase of fresh roses stood in the center of the dining table.

I shed my sandals and ordered ice cream from room service, and Steven added a can of whipped cream to the order as I opened my package. It was some written material that had been sent by courier from Covington Enterprises regarding tomorrow's paintings. The original material had been given to Janice, who was now in Phoenix, so they had sent a copy to the hotel for me. As I perused the papers, Steven came up and started to rub my neck and shoulders. I had trouble concentrating. His massage was meant to be relaxing, but his touch always had the opposite effect on me. I was getting wet considering all the other things he could be doing with his hands. The knock at the door saved me. Room service had arrived, and I needed to read over these papers before he distracted me completely.

Steven brought me my bowl of chocolate ice cream.

I ignored the bowl. "Just give me a minute to finish this.

He started to knead my shoulder muscles again. "I've given you all day."

"Steven, please," I begged.

"I'm done waiting, Sugar." His hands slipped down my sides and under my arms to stroke the undersides of my breasts.

How was I supposed to read anything like this? "It'll just take a few more minutes."

His hands continued to wander and were cupping my breasts and then unbuttoning my shirt.

I tried to finish the reading, but he was killing my

224

concentration. "I need to read this first."

He ignored me. "No arguing." He kissed my neck. "It's time for your lesson." He put his hand inside my bra to tease my nipple. He moved his other hand down to caress my other breast. "Get up," he whispered into my ear.

He clearly did not intend to behave himself. I pushed the chair back and stood.

He kicked the chair to the side and his arms wrapped around me. "That's a good girl," he said into my ear, holding me tightly. "You have two choices tonight."

"Yeah?" I asked, snuggling into him.

"Bad girl, or really bad girl," he said as he moved one hand down inside my pants, teasing my curls while the other cupped my breast.

I tried to turn around, but he wouldn't let me. My man was intent on teaching me something tonight, but I was afraid to learn what *really bad* was.

He moved his fingers down farther to part my slit. "If you don't choose, I'll choose for you."

I chickened out. "Bad," I purred.

He pulled his hand out. "A bad girl does what she's told. Do you understand?"

I nodded.

"Close your eyes, take your clothes off, and don't turn around."

I closed my eyes, finished unbuttoning my shirt, and threw it aside. I reached behind me to unhook my bra, which joined the shirt. I removed my pants while I could hear him taking his clothes off as well. I kicked my pants to the side. I could hear him moving around, but I kept my eyes shut. The moistness between my thighs was undeniable as the excitement of the unknown grew.

He unzipped something that must have been a suitcase. "This will make it easier to keep your eyes closed."

I could hear him walking my way. I winced as a soft cloth touched my face. I put my hands up to it. I relaxed when I realized it was a silk scarf and he was blindfolding me with it. "Are you going to tie me up?" I wasn't sure I was ready for that.

He didn't answer me. He put his arms around me from behind.

I gasped at the touch that I had been yearning for. The rod of his erection behind me told me clearly that I wasn't the only one who was naked. I rubbed my ass sideways against him.

He caressed my breasts before moving a hand lower. His touch was like fire as a trail of heat followed it down my abdomen through my curls and finally parted my slit. He circled my clit, teasing me with slow, light movements. He kissed my neck and cradled my breast while dipping his finger in and out of me. He moved around and picked me up. He carried me into the bedroom.

I nestled my head against his warm shoulder.

He laid me down on the bed. He positioned my hands above my head. "Keep your hands up here. Do you understand?"

I nodded, listening to his breathing as he leaned over me. The heat between my legs kept increasing. His breath was warm against my neck.

"Do you trust me?" he asked as he nipped and kissed the hollows of my neck and circled my breasts with his fingertips.

I trembled as his fingertips lightly tickled my sides. "Yes."

He spread my legs and his fingers parted my folds, gently sliding over my clit and teasing my entrance with tiny circles.

I grabbed for his head to pull him to me for a kiss.

He pulled away, removing the exciting gentle touch of his fingers on my pussy.

I put my hands back over my head again, yearning for that touch to return. I was going to be at his mercy, unable to touch him and hold him.

The bed shifted as he stood. "Don't move."

I could hear him go to the other room.

There was a clink of something as the bed shifted with his return.

"Open up."

A cold spoon touched my lips, and as I opened my mouth, he gave me a small spoonful of ice cream. I shivered as the next spoonful ended up on my bellybutton.

Steven's tongue circled the ice cream and licked at it. He sucked it up.

I quivered as his tongue dipped in and out of my navel. I couldn't keep from laughing at the tickling sensation.

He gave me another taste with the spoon before he dripped some between my breasts and repeated his sensual licking of my body.

My nerve endings were tingling as he licked me and blew on my skin. My nipples hardened to little pebbles as he followed up with the cold torture on the tip of one breast, followed by the other. I got a spoonful of the cold dessert delivered to my mouth between each.

Suddenly, there was a hiss, and I recoiled at a chill between my breasts, not as cold as the ice cream. "Open up," Steven said.

I parted my lips, expecting another spoonful of ice cream. Instead, the hiss of sweet whipped cream filled my mouth.

Steven kissed me, and we shared the sweetness before he moved to lap up the whipped cream on my body. He applied the cream to my breasts and teased my nipples with his lips and tongue as he slowly removed the froth. He circled his tongue around as if licking the top of an ice cream cone.

The ache between my legs grew more unbearable as my entire body itched for his touch, his licks, and his kisses.

He spread my legs.

Finally.

I spread them farther to give him more access.

He worked a finger and then a second into me, stretching and massaging my walls. He removed his hand and the cream covered my pussy with its coldness. His mouth arrived to lap it up with delicate licks all over me, into my entrance, up between my folds, over and around my clit, finally sucking my swollen bud.

I pulled my knees up as he held my hips with one hand and used the other to apply more whipped cream, which he then lapped up in long, slow licks the length of my slit.

With every touch and every lick, the heat in my core grew. He continued to apply the whipped cream with the can and remove it with his tongue, teasing my clit with licks and sucks but denying me the pressure I wanted.

His movements were setting off so many nerve endings in my sensitive little nub that I trembled at his every movement. I couldn't hear anything but the blood rushing in my ears. My heart was pounding so hard it might escape my ribcage. Every time I arched my hips toward him, he backed away, and I was forbidden from using my hands to grab his hair and pull him to me.

The can hit the floor as both hands gripped my

hips and pulled me to his mouth. His tongue flicked and circled and brushed over my clit with increasing pressure. His tongue rubbed and teased in a dance that took my breath away.

The explosion that racked my core came quickly. I couldn't help it. I pulled at his hair, forcing him harder into me as the tremors rattled through me. As the spasms slowed, my legs and arms weakened.

He pulled his mouth away as he climbed up to take my mouth in a kiss, our kiss, the kiss with a taste of me and taste of him, our hot kiss.

The aftershocks of my orgasm gently faded away. My muscles began to gain function again. I pulled myself to him. I moved to grab his cock, but he pulled my hands over my head again.

I sensed it was useless to complain.

"My God, you're gorgeous, Sugar," he said as he positioned himself between my legs. He moved forward and kissed my neck. The weight of his stiff thickness lay against my thigh. He moved higher, placing the tip just above my mound. He ground forward and back, his heavy cock rubbing against my clit.

I inhaled sharply with each movement. I willed him to move a few inches down and bury himself inside me, but he didn't. His stubble scraped against me as he licked and kissed my ear and my neck. I could feel my heartbeat between my legs as my tension ramped up to unbearable levels. The crackle of desire was almost audible inside me.

He rose. "Stay right there," he commanded. The rustling of clothes followed by the rip of foil told me he was sheathing himself.

When he returned, he spread my legs wider and moved between them. He hovered over me, the weight of his cock teasing my abdomen. "Tell me what you want."

The heat of his breath ignited my flame. The raw need in his voice aroused me even more than I thought possible.

He leaned closer. He pinned my wrists above my head with one hand. "Tell me," he demanded again. His stubble scraped my cheek. His tone was scary. The beast lay just below the surface. He reached down between my legs and positioned the tip of his cock at my wet entrance.

I held my breath as I anticipated the coming sensation. I was intimidated by the size of him, afraid he'd split me open.

He pushed the thick tip an inch into my slick opening and stopped. "Tell me," he repeated.

My pussy reacted in a way I never experienced. Just that one inch, and he had ignited a fire inside me that couldn't be doused. I was paralyzed by his power. I wanted to take more of him, but I was pinned, unable to move. "You," I said, finally able to form a word.

"Tell me," he said sternly. He pulled back out

when I didn't answer.

The anguish of losing the sensation rolled over me as I tried to muster enough neurons to respond. "I want you," I said. I needed the cock he was withholding.

He gave me an inch back with a gentle push.

"More, I need more," I pleaded.

"A bad girl can't have what she doesn't ask for."

I wanted him inside me. "You."

He pulled back out.

I wanted the animal, I wanted the predator. "Fuck me, Steven, fuck me hard."

He thrust in rapidly, stretching me with his size. "I'm going to fuck your brains out," he said hoarsely.

I gasped. His dirty talk just increased my desire. I'd found the key words, and I would remember them now. The pressure on my walls was intense as he pulled out a little and drove in farther. The pleasure built with each thrust.

He moved my legs over his shoulders and grasped my hips as he plunged into me again and again, harder and harder. "You are so fucking tight, so fucking wet," he said again and again as he pounded into me. He kept my hands pinned over my head.

Each thrust sent me higher, higher than I'd ever been before. "Harder," I pleaded.

He pinched my nipple with his free hand, sending

a shock through me. He leaned forward to kiss me, bending me with him at the hips. "I'm going to fuck you so hard you can't walk tomorrow." He altered his position, taking my legs off his shoulders.

I wrapped them around him and pulled him into me with my heels behind his legs. I arched my hips into him with each thrust, taking the full length of him, to his moans of pleasure. "Fuck me harder," I pleaded.

He raised up and put his hand between us, fingering my clit. He ground down on it with his full weight with each stroke, and the combination of his hand and his cock sent me quickly over the edge again. He let go of my wrists and grabbed my hips.

The spasms that rolled over me were intense, draining every nerve ending that been holding back for so long. I clawed at his back to pull him closer to me. My pussy spasmed around him, trying to milk him dry.

With a final push, he tensed and rose away from me as he groaned out my name. He shifted my legs down and collapsed down on my chest. His cock continued to pulse inside me.

I had been able to give my man his release, and he had taken me to a place I'd never been before. The warmth radiating from my core relaxed all of my muscles. I was exhausted, spent, and sated. I listened to my man's breathing slowly return to normal and felt his heartbeat on my chest.

He kissed my nose. "Sugar, you are so fucking tight, so fucking good." He pulled the scarf off.

I blinked as my eyes adjusted to the light and found the look of pure satisfaction in his eyes.

"That was your first *bad girl* lesson."

He had taught me to talk dirty, and I looked forward to my next lesson, but I was still reticent about what a *really bad girl* lesson might be.

Being bad can be good.

* * *

Dim morning light filtered around the edges of the curtains as I woke. Steven's warm leg was next to mine. The clock said seven thirty. I slid out of bed as quietly as I could. The tent in the sheets told me morning hard-on was a pretty constant thing for Steven.

The sound of the shower must have woken him, as Steven joined me in the shower. "Morning, Sugar, do you really need to rush off?" He started to wash my back.

"I'm due at the de Young first thing." I turned to face him, greeted by a poke in the belly from his cock as he moved closer.

"Too bad. I was looking forward to having you for breakfast." He shifted to washing my breasts and leaned down to kiss my neck.

His touch was electric and his kiss tingled my

skin. I had to be strong and ignore the desire welling inside me. "I can see that." I grabbed his cock and pulled playfully.

He moaned as his hands slid down to between my legs with the bar of soap.

I shivered as his fingers slid up and down my slit and circled my quickly engorging clit. He knew instinctively how to push all of my buttons. I stroked his cock a few times, teasing him before I moved away. "I really have to get going." I spun around under the shower, rinsing off. He had no idea how difficult this was for me.

He gave me that sulking look like I'd just stolen his Halloween candy. "You know what they say about all work and no play."

I opened the door to leave the shower stall. "Yup, it will keep Emma from being suddenly unemployed." I closed the glass door and turned my back on those puppy dog eyes.

Walking out of the hotel, I was greeted by the cold fog that often blanketed San Francisco in the morning. It was a dingy gray start to the day. At the de Young, they had a larger and more extensive lab than we did down south. The Covington paintings had been delivered to the museum on Friday and had already been cleaned. The technicians were ultra-helpful, and Mrs. Newmark in European Art, who had been assigned to help me, was very nice. She had also graduated from Santa Clara, and we traded stories about a few of the professors there. She recalled quite a few of the ones I had, which probably had to do with most of them being old enough to remember the horse and buggy days.

At midmorning, I checked in with Janice. Her mother was recovering nicely from the accident. She wanted to stay down in Arizona to help out for the rest of the week, though, and asked me to present the full results of our examination to Mr. Perkins tomorrow. We discussed the touchy subject of the Nazi markings we had found on the three paintings from storage, and Janice decided to call Mr. Perkins this morning to go over it with him before tomorrow's deadline. I was glad I didn't have to deal with that sticky issue. Accusing the client of trafficking in Nazi war loot was not an easy conversation to have. I grew nauseous thinking how my conversation with Steven would go on the subject after Janice made her call. There was no right way to broach this topic. Accusing his family of trafficking in looted art was not going to be easy.

I was finishing the last of my notes to wrap up the examination of these paintings when my phone rang. The number had a 212 area code. When I answered, it was the MET in New York calling about a resume I had sent in last month. They called to arrange a phone interview. I explained how I was currently examining some pieces of the Covington collection at the de Young's lab in San

Francisco. We set a time for me to call New York for the interview on Thursday morning. She lingered on the phone, curious about the Covington collection audit, and she was suitably impressed by my explanation of our examination procedures and our findings. I had a warm feeling after talking to her.

As I packed up my things, Janice called back. Perkins had already known about the markings and the Covingtons had paperwork showing they had negotiated with the Rothschild family. Of the five they had originally obtained, the family wanted two back and accepted payment from the Covingtons to keep the three we had seen. Perkins was arranging to get the records updated at the *Commission for Looted Art in Europe*. To say it was a welcome relief was the understatement of the year.

The foggy gray start to the day was rapidly turning sunny. Steven wasn't a member of a despicable family and the MET wanted to talk to me. Me. This was the opportunity I'd been hoping for. I hadn't expected to be considered by them for another few years, at least, but my father had taught me you set a goal and just kept on working toward it, no matter what, so I'd sent in a resume anyway.

The MET.

CHAPTER SIXTEEN
(Three weeks later)

Emma

It had been a wonderful few weeks since our trip to see my parents. Mama had called several times to check and see how Steven and I were doing. I could tell that she was still worried that a lawyer was a mistake for me, and I continued to reassure her that Steven wasn't like that. She also kept asking about Megan and Braydon. She was worried for Megan, and she had been such a pest about it that Megan had stopped talking to her about it. I'd warned Mama to be careful about it, but she hadn't listened. Now she wanted me to be her spy and to tell her what was going on, which I refused to do.

I'd spent the day with Steven. We had gone down to the beach again. This time, we walked instead of biking.

Katie joined us. She swore us to secrecy. She wanted to ask Steven questions about the legal implications of what she suspected she might find in one of her audits. She said it was not the kind of thing she could talk about at one of their dinner meetings at Cardinelli's.

We had lunch at a little hole-in-the-wall hamburger joint in Venice, where we got a table far from anyone else, with some loud music nearby that would keep anybody from overhearing what Katie had to say. I didn't understand the terms they were using, but I could tell Katie was worried. I was humbled that she considered me close enough to family to talk about this in my presence.

She left after lunch, and we walked farther down the beach before turning around.

"She seemed worried," I said, holding Steven's hand as we walked in the sand.

He glanced behind us for a moment. "She is. What I'm most worried about is that she is sneaking around and looking into things that aren't in her area, and that might get her fired."

"So, you think she's on to something?"

"I can't tell yet. Before I met you, she had me go down to her office with her when everybody was away at an off-site meeting. We copied some documents, and she wanted me to look at them from the legal perspective. She thought something was wrong."

I stopped. "And?"

"Nothing strange that I could see. The

transactions were contorted, but nothing that screamed illegal. She obviously hasn't dropped it."

We started walking again. "You think she'll be okay?" I asked.

"Not if she keeps poking around. Sooner or later, somebody will figure it out, and boom, she's out of a job. Once she gets her two years of experience signed off by the firm, she's free. Until then, she needs them more than they need her. Last week, I told her to cool it until she had her time signed off."

I put my arm around my man. "Doesn't sound like she took that advice."

He squeezed me. "When she gets an idea into her head, talking her out of it can be like arguing with a rock. No matter what you say, the rock doesn't budge."

When we got back to the car, it was late, and we headed back to Steven's.

We were walking toward the front door when a car door opened.

Jason.

The toad with the monogrammed seats in his car. He stepped out of his red Maserati and onto the sidewalk a bit ahead of us.

Steven saw him too and took my hand. We continued walking.

Another much bigger man with full sleeve tattoos and missing a few teeth got out of the passenger side to join Jason. The guy was easily as large as

Steven.

Steven slowed me down and pushed me back a bit.

"I told you that you would regret it, Covington," Jason yelled at us. "I'd like you to meet my brother Carl, here, and my other brother, Peter." He motioned to the mountain of man next to him and another one behind us.

Steven and I both looked back. Another large man with a shaved head and a menacing look to him trailed behind us.

Steven pushed me toward the wall, away from the street. "Stay behind me," he said in a low voice. "We don't want any trouble here," Steven said toward Jason, glancing back and forth between the three men.

"I warned you, now it's time to pay the piper, Covington. Did I forget to mention that my two brothers fight MMA?

Tat guy walked toward us from the right and baldy from the left.

Steven pushed me back farther and stood, shifting his gaze from one of the ugly brutes to the other. "I'm warning you, Bigsnot, that if you guys don't turn around and leave right now, your car isn't the only thing getting messed up."

Neither of the brutes stopped.

"You're the one getting messed up here, Covington," Jason shouted. He started following a few strides behind toothless tat guy.

Tat guy made a run at Steven with a bloodcurdling yell.

Steven lowered his stance and then ran at him as well, closing the distance quickly.

I moved to the right. I didn't want to be too far from Steven.

When the two converged, Steven slid on the ground, knocking the legs out from under tat guy. Steven rolled to his feet, and when tat guy started up, Steven kicked him in the gut, followed by a fist to the throat.

The brute doubled over, holding his throat and gasping for air.

I kept moving toward them along the wall because baldy was coming up fast from the left.

Steven moved toward baldy. "Are you as stupid as you are ugly?" Steven yelled at baldy.

Baldy roared and lunged at Steven, swinging and missing.

Steven ducked right and spun around, kicking baldy in the knee.

The big guy crumpled and received another kick, this one to the head.

I shrieked as someone grabbed my arm from behind me.

"You bitch." It was Jason.

I stomped as hard as I could on his foot.

He let go.

I spun around and did what my daddy had taught me. I kicked as hard as I could, and connected with his balls.

Jason screamed out in pain. He went to the ground and curled up in a ball.

Steven ran up behind me and pushed me aside. Tat guy was getting to his feet again. Steven spun around and delivered a kick to the chest that sent him reeling back into Jason's car. He thudded into the door and slumped back down on the ground.

The car had a large dent in the door where the big guy had hit it.

Steven picked Jason up by the collar and threw him toward the car. "Get your brothers and get out of here before I really get mad." Steven put his arm around me and started us back toward his building.

I was shivering. I glanced back. Baldy was still on the ground. Tat guy was struggling to his knees, and Jason was still in a ball, moaning.

"Don't look back," Steven said. "Your life is ahead of you, not behind you. He's a moron and a creep." Steven opened the door of his building for me.

I was still shaking. "What if he calls the cops?"

"Let him." Steven pulled his phone out of his pocket. He stopped the recorder app. "I have the whole thing on tape. They started it. If they call the cops, they end up charged with assault, not me."

I wouldn't have thought of it, but then my man

was a lawyer, and one who had ended up on the wrong side of an assault charge before. My man was smart and strong, and one hell of a fighter. I'd seen a few fights outside of fraternities at school, but nothing like the ass whooping Steven had laid on those two clowns. He was a regular James Bond, or maybe Chuck Norris. Now I could understand how he broke that guy's arm defending Mike's sister. "You a black belt or something?"

"I learned from an ex-SEAL, and they don't like to lose. He didn't believe in letting the other guy land the first punch or the last." He put the key into his door and opened it.

I went through the door, into the safety of Steven's place.

"And what did you do to poor Bigsnot?" He asked. "He's going to need a serious ice bath."

"My daddy told me that if they can't hear the scream in Cleveland, then I didn't kick him hard enough."

Steven wrapped his arms around me and chuckled. "Remind me not to get on your bad side." He held me for several minutes as I slowly calmed down from the frightening experience.

* * *

Steven

It had been a week since the scuffle with Bigsnot and his brothers. Emma had finally felt safe enough to go back to her apartment. The next day, her sister, Megan, had come over after another of her fights with that dipshit boyfriend of hers, Braydon. This time, she had brought along her dog, Horace.

Who names a dog Horace?

That first night, the yappy little mutt had kept us up half the night, and since then, Emma had been staying at my place where it was a yap-monster-free zone.

Sitting in my cube at E&S, something about the way Coulter had answered the questions in the deposition bugged me. While most of the office was at lunch, I slipped into the records room and pulled down a few of the Coulter folders.

The firm did his personal taxes as well as his estate planning and general legal work. I found the answer to my question on his last two years' tax filings. Or rather, the answer was in what was missing from his tax filings. Emma had him dead to rights on purchasing the painting she was after in a group of four he bought from the French art dealer two years ago. That much seemed certain.

If he had the painting and it was looted by the Nazis, why didn't he try to settle and come to some quiet arrangement with Emma and her family? That was certainly better than having his reputation trashed by the local press once this got into a public courtroom. Even if he didn't have the painting, the press would surely sensationalize the possibility that he had it.

He had answered the question about having a Renoir very carefully and very obtusely. Emma hadn't caught it and hadn't asked him to clarify it. His answer was that he didn't currently have one, not that he had never owned one or that he never owned the one she was searching for. The key fact was that he denied owning two of the other paintings on the receipt that she asked him about, and we knew he bought them together.

It left open the very real possibility that he had bought and sold all the paintings. He had picked them up at a price that was a steal. The tax returns showed no sales of art. My bet was that this would be the leverage I needed.

I put the files back where I got them and left the office with a smile.

After lunch, I called Big Tom Coulter from an empty office.

He picked up on the first ring. He remembered me from our prior family meetings. After a few pleasantries, I got down to business. "Tom, I'm calling to give you a warning about the Watson suit."

"What kind of warning?"

"I'm not assigned to the case, but I think you are

taking an unnecessary risk."

"What does that mean?"

"I think this case is going to get a lot worse for you before it gets better."

There was silence on the line. "Monica told me that I'm in the clear. After the deposition, Monica thinks she has enough to get the suit dismissed for lack of evidence."

I needed to take a chance here. "Tom, the reason I'm not on this case is that I know that Watson girl and what she's capable of."

"And?"

"She has hired an attorney, a good one, who also happens to be the son of a judge, and that gives him extra pull in court. They plan to depose your wife and your daughter, so this won't be a cakewalk." I didn't know this for certain, but it was what I would do in Mike's shoes.

"That bitch."

I paused for effect. My hand was shaking. "And file an IRS tax whistle-blower claim against you." This was my big gun.

"What?"

"She thinks that you have been making money reselling paintings like hers and not putting it on your taxes. Are you covered on that front, or could that cause you a problem?" LeMere had told Emma that he had been a regular buyer. I mentally crossed my fingers and hoped for the right answer.

He was breathing heavily now on the other end of the phone. "Do you have a suggestion?" That meant I was right. He was exposed on the tax angle and was now running scared. I silently pumped my fist into the air. I had him, the jerk.

"She just wants the painting."

"But I don't have it anymore." The words I was waiting to hear.

Now, I had one more thing to find out. "Who has it now? We need to point her at someone else."

"I sold it to your old girlfriend, Victoria Palmer. Monica told me to get rid of it before the deposition and she would get the case quietly dismissed." Monica was just that underhanded.

"I think that I can get the Watson girl to back off with that information."

"And she would drop the suit?"

"I'm pretty sure she would. Give me a week to try. Just don't tell Monica. She rubs this girl the wrong way, and she would blow up the negotiation if she got involved. Do I have your permission to work this for you?" It was imperative that Monica not find out.

"Sure, Steven, and thanks for the call."

After hanging up the phone, I put my feet up on the desk and tried to relax. I willed my heart to stop racing. It took a few minutes because I was jittery from the adrenaline. The call had been tense. It could have gone wrong in several ways. He could have denied ever having the painting. He could have not been spooked by the IRS threat. He could have not wanted to tell me where it went, or he could have insisted on getting Monica involved.

Just my luck he would sell it to Victoria, of all people. Anybody else and I could surely name a price that would make the painting mine. Victoria and I had parted amicably enough, but she could be completely unpredictable, and sometimes vindictive. This was going to take some thought.

I need a plan.

* * *

Emma

Last night, Steven had come over and been in a fantastic mood. Something at work had gone unbelievably well, which was quite a change. Normally, whenever we talked about his work, it ended up coming back to what a bitch Cruella was, or The Mistress of Misery, as he called her. He was figuring how many days were left in the countdown to when he would be free of her.

I'd enjoyed telling Cruella to go screw herself, and Steven's friend, Mike, had stopped her little eviction ploy. At first, it had seemed so hopeless, but Steven and Mike turned it all around for me.

Steven was even more convinced than ever that I

would get the answers to my questions "sooner rather than later," he said.

I didn't see how it could be with what Mike had told me about the time frames involved in this legal dance of the deposition, but I didn't understand half the terms they used anyway. I trusted Steven's judgment. Art was my field and the law was his.

His good mood had turned into a desire to celebrate, and that turned into two very long lovemaking sessions last night and another this morning that threatened to make me late for work again. I needed to stop by the ATM to get some money, but I was pressed for time. I had been late once already this week, and that was my limit.

"Steven, can I borrow twenty dollars? It's my turn to buy lunch and I'm all out," I shouted to him from the kitchen.

"Anything my little Sugar wants," he yelled back.

I looked around. I knew I'd stripped his pants off out here somewhere last night. I found them by the side of the couch. I pulled his wallet out and opened it up. This man carried serious cash with him. I searched for something smaller than a hundred and found two twenties behind the big bills. I pulled one out, and a folded-up receipt fell out of the wallet when I did. I picked up the receipt to put it back.

HARRY WINSTON JEWELERS and yesterday's date were printed above the fold.

"Find my pants?" Steven asked, strolling out from the bedroom with just a towel around his waist. "I know they're out here somewhere."

I hurriedly stuffed the receipt back where it had come from and held up the wallet. "Found it."

"Take as much as you need," he said as he opened the fridge and pulled out the orange juice.

"I only took twenty. The kinds of places I go wouldn't know what to do with a hundred-dollar bill." I kissed him quickly on the way to the door.

I got out without letting on that I'd seen anything. Steven had been jewelry shopping, and at one of the most expensive stores in Los Angeles. *Jewelry.*

* * *

We always had our phones on silent while in the public areas of the museum. When I got back from my morning rounds of the exhibits, I found a missed call on my phone. A chill ran through me. It was from Mr. Bonafort at the MET. I'd missed the call while handling questions from guests.

I had thought the phone interview with him three weeks ago went well. We talked after getting back from San Francisco, and now he was calling back. This could be either bad or worse. There were no good outcomes from this call. Either he was going to tell me they had selected another candidate, or they liked me, and I had to choose between Steven and continuing to interview with the MET.

A month ago, the MET would have been the easy choice, but since then, things with Steven had grown so good and so comfortable that I didn't want to give him up for anything, not even the MET. Nobody had ever cared for me the way he showed he did with every little comment and gesture. He wasn't a Todd. That day at the taco stand in Venice with all the bikini babes rollerblading by had been so telling, and every time we had been out since then.

Most men, at least the straight ones, would have glanced discreetly, but not my Steven. He only had eyes for me. Todd wouldn't even have been discreet. His head would have been on a swivel. Why hadn't I seen it earlier? Todd's constantly roving eyes should have told me it wasn't just the girls. It was Todd, the A-hole.

Now, with Steven, I was finally able to see the difference clearly. After the breakup with Todd, I'd wondered what I should have done differently, or what I'd done wrong, or what I hadn't done right. I didn't completely blame myself for his cheating, but I thought I'd somehow contributed to it a little bit, or I could have somehow prevented it. Now, it was clear as day that it was totally him and the little brain in his pants taking control.

I giggled when I considered how a trip to my parents with Todd might have gone. Daddy would have eaten him alive. He probably would have peed in his pants when he saw Daddy holding the old Winchester. Steven just strode up to him and shook hands like a real man.

The way Steven looked at me was such a turn-on. I'd learned how I could drive him nuts just walking up to him with my jiggle walk that bounced my boobs a little bit or sashaying away from him with my exaggerated hip sway. My favorite was doing my jiggle walk up to him when he was making breakfast in the morning, wearing one of his shirts, braless, with a lot of buttons undone. That always got a reaction. Second best was bouncing in braless in one of his tee shirts. They were tight enough to show my nipples and just long enough for him to wonder whether I was wearing panties. He preferred not, and sometimes I preferred the fun of him pulling them off. I was getting excited thinking about it. I needed to stop daydreaming and get back to work.

Mr. Bonafort was probably just being polite anyway and calling to tell me the position had been filled. I didn't have much experience, not big museum kind of experience, and I didn't have anybody to sponsor me. I wasn't related to anybody or had a friend I had worked with before who worked there, so how interested could they be in me? What did I have on my resume to recommend me over the hundred other candidates they must have? I shuddered at the realization that this was likely to be a bummer.

I went outside for some privacy and called Bonafort back. It turned out to be neither of the things I'd expected. He wanted to tell me the process was delayed and he wanted me to hang in there and not be disappointed that I hadn't heard from him yet. It was a thoughtful gesture on his part. The fact that he wanted me to keep them in mind and not give up was encouraging. I'd been afraid I wouldn't make the first cut, much less get to later stages of consideration for the job. This was the MET, after all, the largest museum in the country. The only downside I could come up with was that it was located on Fifth Avenue, right on the edge of Central Park in the middle of the most expensive place to live in the United States.

The job would probably entail quite a lengthy commute. I hadn't even thought about the cost of renting in New York. LA was bad compared to Omaha, but it was nothing like Manhattan. I also had no idea what the salary range was for the job. What a dope. I might be applying for a job that would pay me so little I would have to ride the subway for two hours to afford a place to live. How far did the subway go, anyway? I had the sinking feeling I needed to know a lot more about the job than I did. I could also use more Tylenol this morning, but the supply in my purse had run out.

After lunch with Janice, I stopped off at the drug store to replenish my Tylenol supply. Megan called while I was in line at the register to say she was back with Braydon, and after five days of having her and that mangy little Horace at my place, that was good news. Finally, I could sleep in my own bed again. Steven's place was nice. Well, calling it nice was like calling Jupiter big. It was way better than nice, but it just wasn't mine. It was too spartan and much too neat. I missed my messy little place.

They were across the street as I walked out of the store. It was Cougar Lady lunching with some older bald dude. Apparently, she didn't only go after the young ones after all. I snapped a picture of her as she kissed Mr. Senior Citizen so I could show Megan later what the face of evil looked like. Mr. Senior Citizen was probably loaded. She struck me as the gold digger type.

Driving home from work, one question kept rattling around in my head. What would I do if the MET wanted me, or rather would take me? I rounded the corner to my apartment. I fished my keys from my purse. The paper was taped to my door.

THREE DAY NOTICE TO QUIT.
I'm being evicted.

CHAPTER SEVENTEEN

Steven

She sounded frantic.

"Slow down, Sugar," I said into the phone.

Emma sobbed on the other end. "It says *Three-Day Notice to Quit*. I have to leave, and I don't have any place to go. How can they do this?"

I grabbed my keys from the counter. "I'm coming right over. Just calm down and relax. Let me take care of this for you. It'll be all right."

"But…"

"Sugar, just trust me and let me take care of this."

She calmed down a little. I grabbed my coat and was out the door.

Evening traffic was slow and it took a while to get to her place and find parking.

Emma greeted me at the door. Her mascara had run and her eyes were red. She shivered in my arms.

"Don't worry, Emm, I'm here now." I held her

tightly as we rocked back and forth, sort of a slow dance without the turning. Her sobs slowed and I led her to the couch. "Where is it?"

"On the counter."

I guided her down onto the couch and retrieved the paper from the counter along with some of her favorite M&Ms. Sitting down next to her, I handed her a tissue and the candy.

"Thanks."

It was a standard three-day eviction notice, claiming Emma had violated the terms of her lease. They had filled in the form to claim that Emma had violated the no pet clause.

The bottom of the form caught my eye. My blood began to boil as I gripped the paper. It was signed *Monica Paisley, atty for Date Palm Leaf Properties.*

The bitch.

Monica didn't handle three-day eviction notices. This was fifty levels beneath her. No doubt, the bitch was using this to get leverage on Emma in the Coulter case. This was typical Monica. No counter-move was too low for her. "Sugar, let me call Mike and have him handle this for you."

She sobbed. "But what do I do? Three days isn't enough time."

I took her hand. "Emm, Mike will get this stopped right away. They can't force you out if he takes it to court."

She chewed another M&M. "You sure?"

I hugged her. She was trembling. "Of course I'm sure. What's the use of dating a lawyer if he can't help you with a simple thing like this?"

She laughed. That was a good sign. I needed her to trust me and to know I would take care of her.

"Doesn't that lady down the hall have a dog?" I asked.

She had stopped crying. "Mrs. Gimple, yeah. She has a pug, the stupidest dog you'll ever meet." She wiped her nose. "It took her months to housebreak him, and he pees on anything vertical." She giggled. "So don't let him get near your leg."

That was just what I thought the situation was. "Bring me your copy of the lease, Sugar, and I'll take care of everything."

She got up and went to her desk while I went to the fridge and poured some wine for us.

Back on the couch, I took a sip as I started reading her lease.

Emma sat next to me and snuggled up close, leaning on my shoulder. Her citrusy scent drifted my way. She placed her hand on my thigh. My cock took notice, making it hard to concentrate.

I offered the glass I'd poured for her and she took it. Emma had downed a fair portion of it by the next time I looked up.

Her lease was pretty simple, and the pet clause was what I had expected, given the neighbor on her floor and the dogs I'd seen downstairs. It required an extra one hundred-dollar deposit and fifty a month extra rent to own a pet. This would be easy to fix in court. The property did allow pets, even poorly-behaved ones. The judge would see it as a simple monetary issue. Once Mike got to court, this would be stopped and the worst that could happen would be fifty a month more rent.

I took out my phone. "Sugar, why don't you go change and I'll take you to dinner?"

She kissed me on the cheek and went to her bedroom.

I dialed Mike. I explained things to him while Emma was changing. He agreed with my take on the situation and agreed to handle it in the morning if I brought him the paperwork.

Emma came out changed from her work clothes into jeans and a scoop-neck tee with a leather jacket and sandals. The jacket slid open and revealed a nipple poking against the tee shirt. She was going to tease me by going braless tonight. She bounded over with a smile on her face, a face that had been cleansed of its makeup and was as beautiful as ever. She sported only lip gloss, and those lips were awfully tempting, but if I started anything now, we would both miss dinner and starve, so I took the high road and escorted her out. I carried the lease and the eviction notice with me.

We opted for Mexican down the road. She started by ordering a round of margaritas for us. I would have to limit her alcohol if I was going to keep her upright. She had already downed a glass of wine at the apartment.

Once we took a table, she started right in on the chips. "Why did they do this? Why me?"

She really didn't know. "Did you notice who signed the form at the bottom?"

She gulped some of her Margarita. "No. What does that have to do with it?"

I pulled the paper out of my pocket and unfolded it for her.

Her eyes finally settled on the signature, and after a few seconds, she comprehended who it was. "That's your fucking bitch boss, isn't it?"

I folded the paper back up. "The one and only. I don't know how she arranged it, but this is because of your lawsuit. This is good news." I smiled and stowed the paper in my jacket. I needed it without salsa and margarita stains on it.

"Sure, losing my apartment. Great news. How come you lawyers always think it's good when something bad happens?" She scowled and gulped down the last of her margarita.

I finished my margarita and ordered another round for us. I took her hand. "Sugar, trust me. This is good. It means you have her running scared. She doesn't deal in petty little things like this. She got involved in this to pressure you because she is scared of you in the Coulter case."

"Getting evicted isn't little to me."

"It is to her. She's doing this to get leverage on you. Bet you anything she calls tomorrow and offers to drop the eviction if you drop the case."

She swatted the idea away. "No way."

"I can have Mike wait a day to go to court, and I bet she calls you tomorrow."

Disbelief showed on her face. "Really?"

I finished a chip. "I guarantee she calls to offer to stop the eviction if you drop the case."

She smiled. "But what do you want me say"

"Not me, Sugar. What do *you* want to say?"

"I want to tell her no way." Now her smile spread from ear to ear.

I took another chip. "That's way too polite for her."

"Too polite, huh? How about" —she held up her middle finger with a wicked grin— "fuck you and the horse you rode in on, Cruella."

"That's the spirit. Make her squirm."

We finished off the bowl of chips, trying out epithets for her to use before the food arrived.

Emma traced the rim of her empty second glass. "Cruella. I think I like that." She smirked and giggled. She had thought of several good lines to use on Monica. She just needed to pick one.

"It fits her," I replied.

Her grin had turned mischievous. Her foot traced the inside of my leg under the table, shooting a jolt straight to my cock. My appetite was quickly turning from food to something else. She opened her jacket just enough and bounced in her seat, driving me crazy with the sight of her braless breasts bouncing beneath the tight cotton shirt. She winked at me in an overly exaggerated way. My girl was drunk and getting playful. After dinner, Emma wanted to go back to her place. She was more than tipsy. The girl would have no chance in a drinking game.

Once inside her apartment, she spun around and dropped her coat. Her braless breasts that I had done my best to avoid staring at all night beckoned me as she bounded toward me, her hard nipples showing through the thin fabric. She wrapped her arms around my neck and pulled me down to her, her lips seizing mine, the spicy taste of salsa and the sweet taste of margarita mixing on her tongue. "Take me to bed, my big stallion," she growled. I was quickly learning she was hell on wheels when she was drunk.

Lust rattled through me. I lifted her up, and she wrapped her legs around me as I cupped her ass and carried her to the light switch. I bumped it off. I fumbled my way to the bedroom, carrying her as she pulled at my hair and growled into my ear.

Bumping into the bed, I turned and fell backward with her on top of me. She released her grip on my neck and started to work on my shirt as I wrestled her shirt off and cupped her marvelous tits in my hands. They had teased me all night and I'd been waiting to feel them, to massage them, to knead them, to lick them, to suck them, to worship them. She was a real woman with real breasts. Nothing artificial here. They were soft and supple, and they bounced in the most tantalizing way when she walked. They were topped with amazingly responsive nipples. Perfect works of art, warm and inviting.

She rocked her hips over my cock with a growl. I had a tigress on my hands tonight.

I cradled and massaged her breasts and kissed and sucked her nipples as she rode me through the fabric of our clothes. I started on her pants as she slid down and worked my buckle loose. We frantically raced to get each other naked. I flipped her on her back and planted my face between her legs, working my tongue and my lips over her clit as she whimpered her encouragement. I lapped up her sweet juices.

My secret fuel.

My sweet Sugar was so hot, so wet, so responsive to the slightest touch or lick tonight. I added my fingers to the mix, first one and then two, alternating with my tongue on her clit.

She arched her back and clamped her legs firmly around my head, grabbing at my hair and pulling my head into her with ever increasing moans.

I loved that she'd found what she wanted, what

she needed in this. It was such a turn-on. I increased the tempo and the pressure with my tongue as my fingers massaged her.

She growled for more.

I used my free hand to knead her breast and tweak her nipple. I knew that for some women, the slight pain increased the pleasure and for others, not. Emma was definitely in the *Yes* column.

She pulled at my hair to get my head to come up to hers.

I relented and kissed my way up her abdomen, tickling her belly button with my tongue and stopping at those marvelous breasts on my way up to her neck and finally, her lips.

She kissed me with savage intensity and more growls than whimpers as I worked my hand over her engorged clit. I circled the tiny bud, first one way and then the other.

I pressed on her magic little button with my thumb, earning load moans as she clawed at my back. I moved to her ear and lavished it with kisses and licks and blowing that sent shivers through her. I moved back to tongue the little nub of joy.

She clamped her thighs around my head and rocked her hips against my mouth.

I increased the tempo and the pressure until she was on the verge and then backed off. I increased again and pulled back before she got to her climax.

The third time, she pulled at my hair to get more

pressure. She started to shake, and I kept it up, taking her over the edge.

She screamed out my name as she came with a vengeance, squeezing my head with her legs, pulling at my hair, rocking her hips into me, and clamping down on my head as the tremors wracked her body. Her little moans as she came down were sounds of complete satisfaction. As the intensity of her spasms subsided, I removed my hand and licked the sweet juices from my fingers. She pulled me up to her for a long kiss. "You're my stallion," she said as she grabbed a fistful of hair. "Mount me," she growled into my ear.

My girl was a fiery drunk. I didn't need any more encouragement. I rolled off her.

She quickly rolled over and got on all fours.

I moved behind her and grasped the flesh of her hips.

She guided me in with her hand. The tip of my cock entered her wet heat. She was so tight and so wet and slippery. It was magical the way I glided into her as I pushed in a little.

"Take me," she growled as she bucked back into me.

I leaned forward and grasped her tightly just above her hip bones to give me leverage and pushed into her slowly to stretch her.

"More," she pleaded as she backed into me.

I started to thrust slowly then faster, garnering

soft moans of pleasure from her as I worked the leverage to bury my cock deeply into her tight, wet, slippery center again and again.

She reached between her legs and grabbed my balls and pulled me to her. WAY too hard.

I cried out and spanked her.

She let go with a laugh.

I could hardly take it. She was so naturally tight it was unbelievable, and the way she used her muscles to clamp down on me as I pulled out with each stroke was an indescribable pleasure. "Baby, you're so fucking tight, so fucking good."

She bucked her hips back into me. "More, give me more."

I reached around to grab a breast. "You feel so fucking good, Sugar," I grunted out as I gave her the more she demanded. The tension built quickly as my balls slapped against her with each thrust.

She reached between her legs and grabbed my steely shaft with her fingers, then my balls, gently this time, as I worked myself up to a frenzy.

I could sense her getting close with the whimpers and moans she made. I brought my hand around between her legs to tease her clit. It didn't take long for her to scream out my name as she convulsed around my cock. She trembled beneath me and arched her hips back.

With one last deep push, I came, exploding deep into her. "My God, baby." After a few seconds, I forced her forward to lie on the bed and collapsed atop her back, my cock still throbbing deep inside her. I was spent and fulfilled. My woman, my incredible woman. There was nothing like my woman. I kissed her ear as the throbbing of my cock slowly subsided. I pivoted to take my weight off so she could breathe. We looked into each other's eyes with the smiles that could only come from such a satisfying connection.

She licked her lips. She was pinned under me. She kissed her finger and offered it to me.

I kissed it back.

She giggled. "We forgot something."

Oh, shit.

I shuddered. I quickly pulled out and rolled off her. We forgot the condom.

She smiled and kissed me with the slight lingering taste of margarita. "I'm clean and I'm on the pill. It's okay." She wiggled closer.

"I'm clean too," I whispered to her as she turned toward me and her chest met mine, kissing my neck and spearing her fingers through my hair.

She fell asleep resting on my shoulder with an arm draped over my chest. She snorted a few times before her breathing became slow and steady.

I contemplated what had just happened.

My woman.

* * *

Emma

Last night, we had forgotten the condom, and it was the best sensation as he thrust into me again and again. My man satisfied me so completely, and I decided I wanted to skip the condom from now on. I was on the pill, after all.

I found his shirt from last night beside the bed. I put it on and only fastened the bottom two buttons before I ventured out to the kitchen to see what Steven was fixing for breakfast.

Once at work, I waited until a little before lunch to call Steven's friend, Mike.

Steven had already talked with him, and he assured me that he could handle the situation and I shouldn't worry about the eviction notice. He had already checked the lease Steven had forwarded to him and they agreed it was a no-brainer. He asked for Monica's phone number so he could 'call off the dogs', as he put it.

I had programmed Cougar Lady's office number into my phone from her card and given the contact the picture of a witch, an ugly hook-nosed witch on a broom. I told Mike I would send the number when we got off but to wait on doing anything. They both agreed the notice was easy to deal with, and they should know, right? I wanted to see if

Cougar Lady would call like Steven expected. I sent Mike the contact info after we hung up.

Steven had been right. The office number from Steven's law firm showed up as my phone rang at mid-afternoon. It was Cruella and she wanted to offer me a settlement.

Steven and I had tried out dozens of obscene ways to tell her to stuff it, but he said I need to give her enough rope to hang herself with first, whatever that meant.

"Go ahead, Monica, I'm listening," I said politely, although what I was thinking was more like mayhem.

"I understand that you have had an unfortunate turn of events in your rental situation."

"You mean the three-day notice that you tacked on my door yesterday?"

She huffed through the phone. "Dear, that was not me. It is the management that makes those decisions."

Up yours, Monica. I'm wise to you.

I responded, "I'm just not sure what to do now."

"Might I suggest a solution?" she offered.

"And what would that be, Monica?"

She offered, "Perhaps I could prevail upon the management to overlook this incident."

I paused for effect. "And how would that work?"

"Well, I would be calling in some very big favors with them, so perhaps we could come to some arrangement."

I paused again. Steven had suggested to draw the conversation out. "What kind of arrangement did you have in mind, Monica?"

She hesitated. "Let us say I could convince your landlord to drop the eviction proceedings." She paused. "And we were to pay you a thousand dollars for your expenses, and in exchange, you were to drop the Coulter suit."

The proposal was nearly what Steven had predicted out of Cruella.

"Let me think about that." I waited about ten seconds for her to stew. "Monica, I have a slightly different suggestion."

"Such as?" she asked.

"I think you should go down to Hollywood Boulevard tonight." I paused. "Put a bag on your head and see if they will take your thousand to fuck you."

"You little…"

I interrupted her. "When that fails, go fuck yourself and keep the thousand."

"Better go find another shithole to live in, bitch," she yelled into the phone.

"I may not live in the nicest part of town, but at least I don't have to wake every morning and see your face in the mirror."

She was screaming obscenities into the phone when I hung up. I called Mike Salois and told him it was time to send the court order. I laughed and sat back in my chair. I had really gotten to the bitch.

Sit on that, Cruella, and rotate.

EIGHTEEN

Steven

Monica slammed down her phone and motioned to me to join her in the torture chamber she called an office as she swore at nobody in particular. "What the hell did you do, Covington?" Agitated was her normal state, but this was becoming a Richter-nine eruption. "Don't fucking mess with me." She opened her desk drawer, pulling out that gray recommendation envelope again to threaten me.

I had to suppress my instinct to laugh. Lately,

whatever was bad for Monica was probably good for me. The bitch had been even harder to stomach than usual. I needed her recommendation to be a positive, or at least, neutral one when I left. I'd been stifling my instinct to tell her what I thought of her and be the obedient ass kisser long enough to get to the bar. Today was the hardest yet to keep my tongue under control. I put my hands up in mock defense. "What's the problem, Monica?"

She had tried and failed to land the Covington account and seemed to blame me for it. She had more than once hinted that since I worked at the firm, it made a perfect pairing. What she didn't count on was Uncle Garth's view that my working at E&S was irrelevant.

"Did you know about this?" She shoved the court order at me. It was signed by Judge Samson, and it put Emma's eviction on hold pending a hearing. Mike had no trouble getting the eviction stayed, as I had expected. I read the entire paper. The hearing was set four weeks out. Plenty of time.

"No. If you check down at the bottom, her legal council is Mike Salois."

"I know that, and I also know he's a friend of yours."

"Monica, don't blame me if she's smart enough to retain a lawyer." It didn't hurt that Mike and his dad invited Judge Samson and another fellow judge to join them for a round of golf at their club every few weeks.

I had to work hard to stifle my amusement. "Like I said before, Monica, I think it's best for the firm if I avoid the depositions in this case."

She fumed and told me to get the fuck out of her office. She threw the papers in the trash and slammed the door shut after I left. Her little mess-with-Emma operation had been a failure and had backfired on her.

Once out of sight, I smiled all the way back to my desk. It was a bad day for Monica and she deserved it.

Not an hour later, Jeremy was by with the news that we were going to join Monica on a three-day trip to San Francisco to meet with new clients. We were leaving first thing tomorrow morning. As always, our time was hers to waste.

After lunch, I was finishing up my call with Victoria when Monica appeared again. "Gotta go, Vicky. See you for brunch tomorrow at the Ritz. Love you too. Bye." I hung up the call.

Monica stood over me. "How cute. Getting back together with your ex, Steve?"

I ignored her.

"Don't forget the five o'clock meeting to prepare for the SF trip," she said.

I grunted a reply as she departed quicker than she had arrived.

I was still on track for the bar next month, and it

couldn't come quickly enough. Everything about working for the evil mistress of misery turned my stomach. It was becoming harder each day to keep my words civil.

I went outside where I could talk to Emma without being overheard. It looked like Emma had one hell of a conversation with Monica, and I wanted to tell her that it had worked perfectly. Monica was so mad she couldn't see straight.

One more month.

* * *

Emma

Steven had called to tell me that it had worked and operation screw-with-Cruella had been a success. He filled me in on her fury at the office.

I relayed the phone call with Cruella and which line I had chosen to use on her.

He laughed his ass off at the Hollywood Boulevard bag line I'd decided on. The bad news was that he told me he was now scheduled to go up to San Francisco for three days with Cruella and two others from the office starting tomorrow. He agreed to come by and see me tonight before he left.

We had been together so much the last few

weeks that the idea of three days without him seemed daunting. I was planning dinner at my place tonight. I'd bought the steaks yesterday.

"Sounds great, Sugar. How about I bring dessert?"

We agreed on that and I went on with my day. He had told me he had an early flight, and I thought it meant he couldn't stay. I toyed with the idea of asking for a day off to go up and surprise him. I thought showing up Thursday night at his hotel might be nice.

At the end of the day, slightly after I had gotten home, Steven showed up at my door with luggage and a shopping bag. "We have an early flight, and I thought it might make sense if I left directly from here," he said, rolling the suitcase in the door.

That sounded sensible. I jumped up into his arms for a quick kiss. I wrapped my legs around his waist. "I'm going to miss you," I said as he broke the kiss and nibbled on my neck.

He twirled me around and sat my butt on the counter.

I kept my legs clamped around him.

He pushed me back and pulled my shirt over my head.

I shrieked with joy and ripped open his shirt. A button or two went flying.

He reached around me to undo my bra but was surprised to find no hooks. It was a front-clasp and it took him a few seconds to figure it out.

He grabbed the shopping bag and carried me into the bedroom. We fell onto the bed as I started working on his pants. He ripped open the paper bag. He had two cans of whipped cream and a can of chocolate frosting. "I told you, I'd bring dessert," he said with an evil grin.

We spent an hour having each other for dessert. We showered and had a late dinner.

* * *

Steven

I had arrived in San Francisco on the early flight, along with Monica, her shadow, Lenny, and Jeremy. We had arranged for an early check-in at the Ritz Carlton. Only the best for E&S when the client was paying. My phone dinged as I was unpacking my suitcase.

SUGAR: did she book you adjoining rooms?

SUGAR: Call me tonight?

ME: Y and no

SUGAR: Which is yes?

She was worried. I tortured her, waiting a few seconds before texting her back to clear it up.

ME: Yes to the call no to the room

SUGAR: I hate that woman.

ME: u me both

This trip worked out well for me. I'd called Victoria yesterday and set up a brunch meeting with her. This way, I didn't have to come up to San Francisco on the weekend and figure out how to keep Emma from finding out.

Victoria had agreed to join me in the restaurant at our hotel for an early lunch.

She rounded the corner, beautiful as ever. No wonder she was so successful in Hollywood. Her face was made for the big screen. She had always been self-conscious of her appearance, and that translated into constant applications of creams and lotions, followed by a nose job, a boob job, and who knows what else. She was her own worst critic, appearance-wise. She was accompanied by Penny something-or-other, her sycophant assistant, constantly taking pictures for Victoria's Instagram account. Penny also carried a package.

Victoria waved. "Steven, so good to see you."

Her breasts spilled over the top of a strapless light blue bandage dress with a tight midsection and a medium-short hemline. Her heels were shorter than usual. Her hair cascaded over her shoulders, not a strand out of place, looking like she had just brushed it out. Most likely, it was one of Penny's chores. She had on the sapphire and diamond earrings and necklace combination I had given her at our six-month dating anniversary. Quite a nice touch. The earrings always did look stunning on her, complimenting her eyes, and the necklace pendant was large enough to draw one's eye to just the right spot above her cleavage.

We gave each other a quick hug and a peck on the cheek. I caught Penny taking a quick snapshot as we did.

Victoria did a quick spin for me. "It's a Vera Wang. Do you like it?"

"Vicky, you would make a burlap sack look like a million dollars. You look as lovely as ever." That was no lie, but it was still a good idea to butter her up. Things could go wrong if she didn't accept my proposal.

"Steven, you say the nicest things." She checked her makeup in a small compact and put it away. "You look good. I hope life has been treating you well."

"I've got no complaints," I said. That was true so long as we kept anything to do with the law firm

ERIN SWANN

out of the conversation.

She cuddled up next to me and put one arm around my back and the other suggestively on my chest. "Penny, one or two more."

I put my arm around her and added a sincere smile for the camera.

Penny took shots from two different angles.

"Pick the best one and title it brunch with my handsome ex." She was constantly posting to her Instagram account. "The price of keeping up in my business," she complained as we sat down and I ordered champagne for both of us.

I shifted my silverware. "So, tell me how you've been. I saw you are in the next *Fast and Furious*. Does that come out soon?" I'd checked her credits on *IMDB.com* before I came and knew it was the latest big gig she had landed.

She sighed. "Next summer. Post-production on those takes forever with all the CGI and everything." Her breasts heaved over the top of her dress as she talked. It was a diaphragm breathing technique that she had studied as an actress a long time ago. She thought it helped her land a few parts over the years. The dress was also tight enough to preclude eating anything more substantial than a breadstick.

I studiously kept my eyes up. "Is it a good part?"

Her bright, toothy smile broke a little bit. "Not so much, just twenty lines, but at least I didn't get killed off, so if they like me, I might come back with more scenes in the next installment."

I could tell she was disappointed, but in her business, an optimistic view of things was a good practice.

The waiter arrived with our champagne and started to pour.

"On the brighter side, I'm reading tomorrow for a part in the next *Mission Impossible*."

I didn't have to feign interest. "No kidding, tomorrow?" It truly would be a big break for her. She had pretty constant work, but she hadn't landed a major part in a big film yet. "That's great."

"Sure is. My agent said Tom asked them to get me." She meant Tom Cruise, naturally.

I raised my glass for a toast. "How great is that? To *Mission Impossible*."

She raised hers as well. "To *Mission Impossible*." Now she had a serious glow about her. Her smile grew and her eyes brightened as the thought of landing the role lingered with her. "It sure would be great." She giggled. "And I wouldn't have to wear heels."

I laughed. She was on the tall side for an actress, and we all knew Cruise was a midget, even in his elevator shoes. "I hear he likes 'em tall." I took another sip. "Nicole Kidman and Katie Holmes were both taller than him."

She huffed. "I just want the part. I don't want to

marry the guy."

"Just sayin'."

Her eyes glowed as the thought bounced around in her head. Her face betrayed her. She wasn't as opposed to being the next Mrs. Cruise as she pretended.

I took another sip of my champagne. "I think you would be great opposite Cruise."

She leaned forward and cradled my cheek in her hand. "You are so sweet to say that."

The waiter returned and I ordered a burger with fries.

She chose a salad with dressing on the side. "One of the downsides of the profession," she muttered after ordering. "The old cameras added ten pounds, but with HD it's more like fifteen."

Penny clicked off another picture one table away. She didn't get to sit with us, one of the downsides of being a personal assistant.

After picking at her rabbit food for a while, she asked, "So, what do you have for me?"

I pulled the box out of my pocket and teased her by opening it in my direction so she couldn't see its contents. "It once belonged to the Duchess of Overdale."

Her eyes lit up as she leaned forward. She had always been extremely status-conscious. Only the best for Victoria.

I had her full attention. I pulled the ring from its

velvet embrace, and leaning forward, I offered it to her. I hoped the tidbit about the previous ownership would do the trick.

Victoria's hands went to her cheeks. "My God, it's gorgeous," she shrieked.

The other diners around us looked over at the commotion, and we got quite a few oohs and ahhs. Penny snapped some more shots. I understood how in her business, all this social media crap could help Victoria, but I hated it. Having your whole life out there for everyone to see was not my style.

Victoria took the ring and held it up to her ring finger. "It's just perfect. I love you, Steven." Her voice was loud. She was too good an actress for me to tell if she was making a spectacle for her audience or if she was sincerely overwhelmed by the ring. She put the ring on her finger.

My mouth went dry. "Vicky, will you accept my proposal?" I asked in a low voice, trying not to entertain the assembled audience.

"I will, I will. I love you, Steven," she announced as she rushed around the table to kiss me and hug me.

She sat back down, still quite blushed and teary-eyed. She waved Penny over for more pictures.

My heart was racing from the excitement. I'd done it. Emma needed to know her quest was over. This was going to be quite a shock for her. But I needed to tell her in person. My fingers trembled as

I typed out a text message.

ME: I have some important news to share with you when I get back

SUGAR: What is it?

ME: Something I need to tell you in person

In person was the only way.
Emma will be so happy.

* * *

Emma

Steven had gone up to San Francisco this morning. I remembered last night's dessert and wondered if I should try to surprise him tomorrow night at his hotel.

Janice woke me out of my reverie. She asked me to pass the list I had made up for the Christmas gala exhibit we were working on. I got back into work mode. Steven wouldn't be back until Friday night. I succeeded in putting chocolate out of my mind until an hour later, when Janice brought me a mid-morning Mocha, then the thoughts exploded in my head again. She had no idea why I was smiling and so giddy about getting a simple Mocha.

My phone rang. It was Mr. Bonafort's number from the MET. I excused myself and took the call in the hallway, escaping toward the stairs.

"Miss Watson," he began. "I—no—*we* would like you to come out for another interview at your earliest convenience."

My heart stopped.

They wanted me.

A violent trembling overtook my legs. I leaned against the wall for support. This came out of the blue. "I'm sorry, you said right away?" My stomach turned over.

"Yes, Miss Watson, as soon as possible. I have just gotten my budget approved for your position, and I would like to move forward quickly."

He said 'my' position.

I was going to have to make an impossible decision. "Mr. Bonafort, I'm going to need a few days to figure this out."

He agreed to give me until Monday to figure out a time to come visit. I hadn't told him that what I needed to figure out was whether I would come out.

I needed to talk with Steven this weekend when he got back. What was I going to do? How could I choose between the best man I had ever met, my dream man, and my dream job? I couldn't have both, and I couldn't give up either one. I knew the answer was that I had to give up the job. Another job might or might not come along at some point, but I wouldn't find another Steven in a thousand lifetimes. Not a girl like me. I needed him to understand what I was giving up. I was getting nauseous thinking about it. My head started to spin as I got back to my desk. I almost missed my chair as I plopped into it. I laid my head down on my desk and closed my eyes. How could such good news be so bad?

A little before lunch, my phone beeped with a text message.

STEVEN: I have some important news to share with you when I get back

Maybe he was going to tell me how my little rant was still screwing with Cruella's head.

ME: What is it?

STEVEN: Something I need to tell you in person

I'd learned that I couldn't coax anything out of Steven if he was determined to keep it from me, and that's what this looked like. Maybe he had done something extra to screw up Cruella. I smiled at the thought. The bitch deserved it.

CHAPTER NINETEEN

Steven

Penny put down her phone and brought the package over. Her eyes bugged out at the sight of the ring. She undid enough of the wrapping for me to see for sure that the painting was the one I was searching for, and she gingerly re-wrapped it. Victoria and I signed the exchange papers to make it legal.

Victoria insisted that I tell her all about Emma as we finished lunch.

I was happy to oblige. This had worked out so perfectly.

Victoria admired the ring on her finger every few minutes. We finished in short order and said our goodbyes.

I did it. I'd gotten Emma's painting for her.

I tried to imagine Emma's face when I told her that her mother's dream was going to be realized.

The painting was finally going to be back in the family.

I made my way toward the front desk. The rush of adrenaline had my heart racing. This painting needed to be in a more secure place than my hotel room. Rounding the columns at the entrance to the restaurant, I bumped into Monica, of all people.

She was typing on her phone. "Want to have lunch?" she asked. She knew I had planned an early lunch with Victoria today. Early-onset Alzheimer's, perhaps.

"Sorry, just ate." I escaped to the front desk. I wasn't going to let her spoil my mood right now.

The desk people were quite accommodating. We unwrapped the painting so they could take several pictures of its condition before I handed it over to them for safekeeping. They acted like they handled million-dollar paintings all the time for their guests. It was a relief to get this part done.

I returned to my room to collect my briefcase for our afternoon meeting with the client.

The meeting lasted four hours as Monica kept asking questions, stretching out the billable hours, no doubt. After the meeting, we all got sucked into dinner with the client. Monica was the only one excited by the prospect of spending another three or four hours with the engineering guys from this company.

At the restaurant, they spouted technobabble

none of us truly understood as we nodded every so often like little bobble head dolls. Monica threw in dozens of meaningless questions they were eager to answer in a language that less and less resembled English as the dinner wore on. At least the steak was good, and our guests kept our wine glasses full.

They wanted to initiate a suit against Google. They were certain that Google infringed one of their patents, and in their minds, it was a simple matter of right and wrong. Who were we to burst their bubble and point out how Google had an unlimited legal budget with which to do battle with their tiny company? The mouse was about to bite the elephant and learn that size mattered.

No doubt, Monica was drooling at all the hours the Google counterattack would make them spend with us once they started this unwise little war.

We got out of the restaurant late, and when I called Emma, it went to voicemail. She was probably asleep. I wished her a good night and headed to my room.

Two more days here in San Francisco without my woman would be the price I would have to pay. Come Friday, though, I would be back with Emma, and she would have her painting and I would be that much closer to taking the bar and getting the hell away from E&S and the evil mistress of misery.

I have the painting.

* * *

Emma

I left for an early lunch at Burger King. It would be empty enough for me to get a booth to contemplate my options. When I got there, I decided to treat myself to an apple pie as well.

After a few fries, I took my first hard suck on the straw of my chocolate shake. Nothing came out. Why did these things have to be so hard to get through a straw when they first came over the counter? My phone dinged with a message.

The message was from a number I didn't recognize, but it said *Flash news about S. Covington's engagement*, and it had an attached video. What the hell was that about?

I could see Steven and a blonde in the picture frame. I pressed the play button. The video had just unintelligible background sounds, but the picture was Steven, all right, and I could see now that the blonde was his ex-fiancée, Victoria Palmer, the actress. He opened a small box and presented her with a ring. My heart stopped. Even from a distance, I could see it was a gigantic diamond. A diamond ring. A chill went through me. I couldn't quite make out what he said, but her exclamation was loud and clear. "My God, it's gorgeous," she yelled. That quieted the surrounding tables. She put it up to her ring finger and said, "It's just perfect. I love you, Steven." The crowd oohed as they realized what was happening. He said something I didn't catch and she responded with, "I will, I will." She raced around the table and hugged and kissed him. The video ended.

I found the earbuds in my purse and listened to the video again. Now I could hear him say, "Will you accept my proposal?" I shuddered. The man who yesterday was my perfect man, was now her man.

The asshole.

I pushed my food away. So, this was the important news he had to tell me in person. He had gotten back together with his first love, Victoria. Perfect teeth Victoria, big chested Victoria, famous Victoria, everybody loves Victoria, rich actress Victoria. The wicked, conniving bitch, Victoria. In what fucking galaxy was this fair?

My day had turned utterly to shit.

I hadn't said yes to interviewing with Bonafort when he called because I planned to say no after I talked with Steven this weekend. I wanted him to understand how big a sacrifice I was making for him. I wanted him to know this was not merely an infatuation for me. I could see a real future for us. He had never said he loved me in so many words, but I thought he was one of those men who was just built that way. The kind that thought having a

Y chromosome meant not saying the words. His actions had always shown me how deeply he cared. I could see love in his eyes even if it didn't come out of his mouth.

Until now.

Now I was mad. Now I saw how I was just a means to an end. He had used me. I was just a good fuck buddy that he could come out of his shell with, get beyond hating women, or rather just treating them as fuckable objects that were more satisfying than jerking off. A woman he could use to take the step to being almost human, to being boyfriend material again. All so that getting back together with fucking Victoria would not be such a big leap. How could I have been so naive?

He was the asshole, but I was the fucking idiot here. It was my fault for trusting a lawyer, and a rich one at that. My mother had always told me that rich men only had two uses for poor girls like us. They could either hire us as nannies or bed us until they were bored, or maybe both. We would never be good enough to be wives or mothers to their children. Now it all made sense. On top of that, I had dated a lying, cheating scumbag lawyer and dishonored Elissa's memory. I was the one who was stupid enough to think that he would be different.

My shittiest day ever. Rock, meet fucking bottom.

I sucked on my milkshake that was now warm enough to travel through the straw. I skipped the burger and fries and started in on my apple pie. I was determined not to be a patsy anymore. Steven was not going to deny me my dream job. I shoved away the hurtful memories.

I picked up my phone, took another suck on my shake, willed my fingers to stop shaking, and hit *Call Back*.

By three o'clock, I'd begged off work and was booked on a flight to New York.

MET, here I come.

* * *

I packed a bag and rolled it out the door, locking my little apartment. In the back seat of the UBER on the way to LAX, I tried desperately to settle myself. I had been a frazzled bundle of nerves since lunch. Janice had been very understanding in letting me take some time off with zero notice. Probably a result of having become Mr. Benson's favorite Assistant Curator for securing the pictures from the Covingtons. I didn't deserve it, but a girl's gotta take what she can get.

I dialed Megan. "Sis, I'm on the way to the airport. I'm heading to New York tonight. Wanted to let you know I won't be around for a while."

"So, is this MET?" It sounded like she had been drinking.

"Yup. They called this morning and Mr. Bonafort

wanted me to interview right away."

"That's great, Sis. Is Steven going with you?"

That was a question I didn't want to deal with today. "No."

She was suddenly more alert. "Why not?" She could be so nosy at all the wrong times.

A cold vise clamped down on my heart. I could barely hold it together. "He's working up in San Francisco for a few days, and I need to go tonight." I couldn't bear to tell her what Steven had done, not yet.

"Okay, Sis, good luck." My answer had satisfied her.

My breath caught in my throat. "Thanks." I didn't like keeping this from her, but I couldn't deal with the twenty questions session that would follow, especially with her drunk.

"Call me when you get settled, and good luck," she repeated. She had definitely been drinking.

I wiped the tear off my cheek. "Thanks. Love and Kisses." I hung up the phone. My stomach was knotted like an old rawhide rope. My situation had gotten so fucked up that I couldn't even explain it to my sister.

How pathetic is that?

Because I booked it so late and most of the flights to the east coast had already left, all I could get for tonight was a flight to Chicago and a change of airlines for the last leg to JFK. The plane was late coming in, naturally, and would be late taking off. I was rewarded with a center seat near the rear lavatories for the first leg, between two guys, one of which didn't fit in a narrow coach seat.

The thinner guy in the window seat wanted to talk for the longest time.

I didn't, so I told him I was flying out to meet my girlfriend in the Big Apple.

That slowed him down.

I added that I had to fly right back in a few days for my next meeting with my parole officer.

That stopped him cold, and he even vacated the armrest on his side like I had a contagious disease. That was good because the large guy seated on the aisle side had his shoulder halfway over my seat.

The large guy fell asleep pretty quickly so I didn't have to talk to him, but that didn't do anything about the smell. I hoped he didn't slump over in my direction and crush me. I could see the headline, *Woman found dead of suffocation after jet lands at O'Hare.*

The occasional fart from the large guy didn't do anything to improve my mood. I hadn't relaxed at all on the plane. I'd tried to go over notes on the MET that I had stuffed in my purse, the people, the history of the museum, and the state of the European exhibits, but I wasn't able to concentrate. Thoughts of Steven kept intruding. My mind replayed the vision of him giving that monster diamond ring to Victoria Palmer over and over in my head. *Will you accept my proposal? I will, I will. I love you, Steven.* I couldn't decide who I hated more at the moment, him or her.

Her with the perfect figure, the perfect teeth, the perfect hair, the perfect face, the perfect job, little Miss fucking perfect. How was I supposed to compete with her?

Thoughts buzzed around inside my head like a thousand hornets the entire flight. It made so much sense that I couldn't understand why I didn't see it earlier. I was an assistant curator at a small museum, and she was a famous actress. I lived in what Cruella accurately described as a little shit-hole apartment. She had a house in the Hollywood Hills. I made barely enough to afford Lean Cuisines for dinner after paying my rent, and she made at least half a million a year, maybe way more. I wasn't homely, but compared to her, I was entirely forgettable. She was strawberry shortcake to my oatmeal. She was skinnier, had better skin, was a few inches taller, had perfect hair, the perfect tan, the perfect smile, everything was so fucking perfect about her that I could puke. It was so obvious that I couldn't compare to her. Steven would have to be brain dead to not want her instead of me.

The flight was a non-stop, but with the time difference, it was scheduled to land after midnight. With the late takeoff and the weather, we arrived thirty minutes late and I followed large fart guy off the plane. The jetway shook with every step he took.

The departures board in the terminal told me my connecting flight was about to leave on another concourse, naturally. I started in the direction the signs pointed, and I ran. When I was too tired to run anymore, I half trotted. The signs kept pointing the way, but unlike road signs, they never told me how much farther.

Finally, I got to the right concourse and near the gate. The door to the jetway was still open. I'd made it in time.

I showed my ticket to the gate attendant at the desk. She told me coldly that the flight was overbooked and I had been bumped because I hadn't checked in yet. The expression on her face told me what to expect, but I pleaded my case anyway. A quick argument with Miss don't-fuck-with-me at the gate got me an education in airline rules. The flight was overbooked, I hadn't gotten here the requisite thirty minutes early, I had been selected to be bumped, and any more yelling by me would get me a visit to the airport police substation.

I started to cry.

After a half-minute of my sobbing, Miss don't-fuck-with-me broke down and became Miss slightly-helpful. A flight on a different airline three gates farther down also went to JFK, and sometimes, passengers who missed this flight could get a seat on that one.

Just then, fart guy rolled past me seated on one of those electric shuttle carts.

When I reached the gate Miss slightly-helpful had pointed out, there was fart guy seated, waiting for the plane, boarding pass in hand.

The fellow at this gate said there was one seat left and his flight was fourteen dollars cheaper and he would accept my ticket from the other airline but I wouldn't get a refund for the difference. "Do you want to do that?" he asked.

I couldn't give him my ticket fast enough.

Forty minutes later, I was in the last row of the plane in a seat that didn't recline with a drooling granny on one side and smelly fart guy on the other. Right ahead of us was a nice couple with a three-year-old terror sitting between them. The little guy was already voicing his displeasure at two hundred decibels and we hadn't even started moving. I put in my earbuds and turned up the music. I turned it up even higher.

An hour into the flight, the *Fasten Seat Belts* sign came on, and the captain announced we would be taking a slight detour around some weather ahead.

The weather turned out to be what the airlines classified as moderate turbulence. Which meant no drink service and every once in a while, the seat belts were the only things keeping us from hitting the ceiling. I learned that after the little terror's grape juice box hit the ceiling and landed in my lap, staining my pants. The couple ahead of us had given it to the demonic child in a failed attempt to quiet him.

The juice box was followed a few minutes later by baby spit. I counted myself lucky it wasn't purple demonic child vomit. My stomach rebelled at the roller coaster torture. Right now, it was a good thing I'd been in such a hurry that I didn't have time for dinner, or I might be figuring out how to use the airsickness bags.

My day was getting better by the minute. Fart guy kept elbowing me in the ribs on his downward trips after being launched upward by the turbulence.

We arrived at JFK forty-five minutes late after our weather detour. The place was eerily deserted. I had granny drool on one shoulder, demonic child spit on my blouse, bruises in my side from fart guy, and grape juice stains on my pants, but solid ground never felt so good. The taxi ride into Manhattan was short by New York standards, given the light traffic at this hour. The gloom outside the taxi window matched my mood.

A miracle happened when I arrived at the hotel. The night clerk on duty was able to find my reservation. It would have been a fitting end to this shitty day if they had given away my room. The Holiday Inn was all that came to mind when I had only twenty minutes to make a reservation before I left. Not very close to the museum, but it met my budget. The room turned out to be small but clean enough. I hung my clothes in the closet and set a wake-up call. I felt like shit and needed to get some sleep before tomorrow's interview. I grabbed a package of M&Ms, a vodka, and a rum from the minibar.

When I finally turned on my phone, I felt like my heart had been ripped from my chest and thrown into a bottomless pit, never to be seen again. I found voicemails from Steven.

The asshole.

I deleted the messages without listening. Then I blocked the dickhead's number.

I was cold.

Numb.

I texted Megan that I'd arrived safely and put my phone on silent for the night. I ate a few green M&Ms, opened my two bottles of magic forgetting potion, and drank away the hurt.

Alone.

CHAPTER TWENTY

Emma

Hotel phones had the most annoying rings. The wake-up call jolted me awake, but that was the idea. I rolled over, picked up the phone, and acknowledged it. Four hours of sleep was going to be my ration for today. My mouth felt like I had been eating gravel, and I needed to find my Tylenol. Alcohol always did this to me. Next time, I was going to try melatonin or something.

After three Tylenols, a hot shower, and a quick trip in casual clothes to the breakfast buffet, I felt human again.

I'd studied the route from the hotel to the MET in the taxi and decided to walk it. The exercise would do me good, and I didn't like the idea of making this my first ride on a New York subway. I got shivers just thinking about the subway.

I dressed in a conservative navy suit with a mid-length skirt, a cream blouse, and pearl studs for earrings with a single-strand pearl necklace. *Very business-like*, I decided, checking myself in the mirror for the tenth time.

Once on the sidewalk, I was carried along in a sea of people, completely unlike LA. I had my mental map memorized but checked the route on my phone as well. After three blocks, I realized I had made two mistakes. First, the blocks were much longer than I imagined and I might be late if I didn't pick up my pace. And second, the humidity was stifling compared to California and I was going to sweat right through my suit in no time.

I hailed a cab at the curb. The back seat smelled faintly of sweat and other things I didn't want to think about, but at least it was air-conditioned, and it would get me there early and only a little sweaty.

Exiting the cab, the MET looked even more magnificent than in the pictures. The facade was huge and imposing, set back from the street on the Central Park side of 5th Avenue. I took in the majesty of the place. I was finally here. The MET. The largest and most important museum in the country.

After climbing the dozens of steps to the entrance between the fluted columns, I was inside. I marveled at the towering arched ceilings of the great hall. The nice lady at the circular information counter kindly summoned someone to escort me into the office area.

Seven hours later, I'd interviewed with five people, including an interview over lunch with Mr. Bonafort, and had been given a tour of some of the European exhibits, the restoration area, and some of the basement. It had been overwhelming and exhausting.

The day had gone okay until the last interview. Mrs. Langston kept asking details I had to admit I didn't know. I must have said *I don't know* or *I'm not sure* two dozen times with her, especially when she asked me questions about the MET's history and its organization. When I left, I knew I'd bombed.

I hadn't studied enough before coming out. Originally, I hadn't even expected to have a chance for an interview, much less an offer, but now that I had gotten this far, I was heartbroken that I might have screwed up by not studying more ahead of time. I could only go back to my crappy little hotel room on my way back to my crappy little life in my crappy little apartment that I deserved for letting my preoccupation with Steven screw up my studying for the interview.

I could kick myself.

If I'd kept my focus on the MET instead of Steven, I would have done better, I just knew it. Shuffling back to my hotel amid the late afternoon crowd was my self-imposed punishment for screwing up so royally. I was sweating like a pig, and my feet were killing me in these shoes. I considered taking them off until I noticed the people walking their dogs on the sidewalk. I felt like dogshit, but I didn't want it between my toes.

Steven had fucked me over emotionally, and now, he had caused me to screw up my best chance to get onto the staff at the MET.

Fuck all the lawyers.

* * *

Steven

It was Thursday afternoon and I still hadn't heard from my Emma. She hadn't called or responded to my texts. The museum was no help. I didn't get any more out of them than *She isn't in today.* I didn't have her sister's number so there was nothing I could do to reach her through Megan until I got back.

At a break, I called Uncle Garth and asked him to check with his sources to see if she had been in an accident. He assured me after a quick check that she hadn't been, according to the police. Emma had told me of one time before when she had to stay with Megan to help her deal with her sister's shit boyfriend. Maybe this was one of those times. I hoped it was as simple as that.

My sister-in-law, Lauren, called about five

minutes later to see how I was doing. The family grapevine was working at warp speed. She had already heard of my call to Uncle Garth. She told me to hang in there and have faith in Emma, that a day or two out of touch was no big deal. She had given Bill a similar fright once when she was out of touch for two days.

She admitted she had accidentally dropped her phone in the toilet. Naturally, the phone didn't take to water well and she spent two days trying to dry it out so she wouldn't have to explain her stupidity. In the end, she had to buy a new phone anyway. The story made me laugh, but that was probably the point. I could picture the agony on Lauren's face as she tried to figure out if retrieving the phone was worth sticking her hand in the toilet bowl. I thanked her for the encouragement.

In the meantime, I had to tolerate Monica and her sycophant shadow, Lenny, for another day. Jeremy and I had instructions to sit quietly in the meetings, taking notes, and leave all the talking to Monica. Mushroom duty, we called it. Time progressed at a snail's pace. Swallowing a hundred live frogs would have been easier than sitting through these meetings not knowing what had happened to my girl.

Mushroom duty was an apt description. I was in the dark about my girl and Monica kept shoveling shit on us. Sitting in these meetings four hundred miles away from my woman was eating me alive.

I hope she's safe.

* * *

Emma

My self-imposed hike had been long in the muggy heat. I was hot, sweaty, and tired. I climbed out of my clothes and got into the shower, a nice, long shower. I didn't hear the phone and I didn't notice the missed call until nearly dinnertime. They had called Thursday afternoon after I got back to the hotel. When I checked the message, it was Mr. Bonafort congratulating me on a fine day and asking me to come in again Friday. They wanted me back.

I'd felt sure I had flunked. I couldn't believe it. I played it over again to make sure I wasn't hallucinating. The day took on a whole new luster. It was time to celebrate. I'd passed by a Ben and Jerry's on my way back to the hotel. I could see a nice bowl of Chunky Monkey in my future. After a change of clothes, I was on my way to my ice cream reward. I called Megan. She was in a hurry, getting highlights done, which was fine by me. I didn't want to spend any time discussing Steven with her anyway. I told her quickly that I had passed the first interview at the MET and they wanted me back again.

Megan was both surprised and happy for me.

I explained I didn't want her to tell Steven where I had gone or what I was doing. I didn't explain why. That would have meant explaining how stupid I had been.

She agreed that a job interview in another city was not the kind of thing he should hear secondhand. She would let me be the one to tell him. But she didn't know the half of it, and that was fine with me for tonight.

Nobody knows know the half of it.

* * *

Friday morning, I took a cab back to the MET, and by lunchtime, I had an offer to join the European Art division as an Associate Curator, which was the lowest level, but anything at the MET was a step up for me. I'd confided in Mr. Bonafort that I didn't feel very confident after the interview with Mrs. Langston. He told me my reaction was normal. She always asked questions people couldn't answer, and the real test was to honestly acknowledge your limitations and not try to fake it. He said they wanted people who understood what they didn't know and would ask for help. I had passed with flying colors.

Once outside the building, I scanned over the

printed offer in my hand again. They wanted me to start whenever I could finish up with my museum in Los Angeles. The money was way better than I had expected. It was enough to allow me to get a place within a reasonable commute. I could hardly contain myself. I wanted to jump up and down or yell or do something equally unladylike, but I restrained myself. I was in front of the MET, after all. My dream was coming true. It was just up to me to not screw it up now.

A few days ago, I thought I would have to make a terrible decision and choose between Steven and a possible job here. I should have understood it had been a false choice. A girl like me never really had a chance with a guy like Steven. Now the choice had been made for me, and I ended up on the right track. I shivered at the realization that I'd almost turned down my chance at this a few days ago for the illusion of a life with Steven.

It was late afternoon Pacific time when I called to talk to Janice. She was taking a few days off back in Phoenix to help her mother again. When I explained I had an offer from the MET, she didn't even let me finish before telling me that it was great news and she would let me go right away since I had enough vacation time accrued to cover the two weeks' notice. I could start Monday at the MET if I wanted.

This was not at all what I'd expected. I had

dreaded telling her that I would be leaving, but she was extremely happy for me and supportive. She told me Bonafort had called several weeks ago for a confidential reference and that she had given me her highest recommendation and told him he would be an idiot if he didn't hire me. Heat rose in my cheeks. It was humbling to hear her say that.

I accepted the offer later in the afternoon, and they scheduled me to start on Monday. I called Mama to give her the good news. She was overjoyed, but I could tell she wasn't thrilled about my being three thousand miles away. Megan's shift had already started, so I put off calling her until tomorrow.

I work for the MET.

* * *

Steven

We flew back to LAX late Friday afternoon, which was still two days too late for me. That's how long it had been since I'd heard from my girl. I skipped baggage claim and went straight to hail a cab to Emma's place. I wasn't waiting for anyone or anything. I had to find out what was going on, and the apartment seemed like the best place to start.

I had the cab wait while I knocked and knocked, pounded was more like it, but the result was still no Emma or Megan or anybody answering the door.

A lady down the hall came out to check on the noise with her mangy dog in tow. It was the butt-ugly little pug that Emma had warned me to stay away from. I was ready to drop kick the beast to the next county when it barked and made a run at me, but the tiny monster ran out of leash before it reached me. The neighbor turned out to not have a clue about Emma's whereabouts.

I'd already called the museum this morning and gotten the same lame answer from the receptionist. She wasn't in and neither was her supervisor. I took the cab back to my place. She had a key, and I hoped that maybe she had sought refuge there.

That was a dead end as well. My place seemed cold as winter without Emma to brighten it up. I had become so used to her cheery presence that things were too quiet, too orderly, too dull, too lonely. I had never minded being alone before. I had my workouts, my studying, and my work. It had always been enough.

Until Emma.

The bar was getting closer, but studying could wait. It would have to wait. Everything would have to wait.

I didn't know very much about Emma's sister. I didn't have her number or where she lived, but I did know that she waitressed at a Nathan's something or other restaurant. A quick Internet search gave me two possibilities.

The first restaurant was the closest. The hostess there had never heard of Megan Watson, and neither had a waitress whom I asked. Strike one.

The second was the right place. The hostess said Megan was on duty. I asked to be seated in her section. It only required a short wait.

I took my table and started reading the menu.

Megan did a double-take when she noticed me. "Why, Steven, you slumming tonight?"

"I heard the food here is good and the service is even better."

A genuine smile overtook her face. She didn't seem at all concerned about my being here. "Aren't you sweet? What can I get you?"

"Iced tea to start."

"Okay, take your time. Just let me know when you figure out what you want."

I thought it but I didn't blurt it out.

What I want is to know where Emma is.

She left in the direction of the kitchen and was back with my iced tea and a smile.

I perused the menu for a few moments. "I'll take the Nathan burger."

"How do you want that cooked?" she asked.

"I'd really like to know where Emma is. I have some news for her."

Her mouth froze into a thin line. "I can't say. I'm not her keeper."

"I just need to talk to her and know she's all

right."

She had the look of a cornered animal on her face. She had admitted she knew but wasn't supposed to tell me where Emma was. "She said she was going to tell you when she was ready."

"Ready for what?"

Megan hesitated. She stepped back, her eyes desperate, trapped. "Ready to talk to you, I guess."

A chill gripped my chest. This was worse than I thought. This was no waterlogged iPhone problem. Emma was trying to avoid me, to get away from me.

But why?

"Back in a sec," she said as she scurried off to take care of another table. She went to the kitchen when she finished with them. Strike two.

A few minutes later, another waitress came to take my order. By the time my burger arrived, I'd still not seen Megan emerge from the kitchen. She had gone, and with her, my only way to contact Emma. Strike three.

My heart felt like a rock wedged between my ribs. She was avoiding me, running from me.

Why?

I didn't finish my food, didn't even start it. I dropped two twenties on the table and walked out.

I am so fucked.

CHAPTER TWENTY-ONE

Steven

The dull ache in my chest wouldn't go away. A million questions exploded in my mind, all without answers. How had it come to this? Emma had left. She wouldn't take my calls or respond to my texts. She had instructed her sister not to tell me where she was. What was she hiding from? What had I done or failed to do? I hadn't told her I loved her in so many words, a mortal sin in Katie's book, but how could that cause a blowup like this? I should have seen this coming. What had I missed?

As I sat in my car outside Nathan's, I thought back to the morning we shared on Wednesday before I left for San Francisco. It had seemed so normal. I cooked a breakfast of waffles and sliced fruit. She had asked why I needed to go for so long. Our words and touches and kisses had all been like any other morning. What had I missed? She had planned to leave later that day and I couldn't sense any of it. How could I have missed something so big?

I cringed at the thought that I had so little understanding of my woman that I couldn't tell she was planning to leave. I couldn't answer any of these questions by myself. She hadn't told me any of her misgivings. She had to have big ones to disappear like this, and she had hidden those from me expertly. She hadn't given me a clue in her actions, her gestures, or her words that she had planned this, or maybe I was just too clueless to catch on. Guys were clueless. Katie had always insisted they were. Maybe she was right.

Why do women have to be such difficult creatures to understand?

The only way to hash this out was face to face. I needed to stop trying to call her. If I got her on the phone, it wouldn't be enough. I had to look into her eyes and talk to her to understand her hurt, her problems. I had to tell her how I felt face to face. I now understood the depth of my love for her. She had to look into my eyes and understand it as well. She had to.

I can't live like this.

In person was the only way. To do that, I had to find her, and I had just the person to call. I started up the car and dialed the number.

You can't hide from me, Emma.

* * *

Bill agreed to meet me at his restaurant as soon as I could get there. It wasn't the quietest place to meet and it was a fair distance from Nathan's, but I was the one calling for help, so the location was his choice.

I thought about what to do on the drive over, but I wasn't making any progress.

When I arrived, the staff was expecting me and I was ushered into a small private dining room on the side. Bill and Lauren were both there. I hadn't expected Lauren. This was kind of embarrassing to talk about with my big brother, even without an audience.

We sat, and Bill poured a round of wine for all of us. Bill had ordered antipasto and bruschetta for us. "So, what's the story, little brother? We may not be able to help, but at least we're good listeners."

They listened as I explained how I had gone to San Francisco for this set of meetings and I hadn't heard from Emma since the morning I left. I also explained the tortured path I had taken to locate her family painting and to get it back from Victoria, and how I planned to surprise Emma with it when I got it back. That earned me a broad smile from Lauren. I also gave them a brief rundown of my encounter with Emma's sister, Megan.

"So you traded a ring for the painting?" Bill asked.

I put my wine down. "Yeah, I wasn't sure it was going to be enough, but she loved the ring and so we traded and signed the papers. I put the painting in the hotel safe for the night and I had it couriered down here today. I didn't want to check it in baggage at the airport. With my luck, some TSA clown would take it home with him."

Lauren reached out to touch my arm. "Steven, that is the sweetest thing I have ever heard. That is so nice of you."

"Right now, that and five bucks will get me a cappuccino at Starbucks," I retorted.

Bill shared a knowing glance with his wife. "Looks like this is ripe for Uncle Garth's favorite saying."

"And what pearl of wisdom is that?" I asked.

Lauren smiled at Bill and continued the thought. "Bill's Uncle Garth told him on more than one occasion when he was pouting and feeling sorry for himself..."

"I never pouted," Bill objected.

"You did too. Anyway," she continued. "He told him when things weren't going well, *crisis reveals character, and now we would find out what he was made of.*" Lauren said with a giggle.

It sounded like something corny that Uncle Garth would come up with.

Bill cocked an eyebrow. "So, what's your plan?"

"She obviously doesn't want me to know what she is doing, and I don't know what I did to make her leave," I replied.

Bill leaned forward. "So what? It doesn't matter. You either love her or you don't."

"It's not that simple," I argued.

Lauren spoke up. "Yes, actually, it is."

She was right. It was that simple. "Yes, I love her. I can't stand to be without her," I said.

Bill put his glass down. "Then go get her and tell her again and again, but stronger than you did before, and make her believe you."

I lowered my eyes to the table. I was ashamed to admit I couldn't recall a time when I'd said it straight out.

Lauren caught my gaze. "You didn't tell her, did you?"

I was a complete schmuck. "Not in so many words," I admitted.

Lauren huffed. "You guys are so beyond stupid, both of you. You Covington men have some kind of genetic deficiency going on here. How can you be so smart in business and in school and so utterly inept with women? It's just mind-boggling. You can't just expect her to read your mind. You need to tell a woman that you love her, and a lot more than once."

Bill's face took on an unusually sheepish look for

him. He was obviously guilty of this sometime in the past.

"But I tried to show her every day how I felt about her."

"That's nice," Lauren said. "And I'm sure you did, but she needs to hear it as well as feel it. Telling a woman that you love her is like watering a flower. You need to do it every day."

I'd failed at the most important test of my life. I should have known how to talk to Emma to tell her how I felt, and I had fucked it up. Big time.

Lauren wasn't done with me yet. She huffed, exasperated at how dumb the males of the species seemed right now. "Instead of giving you guys classes on how to undo a bra in the dark, that prep school of yours should have taught you how to express yourself to a woman."

Bill had been waiting patiently to get a word in edgewise. "Back to the problem at hand. Steven, I think that we should call Uncle Garth. He has resources that should be able to locate Emma, but after that, the rest is going to be up to you." He dialed his phone.

While Bill had the phone to his ear, Lauren added, "Just remember what I said. Like watering a flower, tell her every day, and more is better."

Bill started explaining to Uncle Garth what help we wanted. When he hung up, Bill called for the waiter and we ordered dinner.

By the time we had finished the entrées, Bill had gotten a call back from our uncle. "He said that an Emma Watson boarded a Wednesday afternoon flight to O'Hare, and that is where the trail stops. She doesn't have a return reservation at this point." Bill laughed. He tapped Lauren's shoulder. "That's more than I had to go on when this girl disappeared on me. You should get a call shortly from one of Uncle Garth's guys."

So, my girl went to Chicago. I could only think of one reason for Chicago. The Art Institute of Chicago was one of Emma's dream jobs. She had four museums on her wish list and Chicago was one of those.

I wiped my mouth and got ready to leave. "Thanks for dinner and the help. I need to find a plane to Chicago."

"Just a sec, Steven," Bill said. "Uncle Garth also said that they didn't locate a hotel reservation for her yet, but that could sometimes take a few days."

"Got it, thanks again," I replied. I didn't finish my wine. I pushed back my chair.

I left Cardinelli's smarter than I had arrived, but I still needed a plan.

The phone rang as I opened my car door. "This is Steven," I said. The call came from a number I didn't recognize.

"Mr. Covington, my name is Robert Hanson, of Hanson Security and Investigations. Your uncle suggested I call you. We are on retainer to your family's company. Mr. Durham said you might want our assistance in locating a woman." He went on to explain how they had helped my brother in his search for Lauren. He also reiterated they had tracked Emma to Chicago arriving Wednesday evening. "I can tell you that she withdrew five hundred in cash before she left, which is not much if you are traveling to a city like Chicago, so we should get a hit on credit card activity before long."

I thanked him and we set up to call each other tomorrow to discuss any additional information he might uncover. It was a much quicker start than I'd expected. Uncle Garth certainly knew the right people.

When I got home, I packed quickly and put the painting which was still in its box on the dining room table. I would need Bill's help in getting this to me when I found Emma, and I still couldn't risk checking it at the airport. I located a red-eye flight online that had seats available in First Class. A little bit of sleep would be helpful when the hard searching started.

I was in the air by midnight on my way to the windy city.

Here I come, Emma.

* * *

Emma

I woke up late Saturday morning. I hadn't slept well last night. I should have been ecstatic over my good fortune, but my screwed-up relationship with Steven kept intruding on my feel-good intentions. When I opened the curtains, the sun was shining, certainly an omen of all the good things to come. I'd landed my dream job. All I had to do now was not screw up, and things would get better day by day.

But I was alone. I didn't know a soul in this city, and I had nobody to share my good luck with. Why hadn't I fallen for a Smith, or a Jones, or anything but a Covington? And why couldn't he have been a plumber, or a carpenter, or even a nerdy programmer, anything but a scumbag lawyer?

After breakfast, I went looking at apartments. It was still too early California time to wake up Megan. I had no real knowledge of the New York area, but Rachel at the MET had recommended I look in Chelsea or Murray Hill if I could afford it. Checking online, the rents were a lot higher than what I was used to in LA, but this was Manhattan, after all. I decided to give it a try and check out a few. Each unit I looked at had very heavy-duty locks, another difference here in New York, and they were all smaller than they looked online. It was easy to see why they didn't list the square footage in most of the ads.

At lunch, I took a break and called my sister and got the bad news. I'd been putting this off, but now I had to deal with it. Megan told me that Steven had come by the restaurant and asked where I was. She was surprised because she thought I would have already told him. When I explained what he had done to me, she was startled. "You have got to be kidding me, Sis. He just up and proposed to his ex?"

I was still reeling from the whole thing. "I got the video. He gave her a huge ring and asked if she accepted. She, of course, said yes and hugged and kissed him." I blinked back tears at the memory.

"I don't get it," Megan said. "You said he just bought you jewelry."

"Well, I thought it was for me. I saw a receipt from Harry Winston Jewelers and I thought he was getting me something extravagant." The breath caught in my throat. I sobbed. "I thought he might propose."

"You mean he bought the ring for her while he was with you?"

I dabbed at the tears with a napkin. "He was sleeping with me and planning to marry her. How pathetic is that?"

"Oh, Sis, I'm so sorry. I really thought he was the one for you. Can I do anything to help?"

I sobbed. This was so unfair. "No, not right now. I just need to get settled here and then get my things out of my apartment there."

Megan offered to help, and I got off the phone before I completely broke down. I needed to forget I'd ever met Steven fucking Covington. Maybe Megan was right and I needed to set my sights nice and low and find a boring kind of guy whom I could count on to stick with me. I couldn't bear to have my heart ripped out like this again.

By Sunday, I had found a small studio that didn't directly face another building. It was on West 21st street in Chelsea. It was close to the subway, had laundry in the building, and a doorman, which I thought added to the security of the building. A quick signature, a credit check, a deposit on my credit card, and I had keys. All I needed now was furniture. My stuff in California wasn't worth trucking across the country. The rental agent had a list of furniture places for me to check out.

Three cab rides later, I was getting a bed, a desk, a small table, chairs, and a dresser delivered Monday.

I'm officially a Big Apple girl.

* * *

Steven

I arrived and had my bag by six in the morning at O'Hare. The choice to go First Class had not resulted in my getting any sleep. I was too wound up for that, but at least it was a more comfortable sleepless trip than trying to squeeze my long legs into a coach seat. I'd often focused on the downside of being a Covington, the expectations of us, and the presumptions people made about us, but not tonight. Tonight, being born into a rich family definitely had its advantages.

I had worked out my speech for when I found Emma. Actually, I'd worked out five speeches and had no idea which one was best. The thoughts came to me in bursts during the flight. What if she said this? What if she said that? In the end, the exercise only confused me more.

My first stop was to get checked into the Fairmont, which was a bit north of the Art Institute, my only point of reference right now in my search. My first try at the front desk got nowhere. They were booked up for a realtor convention. But Uncle Garth had gotten all of us American Express Centurion Black cards for just such a problem. Flashing the black card got the manager involved, and they magically had a suite available on the thirty-fifth floor for me not ten minutes later.

Being a Covington has some serious advantages.

Room service brought up breakfast. I showered and shaved in no special hurry. The Art Institute was only a few blocks south and didn't open until ten thirty. I had no plan of attack yet, but I needed to get to the Art Institute to start asking questions. It was my only lead right now.

I waited until nine to call Hanson to see what new information he might have gotten. He didn't have a lead on her hotel yet, and he was hamstrung by the fact that some of his sources of information didn't work on weekends. I got the distinct impression that he had people inside the credit card processing companies who sold him information under the table, but he couldn't get anything if they weren't at their work stations today. He said to be patient. Five hundred in cash would mean that Emma would leave a credit trail pretty soon. At ten, I sent a text message to Monica claiming to be under the weather and an email telling her I wouldn't be in on Monday. I would be in when I could was all she needed to know. I started my trek to the museum.

The Art Institute was an impressive structure with giant bronze lions guarding the entrance. I walked in, and at the member services counter, they checked the directory but couldn't find Emma Watson. No surprise. Also, no surprise the curating staff was not working today and I would need to check back on Monday to talk to any of them. I walked the exhibits for three hours on the off chance I would find her here wandering the halls, as she sometimes did in LA.

By lunchtime, my stupidity was apparent. I

should have known she would be interviewing with the Monday to Friday crowd and I wasn't going to find her, or any answers, here on the weekend, but it was the only thing I could do and I had to do something. Sitting on my ass waiting for Hanson might have been the smart thing, but it didn't seem right. I had to try to find my woman somehow.

I went back to the Fairmont and generated a list of hotels to call from the Internet based on the distance they were from the museum. I stopped when my list got to ninety. I started to dial the numbers and ask for a guest by the name of Emma Watson. After about twenty-five calls, I was connected to a room.

The lady who answered turned out to be Emily Watkins from Cleveland. I apologized and went to the next number on the list. By dinnertime, I had worn out my fingers, and all I had learned was that I wasn't cut out to be a detective. This was both frustrating and mind-numbingly boring with a capital B.

Monica had called three times, and three times, I had ignored her. I sent another text saying my throat was acting up and I couldn't talk. The bitch could wait. Her text back just said *gray envelope – don't fuck with me.*

After another fruitless call to Hanson, I decided to veg out in front of the television. Katie called to see how I was doing. I filled her in and tried to sound more optimistic than I felt. I had gone another day without hearing from my woman and it was tearing me apart.

Bill called a little later, and his only useful advice was to eat only pepperoni pizza until I found her. It had been lucky for him and it might work for me too.

I found Sean Connery's *Never Say Never Again* in the on-demand section on the TV and asked the concierge to get me a pepperoni pizza from somewhere, anywhere. The movie was about not giving up in the face of adversity, which I thought fit my situation. I would have preferred the movie be *Diamonds are Forever.* It had the Tiffany Case character, the fake name Emma had given me that first night, but it wasn't in the listings. After four pieces of pizza, I saved the rest for breakfast. I fell asleep halfway through the movie.

CHAPTER TWENTY-TWO

Emma

Monday morning, I was at the MET employee entrance bright and early. The process of getting my badge and filling out the ninety-nine new employee forms went smoothly enough and only gave me mild writer's cramp. They gave me copies of the pages I'd signed, including all seventeen MET policies on this and that to read later. A half-hour training video on how we treated guests kept me busy until ten, when I finally made it to the curators' office area.

Mr. Bonafort introduced me around. I had met several of them in the interview process last week. I was assigned to a two-person office. An office with real walls instead of a cubicle. The last introduction was Marci DeGoote, a bubbly girl a little older than me with short-cropped, chestnut red hair. Marci was my new office mate. She worked in the same department and offered to take me to lunch.

I begged off for today and suggested Tuesday. Mr. Bonafort had nicely allowed me to take the afternoon off to handle the delivery of my furniture. I would start my first full day tomorrow.

I'm now a real MET curator.

After lunch, I called my apartment manager in Los Angeles to give my thirty-day notice. He wasn't surprised. He probably thought I didn't want to fight the eviction notice after all.

My new furniture all arrived in the late afternoon, at least the little bit I had bought to get started with. I went out later to go shopping for some kitchen essentials and bathroom items to tide me over until Megan sent me my first few boxes of stuff by UPS. She had agreed to box up my clothes and kitchen and bathroom items and put the furniture on Craigslist or just get rid of it. I told her she could have my crappy little car, which was better than her crappy little car. By the end of the evening, I was ready to put sheets on my bed and spend my first night in my very own Manhattan apartment. I was now a Big Apple girl. It was exciting and scary at the same time. I'd never spent any real time out of state. I was going to have to deal with snow and muggy weather and all kinds of things that were foreign to a California girl. After Gilroy and Santa Clara and Los Angeles, this was going to be a real change, starting with not having a car.

When I climbed under the covers, I couldn't get to sleep. It wasn't only the street noise, which was a little worse than I had expected. Thoughts of Steven kept intruding. I'd managed to not obsess about him for most of the day. The quicker I realized that it was inevitable that he would go back to his perfect actress girlfriend, with the perfect face, and the perfect boob implants, the quicker I could get over my stupidity and get on with my life. Live and learn, they said. Well, I was going to learn from this experience and go on living. Fuck you, Steven Covington, and your perfect fiancée with the perfect body and the perfect face and the perfect hair and the perfect teeth. I'm done with you. I may not be perfect like her. I'm flawed, but I'm real, and proud of it. You don't deserve me.

You two perfect fakes deserve each other.

* * *

Steven

Sunday had been a complete bust. I called another several dozen hotels with nothing to show for it, and wandering the museum another time familiarized me with the layout but got me no closer to finding Emma.

It was now Monday, and my morning coffee had congealed into a lump in my stomach as I waited to hear from Mr. Hanson. He had told me when business opened up on Monday, he would have access to much more data than he could get on the weekends, and I was smart enough to not ask him how it worked. I didn't need to know about the greenbacks under the table for this information.

Hanson's call came slightly before eleven. California had been open for business almost an hour by now. "Mr. Covington, we have a new lead, sir. Miss Watson made multiple credit card transactions in New York."

"New York? You said she was in Chicago," I said angrily.

"Sir, what we knew last Friday was that she boarded a flight to O'Hare from LAX. What we didn't know at the time was that she changed airlines and took another flight to JFK without a reservation."

Fuck, I'd been in the wrong city for all this time.

"Sir, we don't have the same access to this data as law enforcement does, and it sometimes takes time for us to check everything we would like to."

I needed to cut him some slack. He was obviously doing all he could as fast as he could. "Sorry, Bob. I know you're working this hard. Just tell me what we know now."

"Sir, she checked in to a Holiday Inn in Manhattan and she has made charges at several eating establishments and stores in the city. She checked out yesterday, and she appears to be on foot. She has not rented a car so far, as we can ascertain."

Checking out was not a good sign. "If she checked out, does that mean that she is flying back?"

"Sir, I don't think so. There was a credit report pulled on her in New York by a real estate firm. In my estimation, she has applied to rent or buy something in the New York area. Additionally, Sir, we don't see any activity under her name at any of the airports in the area." She was applying to rent a place in New York. That could only mean that when she left, she didn't plan to come back.

My stomach soured even more. "Thanks, Bob. I'm headed to New York then, as soon as I can get a flight."

He agreed to keep me up to date as he got new information.

I wasn't going to call the MET. This needed to be in person. It would be too easy for her to blow me off over the phone. I was not going to make this easy for her to say no. I needed her, and she HAD to see that we were meant for each other. I had to make this impossible for her to say no and impossible for her to just blow me off.

I booked a flight to LaGuardia and called the Plaza to book a room and get a car to pick me up.

By Monday evening, I was ensconced in a room overlooking the bottom of Central Park. The city around me was so vertical compared to Los Angeles. So many people in such a small area. The sidewalks were like rivers of people, and swarms of yellow colored taxis honking at the slightest provocation filled the streets.

Hanson had sent a text confirming that Emma had started at the MET as an associate curator of Impressionist paintings in the European Art department at the MET, and he gave me her boss's name and a contact number for him as well. Landing a job here was quick work considering she flew out last Wednesday night. Maybe she'd had this lined up for the last few weeks and had just kept me in the dark.

Now that's a scary thought.

I knew the MET was one of her top choices of a place to work, but to accept a job here and not even tell me? That was cold, and Emma wasn't cold, was she? Maybe I didn't really know her well enough to judge. The thought sent a chill all the way to my toes. She had lied about her name the first night with a completely straight face and a second fake name the second night, all without blinking. Was that all she had lied about?

I dialed up a local pizzeria that had a handout in my room and ordered a pepperoni for delivery.

I puzzled out my plan over delicious pizza as I tried to figure out how I was going to get her to sit down with me and talk to me and not be able to just hang up the phone or walk out of the room. I needed time with her, time to convince her that we were meant to be together. Time to convince her that she meant more to me than anything or anybody in the world. She had to understand and give me a chance to change whatever it was about me that was bothering her.

I went over it again. She left without telling me. She wouldn't communicate with me. She told her sister to not tell me where she had gone, at least for a while. Megan had said Emma would call when she was ready to talk. There was an obstacle, some demon she was dealing with that I didn't understand. Because I didn't know what it was, I didn't know how to combat it. Face to face was going to be the only way. I had to make her come clean about it. Only then could I understand her plight and make things right for us. I needed her to listen to me, to talk to me, and not just walk away and leave. I had to trap her.

By ten o'clock, I had figured out an approach that might work. I called Bill and asked for his help. He would need to send some things for this to work. He agreed to put the plan into action and would charter a jet to get me what I wanted once we had the exact list settled. He called back an hour later and we went over the list in detail. He added that Lloyd Benson and Uncle Garth were both onboard as well. He told me about Benson's suggestion.

I called Lloyd Benson and talked over his suggestion. I liked it. He had a better understanding of the people working at a museum like the MET than I could ever have. We agreed to go ahead.

I composed my obligatory email to E&S on my iPhone and sent it. *I quit E&S, effective today* was all it said. I didn't know if Monica would have a cow or be pleased, and I didn't give a shit.

It only took a few minutes for Monica to respond.

MONICA: I'm mailing the gray envelope today – better find another career.

I hardly slept as I kept going over the details of the plan. There were still a few ways this could go wrong, but Lloyd and I both liked the chances of success. For the first time in days, I was optimistic. I'd found her, and I had a plan to make her listen.

I'm here, Emma.

* * *

Emma

Tuesday morning, I found my way to the bus up 5th Avenue and managed to not be late for my first full day of work. I got a tour of our exhibit halls and the adjacent ones in the morning. The museum was monstrously large and I was afraid I might have to use my phone to navigate it for a while. I spent the morning getting a rundown from Mr. Bonafort of ongoing projects in my area. Oddly, nobody ever addressed him by his first name. My specialty was going to be Impressionist paintings. It was obvious from the large backlog of work why he was anxious to hire someone quickly. I was going to be busy. Super busy.

I had lunch with Marci, who was quite the talker. She was a Yale grad and had joined the museum last year. She wanted to know all about Los Angeles and California. Had I met any movie stars? She was disappointed to learn that I had never bumped into one.

I swallowed hard when she mentioned Hollywood. I didn't feel like filling her on my ex-boyfriend and my least-favorite actress just yet. I pumped her on New York life, getting around, shopping, eating, and meeting people. We had to hurry to get back when we realized how much time had gone by. I didn't get to finish my sandwich.

Mr. Bonafort had scheduled a staff meeting for three. I was early and got a seat next to Marci. A half hour into the meeting, a gray-haired gentleman with a bowtie came in and pulled Mr. Bonafort out to talk to him.

"That's Mr. Cromartie, the Director of the

museum," Marci whispered.

"Does he come by often?" I asked.

"Never."

Several of the others in the room were whispering to each other as well.

I could glimpse Mr. Bowtie and Bonafort talking outside through the conference room window, but the conversation was too soft to hear. I noticed my boss point to me, but I could have been mistaken. Mr. Bonafort returned to the meeting with Mr. Cromartie.

The older gentleman spoke first. "We are being graced with a rather significant donation to our collection this afternoon. The benefactor has a Vermeer for us, and he would like us to pick two out of three Rembrandts that he brought for us to examine."

Marci gasped. Those masters of the Dutch golden age would both be in her period of specialization and would be wonderful additions to her exhibit. If Marci hadn't been seated, she would have fallen over.

Mr. Cromartie continued, "As you know, we currently have five of the thirty-five known works of Vermeer, and to get a sixth would be quite remarkable. The benefactor has also offered us several impressionist paintings from Manet, Monet, Renoir, and Pissarro. He would like to have dinner with us this evening to determine the exact donation. Miss DeGoote, you and Miss Watson should join us for dinner."

Marci nodded vigorously. "Yes, sir." Ecstatic was too mild a description of her excitement.

I nodded and raised my hand in acknowledgment.

Bowtie addressed Mr. Bonafort. "Paul, I suppose that is all for now." So there was at least one person here who dared to call Mr. Bonafort by his first name.

Marci raised her hand to ask a question as if she were in school. "When can we see the works?"

"Dinner tonight. The benefactor will have the items available for our inspection at that point. The Vermeer is the only one that I must insist we obtain. I think that Paul, you and your two ladies can choose among the others. Don't forget. The Vermeer is a must." Bowtie excused himself, and Mr. Bonafort continued the meeting as if nothing had happened. Perhaps major donations like this were the norm for the MET.

The Director already knew my name. Bonafort had probably told him when they were outside the room.

Marci and I went back to our little office after the meeting. She sat down. "I don't believe it. Another Vermeer. You know, no other museum in the world has more than four, including the Dutch National Museum in Amsterdam, and we're getting a sixth." She was bouncing in her seat like a little kid.

"Does this happen often? I mean, somebody just walks in with a half-dozen priceless paintings to donate?" I asked.

Marci settled into her chair a little. "Not since I've been here. Usually, what we get is donations of dead people's stuff, you know, like from estates. So we don't get to pick. And we hear about it a few months before things arrive."

Mr. Bonafort stopped by to inform us a limo would pick us all up out front at five thirty. It didn't give us time to go change into anything nicer than what we were wearing. I was happy with my outfit. I had dressed up. It was my first day at work, after all. Marci was upset that she had chosen to wear flats today. Marci and I fixed our makeup and brushed out our hair.

The four of us arrived at the hotel, and Mr. Cromartie took over, checking in with the front desk. We were supposed to meet a Miss Marston. We were escorted to a meeting room, the *Champagne Suite*. The large room contained a single round dining table in the middle and set of easels along two walls. The paintings were all covered.

I wasn't the only curious one here, but none of us dared to peek under the cloth covers.

An older lady entered and introduced herself as Judy Marston and said her boss would be with us shortly. We took places around the table. I was across from the empty seat for Judy's boss. Marci and Judy were on one side and Mr. Cromartie and Bonafort on the other. Waiters brought in bread baskets and offered us a choice of red or white wine. Mr. Cromartie started to engage Judy in conversation, but she had other ideas.

"Firstly," Judy announced. "We would like this to be a completely anonymous donation."

Cromartie straightened up in his chair. "But of course, Miss Marston. You can count on our discretion."

The waiters brought in spinach salads for each of us.

I started on mine while Mr. Cromartie tried again to engage Judy in small talk. We learned she had flown in today with the paintings from the west coast. Also, she didn't get out to New York very often, but not much else of substance.

"While we're waiting," Judy said, getting up, "let me uncover a few of these." She walked to the paintings behind me and pulled the covers off them, one by one. A Rembrandt, a Vermeer, a Monet, and it went on around the room. One painting remained covered.

The door opened and he walked in.

Steven.

CHAPTER TWENTY-THREE

Emma

My heart stopped. Steven was behind this. What the hell was he doing this for? Was he trying to screw up my new job?

"Good evening," Steven said as he strode up to Mr. Cromartie, who had stood. "Steven Covington. So good to meet you, Mr. Cromartie."

He went around the table introducing himself until he got to me.

He offered his hand. "Miss Watson. You remind me of a woman I once knew, a Tiffany Case." He was trying to embarrass me.

The ass.

I didn't respond.

We sat, and Steven and Mr. Cromartie went back and forth as the wait staff cleared the salad.

Steven barely even glanced at me. "Mr. Cromartie, as I said earlier, you and your staff may select any three of the Dutch masters and any four of the impressionist works, and we will take the others back with us."

Mr. Cromartie directed Marci to pick first, which took her all of five seconds. She went up to the Vermeer and the two smaller Rembrandts. The other was large enough that I could imagine it getting too crowded on the walls of her exhibit.

I was growing faint. I didn't understand his game here. He had found me, but I was trapped.

I couldn't very well yell at him in this setting, or kick him in the nuts, which is what I wanted to do. At least he hadn't brought Victoria with him tonight to humiliate me even more. I couldn't understand what his game was. I was asked to select paintings, which I did, even though one of the paintings was still covered. I was moving on autopilot, unable to figure out what he was doing here.

Steven took a sip from his glass. "Mr. Cromartie. I only have one further request."

Mr. Cromartie perked up.

"I would like to dine this evening with the lovely Miss Watson, and Judy will have these paintings delivered to your museum tomorrow morning."

Mr. Cromartie looked at me.

I couldn't screw this up. I was going to have to pay the price. It would blow my dream job in an instant if I refused. "I would love to," I responded. I pasted on the best smile I could muster at this point.

Trapped.

I could get through a silly dinner for the sake of the museum. Couldn't I?

The others said their goodbyes and left.

Alone with him.

I motioned to the rows of paintings. "Where did you get all of these? I thought I cataloged all your paintings."

"Just the corporate art. These are from the family house."

He pulled out my chair and I sat.

"Just the two of us?" I asked.

His smile was soft and engaging. "Just us. I thought it would be good if we talked."

I couldn't hold his gaze. I looked down at the tablecloth. "So talk."

"I've decided to make a change," he announced.

I almost blurted it out.

Yeah, most people would call getting engaged a change.

I didn't say it, but I came close. I glanced up from the table coyly. "Really?"

His smile was disarmingly genuine. "Yes. I've decided to move to New York."

I winced. I would have to be in the same city as them. The A-hole was going to torture me. "But that will screw up your law career, won't it?" He had promised his father that he would pursue law, and he had told me he couldn't practice law in New

York because of the conviction on his record. This was a complete turnaround from the Steven I knew who always kept a promise.

"Yup."

"But you promised your father. I thought that was important to you."

"Sure, it was—and is—but it's less important than supporting the woman I love. I quit E&S. See?" He held out his phone with a simple email to his boss. He had quit.

Now it was out in the open. He loved Victoria enough to move to New York for her career and abandon the promise he had made his father. The gesture made me sick because he was doing it for her.

"What do you think?" he asked.

"That's nice of you," I said. We were dancing around the problem that had come between us and not facing it. "So her work is bringing her out here?"

"It already has." He responded with a chuckle.

I couldn't take his laughing at me. "Why the sudden change?"

"Because I love you," he said.

My heart pounded with rage. His eyes bored into me. I controlled my temper for a moment. He was implying that he still cared for me. He cared about me and proposed to her. He thought I was an idiot. "And what do you tell her?" I wanted to get up and leave, but I'd been committed, or pimped, or whatever, by Mr. Cromartie to tolerate an entire dinner with him. Right now, I was feeling like my salad might come back up all over the table.

He leaned forward. "Emma, I love you and I always have. I..."

I shut him down with a shout. "What about Victoria?"

"What the hell are you talking about?" he barked back.

I pulled out my phone and scrolled down my messages to the video I had gotten of his proposal and started it. I turned the phone toward him. "This," I hissed.

He watched for ten seconds or so without saying a word.

It had surprised the fucker that I'd caught him.

A broad smile tugged at the corners of his mouth. He thought this was funny. "And what did you think was happening?" he asked. A wicked grin grew on his face, like the cat that got the mouse.

He was amused?

I didn't understand the joke. I hesitated. "An engagement, what else?" I shouted back.

He laughed. I'd caught him and he was laughing. At me. The fucking A-hole. "So that's what this is about?" He paused. "Did you know she's gay?" he asked.

In what universe is this fair? I was dumped for a lesbian?

He got up from his seat and trotted to the picture that was still shrouded. "I traded the ring for this." He pulled the sheet off the remaining painting.

As soon as he uncovered the Renoir, my heart stopped. I ran up to the easel. It was my family's painting. He had found it. I had been searching forever, and now Steven had it.

"This is for you, Emma. I wanted to surprise you. I gave Victoria the ring in trade for the painting. I brought it back to LA last Friday, but you were gone."

I almost fainted as it hit me. I'd screwed this all up. I lurched forward.

He caught me and brought me into a hug. "It's for you, Emma."

My head was spinning. I'd fucked up everything. "But I took this job thinking—"

"No worries, Sugar. I quit E&S. It's fine. I meant what I said. I'm moving here to be with you. I love you."

He had said he loved me. Twice. No, three times. I had doubted him, and he had loved me all along. "I love you too, Steven. I thought…"

He stroked my hair and held me tight. "No worries, Sugar."

I pressed my face into the heat of his chest. "But I…"

"Nothing to worry about, Sugar. I'm just glad I have you back."

"But the bar? You can't be a lawyer here."

"Not important. Don't worry. Now sit down and finish your dinner like a good girl. You promised Mr. Cromartie you would eat dinner with me." He was giving up everything for me. He had gone to law school and made all his plans around being a lawyer, and now he couldn't because of me. For me. Because I'd taken this job.

I snuggled against his warmth. "Yeah, pimped for the evening by Mr. Bowtie." I put on a pout. "Can't you just hold me for a while?"

"I can do better than that." He pulled me over to the table, and he punched up a song on his phone. He took me into his arms as Shania Twain's *When You Kiss Me* started. He sang the words in my ear as we slow danced.

I closed my eyes and floated in his arms as Steven sang to me. I melted at the lyrics he had chosen. It was the most romantic dance I had ever had. Dancing in the arms of my man, only the two of us in this giant room surrounded by millions of dollars' worth of precious paintings, and the most important one of all, my great-great-grandmother's painting, painted by the man who loved her, and me, held by the man who loved me.

When the song stopped, he fiddled with the phone again and we danced to another of Shania's songs, *Forever and For Always*, as he sang that one to me as well.

I inhaled his scent as I drifted in his arms, swaying to the music and basking in his voice. I had no idea he was a Shania Twain fan, but I was liking it. No, I was loving it.

"Wanna wake up every morning to your face, always," he sang. He stopped singing as the song continued. "Will you, Sugar?" he asked.

Lost in the moment, I hadn't been paying enough attention to understand. "What?"

"I wanna wake up every morning to your face, always," he sang again over the song's words.

I was still too lost to understand.

"Do I have to spell it out for you? I thought you Santa Clara girls were smart," he whispered in my ear.

My heart raced. Was he asking what I thought he was? "How come you lawyer types can't ask a simple question that a mere college girl can understand?"

He continued to dance with me as the song continued and sang it again when the chorus came around. "Wanna wake up every morning to your face, always," he sang. "Will you marry me, Emma Sophia Watson?"

I felt light as a moonbeam. I couldn't believe it. My heart nearly burst from my chest it was beating so hard. "Yes, YES!" I gripped him tighter. "Even if you are a scumbag lawyer." We kept dancing as the song continued.

"You forgot spoiled rich kid," he said into my ear.

"That too."

He pulled back to gaze into my eyes. "You know, if I wasn't a scumbag lawyer, I wouldn't have found your painting, and if I wasn't a spoiled rich kid, I wouldn't have been able to afford to get it back for you."

"You're not really a scumbag lawyer anymore."

He kissed me on the forehead. "Right. At least now you won't have to worry about Monica hitting on me."

"I wasn't worried. She's got her claws into some older guy." When the song ended, we went back to the table and I pulled out my phone to show Steven the picture I had taken of Cruella with the senior citizen.

A wicked grin formed on Steven's face. "I know that guy." He started the music again.

We kept dancing as he played the songs again. I was lost in his arms, comforted by the lyrics, totally lost. His name was branded on my heart.

Lost in his arms.

* * *

Steven

Dancing with Emma to Shania's music was magical. She melded her body to mine, her red hair catching highlights from the chandeliers overhead. The citrus scent of her hair. The warmth of her soft breasts against my chest as we swayed from side to side. I softly sang the words of the chorus to her as the song came to an end.

When the music stopped, we sat and started on the delicious meal that was getting cold. I couldn't get over how good it felt to have her back.

My woman.

I finished a bite of my potatoes. "Sugar, why don't I tell the boss man, Cromartie, how you talked me into donating the entire group to the museum?"

"No way. You can't do that. That's too much. You said these are your family's paintings."

"Well, not exactly."

"Then what, exactly?"

"I bought the Vermeer from Lloyd Benson. We didn't have one and Lloyd did. He knew it would be the hook Cromartie couldn't pass up. It's the one painting that guaranteed a meeting with the Director himself."

She smiled. "You did your homework, I see."

"Anyway, just think of them as an early Christmas present."

She picked up her glass. "You were planning on giving me four paintings for Christmas? Get real."

"Okay, one then. Pick another one."

She relented and picked the Pissarro. It was like Christmas. I could give the woman I loved a present that she would appreciate. Her eyes glowed with happiness.

I looked up Victoria's Instagram on my phone and found a picture of her announcing her engagement with her partner, Sarah Millhouse. I showed it to Emma. There was also a close-up of the ring I had traded. Victoria had given it to Millhouse, and the caption said *Previously Owned by the Duchess of Overdale*. I knew it would be the kicker that Victoria couldn't resist, the status of the ring.

"Why trade a ring?" Emma asked. "Why didn't you just buy the painting from her?"

"Victoria's father is an accountant," I explained. "He told her that an exchange wasn't taxable, but if she sold the picture to me, she could end up with a big tax problem at the end of the year. Victoria always looks at the bottom line."

"Sensible, I guess." An eyebrow cocked up. "So, how did you find out she had the painting anyway?"

I smiled. "Remember how that receipt you got from LeMere said Coulter had bought four paintings?"

"Yeah."

"He declared in your deposition that he didn't own the three you specifically asked him about."

"So?" she asked.

I took a sip of water. "I checked his tax records

and he hadn't declared any art sales, so I guessed he was reselling them at a profit and conveniently forgetting to tell the IRS about the income. So, I called him and told him I might be able to talk you out of filing an IRS whistleblower claim against him if he came clean about where your painting went."

Her eyes sparkled as she laughed.

I explained how she could get up to thirty percent of the taxes Coulter owed on his under-the-table art sales and how big Tom Coulter was scared shitless at the thought of an IRS audit. He had folded like a wet napkin.

Emma thought it was hilarious. Her laugh was infectious.

"Can I see that video again?" I asked.

"The one about the ring?" Emma pulled it up and it started over again.

It was taken from behind a column near the entrance, based on the angle. Then I noticed the number it was sent from. "This came from Monica," I told her. "The fucking bitch."

Emma's eyes grew angry. "That bitch, Cruella?"

"The one and only." She had sent this to fuck with me. Fuck with us. "I'm going to get her back for this," I hissed. Emma's cell phone picture would do the trick.

Now I was seriously pissed.

* * *

Emma

Megan's call woke us both up. Braydon was being an ass to her again and he was drunker than normal.

Steven was getting the gist of the conversation, listening close to my ear. He grabbed the phone away from me. "Megan, this is Steven Covington, your new brother-in-law. I need you to be quiet and listen carefully."

Steven saying he was going to be her brother-in-law got Megan's attention and got her to shut up, which was no easy feat.

"I want you to call my brother Bill in five minutes. I'm going to call him now to have him pick you up and get you to my place, where you will be safe."

I could hear Megan protesting on the other end.

"Megan, you can even bring that little mutt, Horace. Just don't let him chew anything."

I stifled a laugh.

"You can stay there as long as you need. Okay?"

Megan argued for a minute, but she finally agreed. She didn't really have a choice. Steven was not somebody you won an argument with when he was like this.

Steven gave her Bill's number. He called his

brother. The moment Steven mentioned that we were now engaged and Megan was his soon-to-be sister-in-law, Bill instantly agreed to arrange everything. Family really was important to these guys. He hung up the phone. "Show me a picture of this wanker, Braydon," Steven demanded. "I want to make sure I beat up the right guy."

I opened the photos app on the phone. My laughing stopped when fury rose in Seven's eyes. He was going to fix this and make sure it stayed fixed. I started scrolling backward.

Braydon has no idea what's headed his way.

EPILOGUE

When I saw you I fell in love, and you smiled because you knew. – William Shakespeare

Emma

As I slowly woke, I found Steven's morning hard-on poking me from behind as his arm draped over me. His thumb slowly stroked my breast. This was his favorite way to wake me up when he wanted to get the day started with a little exercise. "Morning," I whispered as I turned over to face him.

He kissed me. "Good morning, Sugar."

I gripped the nape of his neck and pulled him to me for another kiss. My mouth captured his, sliding open and teasing him with my tongue. I pulled back and rubbed my nose against his.

"What is the lady's pleasure this morning?" he whispered.

I raised my head enough to see the clock behind him. We didn't have much time before I had to get ready for work, and I couldn't be late at my new job.

"The lady desires quick."

Steven never really got the concept. His idea of quick was making me come only once before he entered me. Slow translated to more than that, so much more. He pulled the covers down and his fingers parted my folds as he dipped inside me to bring my wetness forward to my clit. He started to work his magic fingers in all the ways that he knew would drive me crazy.

Liquid heat pooled in my pussy at just the suggestion of what he was about to do to me. I'd been learning how I could turn the tables and drive him crazy by pulling and twisting in just the right way on his cock. He was rock hard this morning. Pure lust. I inhaled his scent as I held his head close with my other hand.

He pulled down to kiss and lightly bite at my nipples, sending shocks through me. He trapped my leg, pushing his thigh up against the hand working my pussy and my sensitive nub. He made sure I never lacked for foreplay. He circled my clit and teased me, increasing my yearning for his touch. He nipped at the hollows of my neck and returned to my breast.

I ached with desire. All the things he did while denying me his cock made me want him in me even more. I needed to feel him thrusting into me with his raw passion. I worked his cock harder as I rocked my hips into him for more friction, more action. I begged him for more.

It was not a record, but my climax came quickly and hard as Steven manipulated all of my buttons and sent me over the edge by telling me he loved me, which was the most stimulating thing of all. As my convulsions subsided, he brought his fingers up and licked my juices from them, following up with a kiss, our hot little ritual.

I rolled over on my stomach and poked my ass up, putting my hand between my legs to guide him in. As his tip found my entrance, he pushed in slowly, still gentle after all this time. He filled me completely as I arched my hips up and thrust back into him. I liked this position sometimes because I could play with his balls as he pushed in. The sounds that he made when I did that were delicious. I could get rough with him sometimes if I didn't mind getting myself spanked. I pulled my hand out and squeezed my legs together, giving him more friction as he speared me from behind. "More," I begged him. "Harder."

I'd learned how it turned him on when I talked dirty. I rocked my hips back with each thrust as his tempo increased and his breathing became shorter. He finally pounded out his release and collapsed on top of me, panting and kissing my neck and licking at my ear.

My man gave me so much more pleasure than I

had ever imagined in my hottest fantasies, and I tried my hardest to give it back to him in equal measure. I had learned how good he tasted and how good I felt when I teased him with my mouth almost to the point of coming and driving him nuts, keeping him on the knife edge, but not quite there, controlling his pleasure and drawing it out till he begged me to make him come. Sometimes, when I had teased him enough like that to bring out the beast in him, I would tell him to mount me and his raw power and lust would take us both over the edge. We hadn't had time for it this morning. Maybe tonight.

"I love you, Mrs. Covington," he panted.

I loved it when he called me that. He had given me his name and everything I'd ever wished for. I had been Mrs. Covington for two months now, and it seemed better every day. I squirmed out from under him and headed to the shower. I had to get to work earlier than he did.

It didn't seem fair, but since he was the boss of his new startup, he got to make the rules, and the software types he worked with were mostly the night owl types who seemed allergic to early morning sunlight.

We had moved to San Francisco. Between Uncle Garth and Lloyd Benson, I had gotten the right introductions to get me an interview at the de Young Museum here. It wasn't as big as the MET, but no other museum in the country was. Uncle Garth's connections at city hall got me put in charge of an after-school art program in the city that meant I could work at the museum and teach art to children as well, without having to choose one over the other. The perfect situation for me.

Moving here had also let Steven take the bar, and he was now a licensed California lawyer, but he didn't want to practice with any of the city's law firms. He had started a company here that was aimed at providing online legal services and advice to tenants throughout the state. He planned on expanding it to other states later. He had been moved by how my eviction could have turned out badly if I hadn't had access to him and his friend Mike Salois. He was determined to find a way to help others in my kind of predicament. It was exactly the kind of helping people that Steven had in mind when he promised his father he would use his law degree to help people.

I was so unbelievably proud of him.

Living here also meant that we could visit my folks, which we did every few weeks on Sundays. Daddy had been practicing behind the barn with the Winchester, and the score was now Steven two and Daddy two in their shooting contests. When I asked Steven if he was letting Daddy win, he told me that a Marine didn't want charity. He wanted a challenge. Mama and I would cook while they did their manly things like arm wrestle, which Steven always won, and dart throwing, which Daddy usually won.

I was so happy for Daddy. He loved Megan and me, but I knew he had always wanted to have a son to do these kinds of things with, and now, having Steven around gave him that chance.

Our wedding had been small and intimate. We decided to have it in the evening at my old museum, centrally located to make it easy for everyone to attend. Daddy walked me down the aisle in his Marine dress blues.

Mama had loaned our painting to the museum, for safekeeping, she said, but she didn't know until the wedding what Mr. Benson had done. He had moved it a special display near the front entrance with a large panel explaining the painting's history and Great-great-grandmama Marie's place in Renoir's life. It included a love letter the painter had written her, which Mr. Benson had located in France. Mama was completely overcome when she saw it. She cried and cried. We both did.

Janice and my other coworkers came. Steven's entire family was there with the exception of his mother. I'd never met her, and I hadn't understood Steven's refusal to invite her until I heard Lauren's description of the woman.

Megan had come stag. She hadn't landed a new boyfriend since Steven had scared Braydon off the day after the call from Megan that we got in New York. He had flown back to LA the next morning to fix the problem.

Steven had read Braydon the riot act when he took Megan back to her place to get some things. Megan said Braydon made the mistake of throwing something at Steven and got himself kicked into the wall for his effort. Steven then threatened to kick his sorry ass all the way to Kansas if he ever saw him again. Braydon was gone the next day.

I couldn't contain my delight when I heard the story. Braydon had learned the hard way that you didn't mess with a Covington. It had been late in coming, but Braydon had finally gotten what he deserved.

The most recent news from LA had come yesterday when Jeremy from Steven's old law firm had called with news about Cruella. The picture that Steven was happy to find on my phone turned out to be Cruella kissing a Judge Vinson, who was on a case she was defending. That was a big no-no in legal circles. Steven and his friend Mike had sent a complaint to the State Bar Association. Cruella had been fired from E&S and Jeremy had called to tell us that her law license had been suspended. It couldn't happen to a more deserving bitch.

I got dressed for work as Steven cooked me pancakes. I had a scare as he drew a smiley face on my pancake with a whipped cream can. "That had better not be the one we used last night," I warned him.

A grin grew on his face. "Now would I do that to you, Sugar?"

I gave him the evil eye. I had a thing about keeping play food and eating food separate.

He put his hands up. "It's fresh, scout's honor."

I scarfed down two pancakes along with some orange juice and grabbed a few M&Ms from the bowl on the counter.

Steven had ordered bags of custom M&Ms from the company, all the standard colors except yellow, and with *I love Steven* on half and *I love Emma* on the rest. The best part was that each one had a miniature image of Great-great-grandmama Marie's painting on the other side. Who knew you could do that?

I checked my purse again for the envelope with the check. I smiled as I found it. Nine hundred and twenty-three thousand dollars from the IRS for turning in that cheating ass Coulter.

I kissed Steven and pinched his ass on the way to the door. I looked back to blow him a kiss.

He winked back at me with those deep green eyes. *My man* wasn't wearing anything but an apron as he blew me a kiss back, an image I would cherish for the rest of the day.

My man.

THE END.

SNEAK PEEK:
THE SECRET BILLIONAIRE

CHAPTER ONE

Pat

"Mister Patrick, what kind of woman wear a thing like this?" my housekeeper, Juanita, asked.

She held up the pink thong Lisa had left last night at the end of her pick-up grabber, the kind of tool they used to pick up trash on the freeway. She'd bought the tool specifically for this weekly undies game. She was scared shitless to touch the panties.

"A pretty one," I answered.

Each week, I made a point of placing the panties out in the open, where Juanita would find them on cleaning day, my little game. She normally came on Monday, but this week, Juanita had family in town, so we'd moved the cleaning forward to Sunday.

She shook her head. "This *chica* no good."

Juanita said the same thing every week without fail.

"You need to find you a nice *señorita*."

I smiled. I knew what women were for, and what they weren't. Obsessing over one woman wasn't for me. My work didn't allow time for that. *Variety is the spice of life*, a wise man once said. Variety in women was the right thing for me, and I certainly didn't need someone telling me to pick up after myself.

Juanita was half right this morning, though. Lisa was no good for me, just not for the reasons Juanita thought. Most girls lasted at least a week or two with me. It took that long to sample the pleasures they had to offer, but not Lisa. One helping of Lisa had been enough. She had all the right equipment but was cold as a fish.

Juanita wagged her finger at me. "You need to settle down with a real woman, Mister Patrick. One that make babies for you. These *chicas*, they no good. I can tell. You going to catch something, make it fall off. Then you have no *niños* and you wish you listen to Juanita."

I loved these weekly lectures. It was our little game.

"Where you want me put it?" she asked as if she didn't know, holding the thong away from her with the grabber.

"In the laundry," I said.

I had a dresser drawer reserved for forgotten ladies' panties, and a bra or two, which was getting full. A few were ripped, most not. Most weren't forgotten either. They'd gotten tangled up in the sheets at some point or lost under the couch. But if I told my guests the cleaning lady was due soon, they usually gave up looking pretty quickly on their way out the door.

There was nothing quite as hot as a girl leaving in the morning going commando. And if one got a little too clingy, leaving the drawer open one morning usually solved the problem.

As she left the room, Juanita repeated her warning about it falling off. Not what I wanted to hear before breakfast.

I finished buttoning up my work shirt and headed downstairs to meet Phil at Starbucks, leaving Juanita to mumble to herself as she cleaned the kitchen.

Settle down with a nice señorita. *Fat chance.*

* * *

Phil was waiting for me inside when I arrived. Phil Patterson was my Sunday workout partner, and we often hit this place after an hour on the machines, but today we were headed over the hill.

I got in line behind the Gladys twins. "Morning Gladyses."

"Good morning to ya, Patrick," the taller Gladys replied. They weren't actually twins, just two older ladies both named Gladys. They rolled in with their walkers and sat at the table by the window almost every morning. The shorter of the two smiled and echoed the taller one's greeting.

In a conversation with them a few months back, I'd learned that they both lost their husbands last year. Since then, I'd made a point of saying hello every time I saw them. They'd told me Gladys was a Welsh name that meant princess, and they were both proud of that.

I pulled out my tattered brown wallet, and a picture dropped to the floor. I really needed a new wallet, but I couldn't bring myself to get rid of this one, a gift from Dad. It was my link back to him.

It was so like Dad to give me a simple gift, something practical that I would use every day. The wallet was embossed with the Covington Industries logo——his subtle, daily reminder that he expected me to join my brothers in the family business. The other side was embossed with FCF, our first rule: *Family Comes First.*

"Pardon me." I stooped down to retrieve the picture my worn wallet had released.

It was the last picture taken of my dad before his accident. Living overseas, I hadn't seen much of him in the two years before he died. This image showed him at his birthday party, the last one I'd been able to attend. He was smiling brightly, opening a present from my sister Katie.

He had been my role model. He'd taught me how

to be a man. Always give, never take; always compliment, never brag; always protect, never hurt; and always be strong, never cry.

And I hadn't cried, until the day I got the call telling me he was gone.

"I'm sorry, ma'am, but there's not enough on this card," the barista behind the cash register said to Gladys, waking me from my reverie.

Short Gladys shrank a few inches and started fumbling with her wallet. "Oh, dear."

I moved up to the counter. "Let me take care of this, ladies. You just go sit down."

"But Mr. Patrick," short Gladys protested.

"No arguments, ladies. My treat this morning."

They begrudgingly turned and wheeled over to their usual table.

I picked up the Starbucks card short Gladys had left on the counter and handed it to the pretty coed behind the register along with a Benjamin. "Put the change on her card, and I'll have a grande mocha, extra shot, please, with a bacon, cheese, and egg sandwich."

Poor short Gladys had looked so ashamed when she'd come up short for their hot chocolates. I pulled a second Benjamin out of my wallet.

"And put this on the card as well." Her name tag said *Jamie*. She was at least an eight on my scale. "You're new here, aren't you, Jamie?"

She blushed, marking my cup with a smile. "No,

just a different shift." She returned a warm, inviting smile, tucking a stray curl behind her ear.

I would add her name to my list later. Phil and I were running late and would have to scarf down our sandwiches while driving over the hill to the project in the valley. I walked the card over to the Gladys twins with my warmest smile and added an admonition to keep it safe because I had put a few dollars on it. I grabbed some napkins and waited for my order at the end of the counter while Phil ordered.

"Don't look now, bud, but your soul mate is right outside," Phil said after giving the barista his order and a wink.

I turned to see Tiffany, of all people, opening the door. Her figure was striking, backlit by the bright Los Angeles sunshine.

"Maybe she's here to see you," I offered.

"No fuckin' way, Romeo. My bank account is a half-dozen zeros short of interesting to her."

Tiffany Lawrence was one woman I had hoped to never meet up with again, but today was not my lucky day. She'd already spotted us and was sashaying in our direction with a hip swivel that was exaggerated even for her. For a moment, I was reminded of what those hips did when I put her on top.

She made an alluring picture in black yoga pants with a wide diagonal pink stripe and a black spandex crop top with a Nike logo on it, which hugged all of her surgically enhanced curves. The crop top accentuated her tanned, bare midriff, and the outfit was likely meant to look like she'd just come from yoga or a spin class, which was such a joke.

The only exercise she ever did outside the bedroom was the two-finger lift of taking her credit card out of her wallet. She was only five foot two, so she wore high heels everywhere. She seemed to have no idea how incongruous this morning's outfit was with five-inch stilettos.

She bounced her ample assets our way and placed a hand suggestively on my arm when she arrived. "Patrick, fancy running into you here," she said with a smile as fake as her surprise.

She knew my routine and had obviously planned this meeting. She was back like a bad rash. Her problem was not how she looked or her bedroom skills. And she wasn't stupid, or at all mean. Instead, she was incredibly self-absorbed. Tiffany was on the hunt for a sugar daddy and not at all bashful about it. I had been her target a few months ago until I cut it off.

There was no spark. The spell had been broken.

"You remember Phil," I said.

She offered Phil her hand, palm down and bent at the wrist like he was supposed to kiss it or something.

"Sure, I do."

Phil had been right. Her tone indicated she knew he didn't have enough cash to interest her.

Phil had always disliked her, but he shook her hand with a smile like the gentleman he was. "Miss Lawrence."

She glanced at Phil only momentarily before returning her focus to me. "Patrick, I was thinking we could…" She traced a finger up my arm.

Her thinking had always resulted in me taking out my credit card somewhere. I had to concentrate to keep it civil and avoid swearing at her.

"Tiff, there is no '*we*'. There is no '*us*'."

"Can't we just talk privately for a minute?" she pleaded as she stroked her fingers up my arm.

The grin on Phil's face told me he wasn't going to come to my rescue. He was enjoying this way too much. He'd had Tiffany figured out from the first night I met her and had reminded me of that more than once.

Tiffany brushed her ample breasts against me as she leaned in close. "It will just be a minute, darling," she added with syrupy sweetness.

"I'll leave you two lovebirds alone for a moment," Phil said wryly as he turned away.

I was raised to be polite, so I gritted my teeth as he ambled a few steps away, and I tried to keep a semblance of a smile on my face, which was not easy.

Tiffany leaned in closer. "I think we should give ourselves another chance, Patrick. We are so good together."

There was no denying she was enjoyable in bed, but there wasn't enough below the surface. Shopping and high-brow social functions were the only things Tiffany found interesting. She was exceptionally pretty arm candy, but that was all.

I thought back to the day I broke it off with her. We'd been at a barbecue a few months ago when I noticed an attractive blonde walking by.

"Patrick, don't be so obvious. I don't care who you play with in your spare time after we're married, but it's just uncouth to look around when you're here with me," she'd said. *"It's embarrassing to have such bad manners, don't you think, darling?"*

Where she'd ever gotten the notion that she would someday be Mrs. Patrick Covington was beyond me. We'd been dating for less than a month. I'd told her we wouldn't be seeing each other any more when I dropped her back at her place that evening.

She moved in close. "You've had your break, and now I think we should be together again." She used her practiced sultry voice.

I met her eye. "Tiff, I thought I made it plain. It's over." I spoke as calmly as I could.

Her plastic smile was replaced by her equally plastic pouty face. "But darling, we are so good together."

She was persistent, like the mosquito you swat at and miss that comes back again and again.

The barista called our orders, and Phil picked up the coffees and sandwiches at the end of the counter.

"No, we weren't good together. I want someone who loves more than just my money or my name, and we both know that isn't you," I told her quietly.

Her eyes narrowed. "How silly, Patrick. Every woman you meet is going to be with you for the money."

I made a move to join Phil. "No means no, Tiff. You will make a fine wife for the right guy." I wanted to say *trophy wife* but held my tongue. "But I'm not that guy."

Anger flashed across her face. "Patrick, you're going to regret this someday. You'll marry a girl thinking she's in love with you and be crushed when you find out all she loves is your wallet."

"Like it's any different with you?"

She huffed. "Well, at least I'm honest about it." She scowled and left as quickly as her expensive red-soled Louboutin heels would allow.

Phil handed me my coffee. "You know, I think she friggin' nailed it."

I followed him toward the door. "So you caught that?" I waved goodbye to the Gladys twins, who waved back.

He took a sip from his cup. "The whole fucking place heard her."

"Nailed what?" I asked quietly as we exited into the bright sunshine and turned toward our cars.

"Being a Covington, you'll never know if the girl falls in love with you, or your name and your money, until it's too fucking late."

"I'll know."

"Bullshit, you will."

"Well, I know it's not her."

"Just sayin', once you whip out the black Amex card and she finds out you're one of THOSE Covingtons, you can't fuckin' know for sure. No way."

I walked along with Phil as I pulled my keys out of my pocket. "Thanks for the pep talk."

Phil had been one of my best friends since high school. He had a thriving construction business and a sideline string of rental houses he'd accumulated by buying rundown single-family homes and renovating them. Today he was joining me at the Habitat for Humanity project where my family volunteered. Today's house was in Reseda, a bedroom community in the valley. The previous house on the lot had burned down, and the land had been donated to Habitat. We were putting up a duplex, and two deserving families would shortly have brand-new homes to live in.

Phil stepped up into his pickup as I settled into

my Corvette, parked right behind him. I noticed the extra writing on my coffee cup as I went to put it in the holder.

Jamie had written her number on it.

Things are looking up.

I pushed the *Start* button, and the supercharged engine rumbled to life. Phil's words rattled around in my skull.

"Bullshit, you will. You can't fucking know for sure. No way. Not until it's too fucking late."

Printed in Great Britain
by Amazon